EXHIBITING ATROCITY

Memorial Museums and the Politics of Past Violence

AMY SODARO

RUTGERS UNIVERSITY PRESS
New Brunswick, Camden, and Newark, New Jersey, and London

978-0-8135-9214-5
978-0-8135-9213-8
978-0-8135-9215-2

Cataloging-in-Publication data is available from the Library of Congress.

A British Cataloging-in-Publication record for this book is available from the British Library.

∞ The paper used in this publication meets the requirements of the American National Standard for Information Sciences—Permanence of Paper for Printed Library Materials, ANSI Z39.48-1992.

www.rutgersuniversitypress.org

Manufactured in the United States of America

CONTENTS

ACKNOWLEDGMENTS

This book has been many years in the making. The journey began more than a decade ago with two courses at the New School for Social Research (NSSR): one on Holocaust Memory with the incomparable late Geoffrey Hartman and a summer course on collective memory in Krakow, Poland, taught by Jonathan Veitch and Elzbieta Matynia. The seed that was planted by those courses eventually grew into a master's thesis, then a dissertation on memorial museums, and finally, this book.

I was extraordinarily fortunate to embark on the study of memory as memory studies was burgeoning at NSSR. With NSSR's roots as a University in Exile, it is not surprising that memory became a key area of academic interest, and I benefited tremendously from the strong community of fellow graduate students and faculty working on issues of memory. I am especially indebted to my dissertation committee, Elzbieta, Jeffrey Goldfarb, and the late (and very dearly missed) Vera Zolberg, whose wonderful insight into memory as an object of study helped shape my nascent interests into a worthy academic endeavor. And I am particularly grateful for the NSSR Memory Group, especially Adam Brown, Rachel Daniell, Lindsey Freeman, Yifat Gutman, and Benjamin Nienass. This group was a steady source of intellectual support and companionship during my doctoral work, though I still marvel that any of us were able to finish our studies with the tireless effort we put into organizing conferences and events, publishing books and journals, and working to build a memory studies network.

One of the best things about my research on memorial museums has been the opportunity to travel the world to visit memorial museums, and I must extend special thanks to the many individuals associated with the museums in this book who generously shared their time and knowledge. In Budapest, Hungary, this included House of Terror director Maria Schmidt and researcher Aron Mathe. In Rwanda and the United Kingdom, James Smith, director of Aegis Trust; Freddy Mutanguha, director of the Kigali Memorial Centre; Steven Robinson, Aegis's Rwanda development officer; and Honore Gatera, head guide of Kigali Memorial Centre. And in Santiago, Chile, and the United States, Katherine Hite, professor of political science at Vassar College; Carolina Aguilera, PhD candidate at Pontifical Catholic University of Chile; Ricardo Brodsky, director of the Museum of Memory and Human Rights; Maria Jose Bunster, general coordinator and head of museography and exhibitions of the museum; Mireya Davila, of the Instituto de Asuntos Públicos, Universidad de Chile, who wrote the museum script; Daniela Jara of the Center for Social Conflict and Cohesion Studies in Santiago; and Manuela Badilla, PhD candidate at NSSR who put me in touch with all these wonderful resources. I would also like to extend my gratitude to the Professional Staff Congress/CUNY Research Foundation, which generously funded my travel to Chile in 2015, enabling me to expand my research to include this important museum.

In addition to the many individuals who assisted me in my travels, I have had the valuable support of many people here in New York. I am grateful to my wonderful colleagues at the Borough of Manhattan Community College for their ever useful advice and support, in particular helping me find a balance between teaching, service, and scholarship. I am also deeply indebted to New York University's Faculty Resource Network. In addition to attending two stellar summer seminars at NYU, I would never have finished this book without my participation in their Scholar-in-Residence program in June 2016. Not only did the program afford me access to NYU's vast library and an inspiring group of fellow scholars, but it also gave me the opportunity to work with Dr. Joyce Apsel of NYU's Liberal Studies program, whose encouragement and expertise have been immeasurable. I am also grateful to Marlie Wasserman, now retired from Rutgers University Press, whose initial feedback on parts of the manuscript was extremely helpful, and Rutgers editor Lisa Banning, who has been simply wonderful to work with.

I must also thank my family for their enthusiasm for my interest in such "depressing" museums. In particular, I thank my sister, Sally LaPorte, for her careful and thoughtful reading of the final manuscript. And without Jonah Kokodyniak, who has been by my side for this entire journey, this book would never have happened. His support for the project has never wavered, and for years he has happily read drafts, talked over ideas, and never once complained about planning vacations to places with violent pasts! Sweet little Stella has only been around for part of the journey, extending it in the best possible ways.

In the last few months, as I finished the manuscript, the world has changed, becoming a much darker and more frightening place. I know that memory and memorialization will play a role both in the dangerous retreat from globalization, cosmopolitanism, and democratic ideals that we are witnessing and in resistance to this movement. However, it is too soon to have a clear idea of what role memory scholars and memory workers will play as we grapple with this changing political and social landscape. I have presented some tentative thoughts throughout the manuscript on the relationship of memorial museums to this changing world order, but much remains to be seen. In the meantime, I hope that my two fields of memory studies and sociology can contribute, in some small way, to the fight against creeping authoritarianism, intolerance, and division.

INTRODUCTION

In Montgomery, Alabama, a new museum called From Enslavement to Mass Incarceration is slated to open in April 2018 in a former slave warehouse. Created by the Equal Justice Initiative (EJI), the museum is intended to explore "the legacy of slavery, racial terrorism, segregation, and contemporary issues of mass incarceration, excessive punishment, and police violence" (Equal Justice Initiative 2016). Designed by Local Projects, an "experience design" studio that was one of the lead exhibition designers of the National September 11 Memorial Museum and claims as its mission to "push the boundaries of emotional storytelling" (Local Projects), the new museum will confront the violence of African American history in a way that is interactive and deeply experiential. Using virtual reality technology, re-creations, sounds, and images, the goal of the museum is to "immerse visitors in the sights and sounds of the domestic slave trade, racial terrorism, and the Jim Crow South" (Equal Justice Initiative 2016). In connecting visitors to the past in a visceral way, it also intends to help them make connections between the violence of the past and the continued inequality and violence of the present, seeking to use the past to work toward a better future.

The museum is part of a larger memory initiative by the EJI that also includes the Memorial to Peace and Justice; located on six acres of land overlooking the city of Montgomery, it will be the first national memorial to the more than four thousand victims of lynching in the American South. The memorial is designed by MASS Design Group, which aims at "design that heals" and is also designing the new African Center for Peace at the Kigali Genocide Memorial Centre (MASS Design). The memorial will be an interactive space intended to help confront this exceedingly dark aspect of US history. Underpinning these two projects is the firm belief of EJI that "public commemoration plays a significant role in prompting community-wide reconciliation" (Equal Justice Initiative 2016); without these sites of commemoration, this violent past may remain in the dark and the wounds will not heal. The Montgomery museum and memorial open on the tail of the new Smithsonian National Museum of African American History and Culture. This wildly popular newest museum on the National Mall is intended to be not just for African Americans but for all Americans, telling a dual narrative of "uplift and tragedy seemingly on a fixed collision course" (Cotter 2016) that echoes broader social and political tensions in a nation passing the torch from its first black president to one unashamedly connected to white supremacist movements. The violence of the past that is contained in these new museums and memorial continue to simmer just beneath the surface, and these memory projects are intended to use memory to help heal the ongoing divisions within American society.

On another continent and in a no-less-complex political and social context, Colombia is breaking ground for its National Museum of Memory to be located in downtown Bogotá. Under the auspices of the National Center for Historical Memory, created by Law 1448 also known as the Victims' and Land Restitution Law, the museum is intended to "carry out actions aimed at restoring the dignity of the victims and spreading the truth about what happened" during the decades of violent armed conflict in Colombia (Centro de Memoria Histórica 2015). The museum has three primary functions: restoration, as a form of reparation to victims; enlightenment, in its contribution to knowledge and understanding of Colombia's past violence; and pedagogy, in its effort to "contribute to the construction of a culture of respect for difference, diversity and plurality" and, ultimately, the prevention of future violence (Centro de Memoria Histórica 2015). Like the Montgomery museum and memorial, the Colombian project is intended to harness the memory and history of the violent past in a way that shapes the present and future. And like the Montgomery projects, it is being created in a complex social and political context.

Decades of armed conflict in Colombia between government forces, paramilitaries, and left-wing guerillas finally ended with the signing of a historic peace accord in summer 2016. Just a couple of months later, Colombia's leaders were surprised and humiliated when a national referendum narrowly rejected the accord, only to be followed that month by the announcement that Colombia's president Juan Manuel Santos Calderón was being awarded the Nobel Peace Prize for his efforts to bring about an end to the violence. A revised peace accord was approved by the Congress in November 2016, but the massive project of coming to terms with Colombia's violent past is just beginning. At the center of this effort to "make visible the magnitude of the tragedy" and remember the more than two hundred thousand people killed, the millions who were forced from their homes, and the many individuals kidnapped or forced into combat is the creation of a national memorial museum (Centro de Memoria Histórica 2015). Like other similar initiatives in the region, such as Lima's Place of Memory and Social Tolerance, Santiago's Museum of Memory and Human Rights, and Buenos Aires' Space of Memory and Human Rights, and working with and drawing inspiration from these museums and their creators, Colombia's new museum reflects the centrality today of memorial museums' efforts to come to terms with past violence.

These are but two from many examples around the world reflecting a new approach to remembering and teaching about the past: the memorial museum. Memorial museums focused on past violence, atrocity, and human rights abuses reflect a demand today that those darkest days in human history are not only preserved but musealized and interpreted in a way that is widely accessible to present and future audiences. They are part of the ever-growing trend of "dark tourism"[1] and reflect a significant shift in the late twentieth century in how societies, nations, and groups memorialize past violence. Both Colombia's National Museum of Memory and the From Enslavement to Mass Incarceration Museum are intended to reveal the truth about what happened in the past, preserving that past in a museum so that the present and future can learn from it. They also seek to harness the perceived power of memory to heal communities and promote reconciliation. The impulse to preserve and remember so that atrocity will "never again" happen has driven memorialization from the second half of the twentieth century through today. And both museums, in their international connections to other memorial museums and the increasingly transnational flow of memorial museum aesthetics and design, reflect the global, transcultural nature of this new commemorative form. Around the world, memorial museums, intended to commemorate and educate using cutting edge museological techniques, are being constructed: from the United States and China to Cambodia, Uruguay, and South Africa. But as the complex political and social contexts in which these museums are negotiating difficult memories suggest, memorial museums are deeply political institutions and their utopian goals are often challenged by their political genealogies.

WHY MEMORIAL MUSEUMS?

This book addresses why and how societies attempt to come to terms with past atrocities and trauma through the creation of memorial museums, a new "hybrid" cultural form of commemoration. Memorial museums emerged in response to the violence and atrocities of the twentieth century and are intended to translate the suffering of the past into ethical commitments to creating a better future through education and commemoration. As such, memorial museums appear to be products of a shift in the way that societies relate to the past: from the nineteenth-century nation-state's celebratory—and often forgetful—emphasis on past triumphs, to a reflective effort to come to terms with the negative legacy of the past. Memorial museums' focus on learning the lessons of history points toward a firm adherence to Santayana's overused (and underthought) maxim that "those who cannot remember the past are condemned to repeat it." Around the world today, it is increasingly a political and moral expectation that societies will confront past violence as a way of moving forward, indicating a new temporal orientation toward the past in political and social life.

This new orientation toward the past has necessitated new commemorative forms that can express a more ambiguous relationship to the violence of the past and apply its lessons to the strengthening of a culture based on democratic values like freedom, tolerance, human rights, and the prevention of future violence. In the contemporary world, political legitimacy for regimes emerging from conflict and transitioning to democracy increasingly relies on coming to terms with the past (e.g., Torpey 2006; Olick 2007; Levy and Sznaider 2010). Museums are frequently used as central mechanisms for addressing past injustices and legitimating nations or groups in the eyes of the international community—by recognizing past victimization and demonstrating a new regime's willingness to learn from history.

As mechanisms of political legitimation, memorial museums are created with the goal of instilling in their visitors and societies democratic values by demonstrating the violence that results from the lack of these values.

They are meant to be inclusive institutions—public spaces in which the past can be confronted, discussed, and debated by its many different stakeholders.[2] They also serve as centers for education, research, documentation, and truth-telling that can expand society-wide knowledge about the contexts and situations in which violence and injustice occur. They further seek to morally educate their visitors, using experiential, interactive, and affective strategies to give visitors an impactful encounter with the past and inspire empathy in them. Ultimately they are created to be spaces that promote human rights and an ethic of "never again." By showing the catastrophic effects of intolerance, exclusion, repression, and dictatorship, they work to promote an opposite set of values that the visitor will take away from the museum with her and apply to her everyday life. Because of their seemingly vast potential to confer legitimacy, enact social change, and promote liberal democratic values, memorial museums have become a truly global form: they appear to be the embodiment of what Astrid Erll terms "travelling memory," exemplifying the movement of "carriers, media, contents, forms and practices of memory" between and across national and cultural borders (2011, 11).

All this makes memorial museums unique new cultural forms intended to work toward the creation of a more democratic, inclusive, and peaceful culture and to put the violence of the past to use in creating a better future. However, they are also political tools, often created and utilized with specific political agendas that can and often do compromise their declared efforts to openly confront and learn from the past. And on closer examination, as this book entails, it appears that the concerns of the present loom much larger in these museums than the difficult memories of the painful past.

A GLOBAL TOUR

To document the emergence of the memorial museum as a new form of commemoration, this book examines five in-depth case studies of exemplary memorial museums that trace the evolution and worldwide spread of the form, as well as highlight the divergent political and cultural contexts in which memorial museums are created. Through these case studies, I explore the questions of why and how societies today use memorial museums as mechanisms for dealing with the past. This study is not intended to explain or address how visitors experience and perceive the museums but instead focuses on the intention behind their creation.

My examination of each museum is what might be called an institutional ethnography, in which I document the creation of an institution centered on three points of comparison and analysis. The first is the cultural and political context in which the museums were conceived, with a focus on the debates, discussions, and intentions behind each museum's creation. For this I have relied on archival sources provided by the museums, secondary sources, and interviews with individuals involved in the conception and construction of each museum. This reveals the political motivations that drive the creation of the museums and determine the interactions between their primary stakeholders, creators, and intended audiences. It also tells us what sort of experience the museums intend to provide for the visitor, how they work to come to terms with the past, what role they intend to play in building a democratic culture, and how memorial museums around the world are in dialogue with one another.

The second point of analysis and comparison is a close reading of the museums' exhibitions, with a focus on their presentation of the past through narrative, exhibition design, artifacts, photographs, documentary footage, testimony, and other exhibitionary strategies. I have visited each museum and spent extensive time in each exhibit. I have also examined the exhibition guides and have used primary and secondary sources related to the design and construction of the exhibitions and their popular and critical reception upon opening. Again, a comparative study highlights the methods used by memorial museums for imparting knowledge and understanding of the past and its memory. My analysis of the exhibits' content and form shows how different societies attempt to assimilate the past into their present understanding of themselves and the ways in which their present concerns are reflected in their representation of the past. This analysis also demonstrates how memorial museums, as new and unique cultural forms, work to engage and educate the public to be moral citizens through the use of experiential and affective strategies intended to encourage an emotional response, identification with the victims, and empathy.

The final point of my comparison examines the museums as public institutions in order to understand how they attempt to engage communities in discussions about the past and in this way contribute to public dialogue and democratic culture. By examining their external programming, projects, websites, and other activities and speaking with individuals responsible for such programming, I look at how they use a range of public programs to contribute to public acknowledgment of past injustice, work with communities to right past wrongs, attempt to prevent future atrocities, and aid in the effort to heal a nation or collective. However, as they are political institutions, I also consider what sort of publics these museums seek to create and what the limits of their ambitious goals are.

In the first chapter, I trace the emergence of the memorial museum form as it parallels the "memory boom" of recent decades and a developing normative demand that societies across the globe work to come to terms with past violence and atrocity. The second half of the twentieth century saw a shift that started in the West, but has spread around the globe, from a focus on the glorious future of the nation, to an effort to reckon with past violence and atrocity as a prerequisite for political legitimacy. With this shift appeared a range of new cultural and political forms intended to help societies around the globe with this reckoning, including memorial museums. However, while several key sociological theories of this rise of coming to terms with the past argue that this marks the emergence of a post- or transnational or cosmopolitan memory culture, the case studies in this book suggest that memory—even that of the negative past—remains firmly in the control of the nation-state.

In the second chapter, I examine the US Holocaust Memorial Museum (USHMM), which opened in Washington, DC, in 1993 and in many ways is the model memorial museum. A number of memory theorists have argued that the Holocaust has set the ethical and legal precedent for societies around the world dealing with past violence (e.g., Levy and Sznaider 2010; Olick 2007; Rothberg 2009). It has also presented today's societies with new forms of commemoration intended to help them come to terms with the past (Young 1993). Because of the particular political and cultural context of its creation—a Holocaust museum in the heart of the US capital—the long, embattled process of developing an appropriate and acceptable Holocaust memorial led to the creation of the hybrid form of a memorial to the victims and a museum that tells the history and story of the past. Thus, as one of the first self-described memorial museums, the USHMM has become a model for others around the world.

The third chapter examines Budapest's Terrorhaza, House of Terror, a museum dedicated to telling the story of Hungary's violent twentieth century under first fascist and then communist occupation. The House of

Terror opened in 2002 as a pet project of right-wing leader Viktor Orbán under his first tenure as prime minister. He returned to power in 2010 and remains a controversial figure today. The House of Terror is one of dozens of museums of communism (and often fascism as well) created in Central and Eastern Europe following its fall in 1989 and the upsurge of memory that accompanied the crumbling of the ideology and its totalitarian rule. As a political project of Hungary's right-wing Fidesz Party, the House of Terror is a deeply political—and problematic—institution. It has embraced many international memorial museum tropes to tell its story of Hungarian suffering in a way that demonstrates how blatantly the memorial museum form can be exploited for political use. However, while the House of Terror's politics are worn on its proverbial sleeve, it is not alone in being driven by a political agenda and importantly reminds us of the deeply political nature of *all* memorial museums.

The fourth chapter focuses on the Kigali Genocide Memorial Centre, which opened in 2004 to mark the tenth anniversary of the 1994 Rwandan genocide. Created under the auspices of the Aegis Trust, a British antigenocide organization, the Kigali Centre clearly shows the internationalization of the memorial museum form. The museum was inspired by Holocaust museums, including Yad Vashem in Israel and the USHMM and not only utilizes increasingly common memorial museum components but also contextualizes the Rwandan genocide among others in an exhibit on twentieth-century genocide, a seeming example of the transnational, "multidirectional" nature of memory today (Rothberg 2009). In Rwanda, the effort to promote peace, reconciliation, and "never again" remains real and urgent, and the museum takes seriously its role as a site of moral education. However, its ambitious work to prevent future genocide and ethnic conflict is undermined by the troubling politics of Rwanda under the powerful leadership of President Paul Kagame, at once praised for rebuilding a broken nation and harshly criticized for his antidemocratic policies and practices. At the moment of writing, Kagame has changed the nation's constitution to allow him to serve a third term, threatening Rwanda's fragile democracy and peace. And Kagame justifies each of his antidemocratic acts by using the memory of the genocide.

The fifth chapter follows the memorial museum form to Latin America where, despite being at the vanguard of the contemporary human rights movement, relatively few memorial museums have been constructed. The recent, most high-profile exception is the Museo de la Memoria y los Derechos Humanos, the Museum of Memory and Human Rights (MMHR), in Santiago, Chile, which opened in January 2010 as the national site for remembrance and education about the dictatorship of Augusto Pinochet from 1973 to 1990. The MMHR was a project of Michelle Bachelet's first presidency from 2006 to 2010. Bachelet was herself imprisoned and tortured under the junta, and the museum likely would not have been realized without her strong political will driving the project. The museum is an excellent example of the crystallization of the memorial museum form in that it adheres to all the norms and expectations of commemoration using this cultural form. However, because of the museum's political provenance and the still-divided politics of Chile today, the museum fails to give sufficient historical context for Chile's recent past in a way that is deeply problematic. Without this context, the museum seems a somewhat empty gesture.

The book's global tour of memorial museums ends in New York City with the National September 11 Memorial Museum, which opened in May 2014. In one of the most deliberative and planned memory processes, the museum was the result of numerous consultations, focus groups, community meetings, and a multiyear "Conversation Series," becoming a twenty-first-century model of the internationally agreed-upon best practices in the creation of a memorial museum. Its debt to Holocaust memorialization is evident in everything from its monumental memorial architecture to the minutiae of artifacts on display (eyeglasses, ID cards), and the museum echoes memorial museums around the world in the set of tropes now commonly recognized. However, 9/11 as an act of twenty-first-century terrorism that was witnessed by an estimated two billion people around the globe, coupled with the museum's location in the heart of the financial center of NYC and its status as a premier tourist destination all greatly challenge the memorial museum form. This chapter thus brings the memorial museum form into the twenty-first century, examining how the form changes in response to a changing world.

The final chapter analyzes my findings and outlines the three primary functions that memorial museums are created to fulfill. First, they are a form of historical truth-telling, intended to preserve the past and serve as a record, complete with material and documentary evidence, of what happened. Second, they are meant to be places of healing and restoration. They are memorials and, as such, serve as symbolic reparations for the individuals, communities, and nations that were injured. Finally, and most importantly, they are intended to be spaces for the moral education of their publics. Not only do memorial museums intellectually educate their audiences about "history," but they also seek to emotionally reach their visitors in order to transform them morally so that they embrace the ethic of "never again." Behind each museum is the claim that it is an essential part of building democratic culture and preventing future violence and atrocity through its creation of a more informed moral public that will work toward these goals. However, the politics behind each museum belie these utopian goals.

PROMISES AND LIMITS

This project began with an effort to identify and describe how the new, global memorial museum form addresses and deals with a pressing normative challenge: the trauma and lasting impact of past violence, genocide, and atrocity on present societies. Memorial museums are new in both content and form. Their focus on what is most painful in the past reflects an effort to critically engage with past violence to build a more tolerant, democratic culture through the promotion of human rights and an ethic of "never again." That this particular cultural form of commemoration is increasingly being used globally as one of the central mechanisms for addressing past violence suggests that it is believed to be an especially effective mode for critical engagement with the past that can translate into a more democratic and peaceful present and future. However, my research reveals that the reality behind the creation of memorial museums is much more complicated than those initial assumptions suggest. In fact, memorial museums reflect much more on the present regimes that build them than they do actually confront the past.

The existence of memorial museums suggests that memorials alone are insufficient and that memory of the past must be supplemented with history in order to come to terms with and understand the past. This raises the questions of what demands the past makes on the present that necessitate such a robust form of remembrance and what these new commemorative forms tell us about present societies' relationships to the past and the future. Memorial museums' goal of preventing future violence reflects the prevalent assumption today that there is a causal relationship between learning about past violence and preventing it in the future. But there is no evidence to suggest that this is the case; genocide and political violence continue, though monuments, museums, and memory projects vowing "never again" proliferate. Nevertheless, memorial museums have become important transitional justice mechanisms in societies undergoing democratic transformation, suggesting that confronting and remembering the past is imperative for building democracy. This is why memorial museums bestow legitimacy upon the regimes that build them and are so popular around the world. However, as the five examples in the following pages demonstrate, there are fundamental flaws to these assumptions and serious limits to what the form can deliver. Rather than educating about the past, memorial museums reveal the political priorities and goals of the regimes that build them, reminding us that memory remains very much in the domain of the nation-state, with the past being simply another arena for enacting present politics.

1 · MEMORIAL MUSEUMS

The Emergence of a New Form

In Ggolo, Uganda, ground has been broken for a new memorial museum focused on the 1994 genocide in neighboring Rwanda (Muramira 2016). Though Rwanda has an active program of genocide memorialization, including the national memorial museum discussed in chapter 4, the Ugandan museum will be the first of its kind outside of Rwanda and reflects the desire for memory and education about the genocide to extend beyond national borders, much like how the bodies of genocide victims that were tossed into Rwanda's rivers and ended up on the shores of Uganda's Lake Victoria had crossed national borders. Across the globe, in Phnom Penh, Cambodia, the Documentation Center of Cambodia (DC-Cam), the leading organization in documenting and preserving the history of the Khmer Rouge genocide, is creating the Sleuk Rith Institute, a permanent memorial museum, documentation center, and campus for research, study, and memory of the Cambodian genocide in a stunning building designed by Zaha Hadid. Though Cambodia is dotted with grim sites of detention and massacre, where bones and other remnants of violence are visible reminders of the genocide, DC-Cam clearly finds it necessary to supplement these sites of memory and preservation in a way that provides a more permanent and robust space for mobilizing memory of Cambodia's suffering for purposes of education for the present and future. And on another continent, plans are under way to revamp the Memorial 68 in Mexico City, a small museum commemorating the 1968 massacre of hundreds of students and other civilians by the police and military. The renovation comes at a moment when many Mexicans are calling for justice and recognition in response to the political violence that has gripped the country in the last decade; driven by the need to connect political violence of the past to that of the present, the renovation reflects the belief that remembering and understanding past violence is necessary for staunching it in the present and preventing it in the future. These are just a handful of examples of memorial museums that have recently opened or are being planned or renovated around the world, demonstrating how the memorial museum has firmly established itself as a cultural form par excellence for remembering and teaching about past political violence.

The global proliferation of memorial museums is part of a recent, broader interest in the past that emerged in the second half of the twentieth century. With, and driving, this interest in memory came a shift in how societies relate to the past, from seeing the past as merely precedent to the nation's glorious future toward an emphasis on coming to terms with past violence and oppression. In response to the political demands of the negative past, memorial forms have been changing to more adequately address the past, contain its memory, and learn from it. Throughout the twentieth century, the paradigm of memorialization has evolved, and the new cultural forms of remembrance are not like their predecessors that dot the memorial landscape of the late nineteenth century—triumphant reminders of the glories of the nation-state. Rather, these new memorials are intended to remember and teach the lessons of the horrors of past conflicts, violence, and genocide, to ensure that that which society might most like to forget is never forgotten. And they appear, indeed, to be increasingly global in form and in content.

It is the purpose of this chapter to trace the emergence of memorial museums as new commemorative forms that reflect this new imperative that societies address past violence and human rights abuses. But looks can be deceiving. Written into the missions and goals of memorial museums are some fundamental tensions that exist in our desires and expectations vis-à-vis past, present, and future. The emergence of new memorial forms and the expectations of the memory that they contain are often at odds with the reality of the present in and by which they are created.

MEMORY AND MODERNITY'S CHALLENGES

Memorial museums are part of a larger "memory boom" that has characterized recent decades. An interest in memory has swept academia—with a proliferation of books, conferences, journals, and centers focused on a new interdisciplinary field of memory studies—and civil society with the rise of nongovernmental organizations (NGOs) and other institutions aimed at confronting past violence, enacting transitional justice, and commemorating the past. It also pervades popular culture in the form of museums and memorials, autobiographies and memoirs, and documentary and feature films and television shows on historical subjects. Memorial museums are one such manifestation of this memory boom—an extremely popular one. Almost everywhere memorial museums are created, they become one of the most popular tourist destinations, demonstrating that it is not just academics but the general public that is interested in memory of past violence.[1]

While memory as an academic field and subject of popular interest surged only recently, memory has been of interest for as long as humans have been self-aware, though it was often framed as tradition, heritage, or identity. With Maurice Halbwachs's groundbreaking theory of social memory in 1925, traditional views of the past as an existential reality that lives within individual memory and shapes the present were radically challenged.[2] Halbwachs argued instead that memory is acquired, recollected, and articulated solely within society and that without social frameworks, such as language, individuals are not capable of memory. Because of this, the past is always reconstructed by and in the present, and memory is simply "a reconstruction of the past achieved with data borrowed from the present" (1980, 69). Though Halbwachs's work remained dormant for many years as the Western world was rocked by World War II and its aftermath, it is his concept of collective memory and the past as a social construction that has largely shaped studies of memory today. However, Halbwachs never qualified his concept of collective memory and instead was more concerned with collective memory as a day-to-day social experience; so perhaps even more important than the rise of interest in memory is the focus of much of it on past violence.

Today's focus on the negative past has become a centerpiece of several important contemporary sociological theories of collective memory that together place a normative demand to confront past political violence at the center of national and international politics. Jeffrey Olick has termed this focus on the negative a "politics of regret." Observing the recent rash of public apologies, the spread of reparations, and the emergence of mechanisms that work to address past conflicts and atrocities like truth commissions, he concludes that "the past is very much on the public agenda, but it is more often a horrible, repulsive past than the golden ages so often the part of public discourse in previous centuries" (2007, 121–22). John Torpey similarly conceptualizes a "reparation politics," arguing that future-oriented, progressive politics have been replaced by the effort to "come to terms with the past" (2006; 2015).

Daniel Levy and Natan Sznaider (2006) go further, arguing that while this focus on the negative past began with attempts to come to terms with the Holocaust in Germany, the United States, and Israel, it has since evolved into a "cosmopolitan memory" that creates a transnational and transcultural "memory imperative" that shapes how individuals, groups, and societies around the world remember their own violent pasts and those of others. According to Levy and Sznaider, "The Holocaust sets the parameters for de-territorialized memoryscapes in Second Modernity, provides a model for national self-critique, serves to promote human rights as a legitimating principle in the global community, and plainly offers a negative example of dealing with alterity" (2006, 201). The memory imperative created by the Holocaust presents a set of normative expectations that shape how societies around the world confront their negative pasts, and it is increasingly global. The shared memory of the Holocaust created "a universal imperative, making the issue of universal human rights politically relevant to all who share this new form of memory" (Levy and Sznaider 2006, 132).

The centrality of memory focused on violence that is captured by these theories and evident in cultural forms like memorial museums is thus deeply linked to the emergence and global spread of a powerful human rights discourse that today dominates local and global politics. In the wake of the violence of World War II and the Holocaust, the Universal Declaration of Human Rights was adopted and began to lay the groundwork for a global human rights regime. Memory has been at the heart of the promotion and advocacy of human rights, especially in the aftermath of atrocity and mass violence. Andreas Huyssen traces the history of these two discourses as they intertwine through some of the key moments of the twentieth century: an awakening awareness of the atrocities of World War II and the Holocaust, the fall of communism in the Soviet Union (USSR) and Central and Eastern Europe, the end of the Latin American dictatorships and apartheid, and the late twentieth-century atrocities and genocides in the former Yugoslavia and Rwanda (2011, 610). Throughout the course of the century, human rights discourse emerged and consolidated, and with it, memory discourse as parallel ways of addressing past human rights abuses with the goal of preventing them in the future. As Huyssen argues, "The continuing strength of memory politics remains essential for securing human rights in the future" (2011, 621).

There are two assumptions about the ethical and moral obligation to remember that are at the heart of this connection between memory and human rights and form the basis of memorial museums' raison d'être. The first is what moral philosopher Jeffrey Blustein (2015; 2008) has referred to as the deontological or expressivist ethic of memory; that is, the idea that acknowledging human rights abuses and recognizing victims through memory is morally the correct and necessary response to violence, regardless of the outcome of this remembering. Memory has become a claim for recognition by groups that have been victimized, silenced, or oppressed and is increasingly considered to be a right for those who have suffered in the past and an obligation on the part of those who have not, whatever the consequences of that memory may be. Memory is thus considered to be healing and restorative when rights have been abused. The second assumption connects memory even more tightly to human rights and is what we can think about as memory's utilitarian or consequentialist function: the memory of past violence is considered one of the surest inoculations against future violence. As Blustein writes, "Remembering the victims of wrongdoing may be an essential part of the process of building and sustaining political structures that safeguard against a return to the wrongs of the past" (2008, 262). Confronting the past through remembrance provides the framework and standards for our understanding and promotion of human rights, meaning that there is a moral obligation to remember in order to protect and promote human rights. Of course, there is at the same time the very real possibility that "memory may also nurture human rights violations" (Huyssen 2011, 621); as history demonstrates, memory has been mobilized to incite violence perhaps almost as often as to prevent it (Barkan and Bećirbašić 2015; Rieff 2016).

Memorial museums, however, assume the positive functions of memory, and in them, we see both the expressivist belief that remembering is the good and correct thing to do as well as the consequentialist obligation to remember in order to prevent future violence and reinforce a culture that respects human rights. In this sense, memory is linked to democracy. In the words of Barbara Mizstal (2010), paraphrasing Adorno (1986), "Without memory, that is, without the checking of, and reflection upon, past records of institutions and public activities, we will have no warnings against potential dangers to democratic structures and no opportunity to gain a richer awareness of the repertoire of possibly [*sic*] remedies" (29).

With the spread of liberal democracy and the strengthening of a global human rights regime over the course of the second half of the twentieth century came a new set of demands from populations that had been marginalized or silenced in the past. The new "history from below" demonstrated that "focusing on the history of everyday life has not surprisingly illuminated the ongoing victimization of large segments of humanity along the lines of gender, class, and race discrimination" (Barkan 2003, 101). The new political power of minorities and marginalized groups also meant a new public validation for victims of various historical injustices. The emergent strength of victims, who today increasingly "write the history" in their demands for recognition and reparation, is clearly due to the growing emphasis on human rights throughout the twentieth century, but it also points to an important function of collective memory and identity. Today, many groups build their collective identities on a shared past of victimization, though often underpinned by the problematic notion that "victimization equals virtue" (Barkan and Bećirbašić 2015). This shift in political and moral power from the victors to the victims puts the negative past squarely in the center of present concerns. It also increasingly defines collective identities and present relationships and responsibilities to the past.

It is not surprising that victimization has become an important political, moral, and social tool, for the twentieth century created many, many victims. The numbers of victims of political violence alone are staggering (and this is to say nothing of structural violence)—an estimated 11 million in the Holocaust, 20 million under Soviet communism, 1.5 million in the Cambodian genocide, 800,000 in the Rwandan genocide, and the list goes on and on. An estimated 187 million people were killed or allowed to die throughout the war and conflict of the twentieth century (Hobsbawm 1994, 12). Granted, the abominations of slavery, colonization, and other violent wars and practices that preceded the twentieth century were no less and often far more terrible, but it was the mobilization of new technologies and powerful ideologies that made the wars and genocides of the twentieth century particularly destructive and that helped make it, in Hobsbawm's words, "the most murderous" (1994, 13).

What is most frightening about the horrors of the twentieth century is that those pillars of modernity that seemed most sacred—progress, science, technology—were precisely the weapons turned against civilian populations. If World War I was devastating because of the new technologies and weaponry that wrought destruction never before imagined possible, then World War II, with the lethal and particularly modern ideology underlying the fascist project, was even more devastating in its murder of the fundamental principles of modernity.[3] At the same time, unlike ever before, history and technology made the events much more accessible and available to the global public; it is not just that atrocities were taking place but that they were taking place before our eyes. As technologies and wars became deadlier, media and information became more widely available. While it seems that we might want to forget the horrors of that murderous century, in our particularly modern dilemma and despite all our knowledge and information about the past, we have been seized with the fear that it will disappear into oblivion.

The fear of forgetting underlines Blustein's notion of our moral obligation to remember. In many ways, remembering seems like the only thing that we can offer the millions of victims. Geoffrey Hartman writes about an "ethical impasse" that results from an excess of information, which "removes all excuse by taking away our ignorance, without at the same time granting us the power to do something decisive" (1996, 103). It is, in part, this moral helplessness in the face of tragedy that drives our incessant need to remember the negative past. Remembering is all we can do. This notion of a moral obligation to remember is at the heart of Daniel Levy and Natan Sznaider's theory of a cosmopolitan "memory imperative" shaped by the Holocaust; the demand to remember and confront the past is not just for victims but also for society and its future. They are not alone in arguing that the Holocaust has determined how societies relate to the past today and provided the tools and ethical framework for confronting violence and preventing it in the future. The Holocaust and World War II did, after all, result in the Universal Declaration of Human Rights and the UN Genocide Convention in 1948, and the trials of Nuremberg set the standard for international justice that has evolved over the course of the second half of the twentieth century, resulting in the establishment of the International Criminal Court in 2003. These mechanisms for recognizing and addressing human rights abuses and other injustices shape national and international politics today, and coming to terms with the past and this preoccupation with the negative past is increasingly viewed as "a positive transitional phenomenon" tied to liberal democratic norms (Cairns 2003, 66).

These norms that have emerged vis-à-vis remembrance and confrontation with past violence have "travelled" around the world (Erll 2011), suggesting that there is in fact a cosmopolitan or transnational memory culture that transcends national borders and connects people and groups from widely divergent backgrounds. In the field of memory studies, a dominant trend of the last few years—what Astrid Erll terms its "third phase" (2011)—has been to depart from what has been seen as its "methodological nationalism" and instead to focus on the movement of memory across nations and cultures. Variously described as "travelling memory" (Erll 2011), "transnational memory" (de Cesari and Rigney 2014), "multidirectional memory" (Rothberg 2009), and Levy and Sznaider's "cosmopolitan memory," these theories surmise that memory—its forms, contents, and modes—circulates across and beyond national borders, reflecting and producing a new form of global interconnectedness. These "transnational [memory] processes can unsettle established memory regimes, especially nation state-sanctioned ones, and can involve the production of new forms of remembering, forgetting and nostalgia, as well as novel modes whereby different types of actors select what to remember . . . and thus the generation of new forms of solidarity and division as mediated through memory processes" (Inglis 2016, 145). Thus our "moral helplessness" is turned into a positive construct for the present and future. The driving principles behind our relationship to the past like regret, responsibility, and coming to terms are envisioned to be a constructive new basis for how global, cosmopolitan citizens deal with the negative past in a way that transcends the nation-state and other hegemonic narrators of the past and works toward a better future. It is this very principle that is behind the creation of memorial museums: the belief that we can learn from past wrongs to create a better, more peaceful and democratic future.

However, it is clearly naïve to assume that we can learn—or have learned—from the negative past or that memory has indeed become denationalized in a way that is more democratic and inclusive and indicates a better future. "Never again" remains an empty ethical imperative in the face of new and changing forms of political violence occurring ceaselessly around the globe. As Astrid Erll cautions, "The global circulation of mnemonic media . . . may indeed effect a change of perspective in viewers from other parts of the world, lead to empathy, and trans-ethnic solidarity. But there is of course also the option of misuses, the hijacking, or distortion of transcultural memory" (2011, 15). Thus in some cases, memory of a negative past can help perpetuate violence in the present and future (e.g., chapter 6 on the 9/11 Museum; Barkan and Bećirbašić 2015). Or, as in the case of the Kigali Centre (chapter 4), collective remembering of negative pasts can silence alternative narratives and versions of the past and in this way further disenfranchise individuals and groups. Remembering according to today's "memory imperative" and the "politics of regret" is often simply a way to attain political legitimacy and appease the international community.[4] James Young warns us that "the motives of memory are never pure" (1993, 2). As tempting as it may be to imagine that there is a truly cosmopolitan memory culture that holds the potential to bridge difference and distance and bring people and groups around the world closer together, this overlooks the instrumental and often self-serving motives of collective remembering of violence, especially as it is embodied in institutions and cultural forms created and run by the state.

FORMS OF REMEMBERING

The shift to an emphasis on the negative past has led to the emergence of new mechanisms for dealing with the past and its victims and perpetrators, such as truth commissions and reparations. In fact a whole new field of study and practice related to dealing with the negative past—transitional justice—has emerged and become a popular enterprise around the world. The shift has also changed the cultural forms that our memories and commemorations take. In response to the many difficulties that the past has posed to the present, commemorative forms have been changing as societies struggle to find appropriate ways to remember. The memorialization process itself has become a subject of substantial scholarly and practical inquiry; debates abound about the proper way to remember the past, and many new organizations are working in the field of memorialization—what we might call an international memory regime—seeking to harness the most effective memorial practices. And increasingly, memorials and other commemorative forms are considered integral parts of the transitional justice "tool kit."[5]

Monuments from the nineteenth and early twentieth centuries were blatantly built for the nation-state, an integral part of what Benedict Anderson calls "official nationalism" (1991). They were triumphant and celebratory symbols of a nation's courageous past, erected to memorialize the nation's heroes in order to create an imposing sense of shared history for a population being consolidated around the idea of the nation. Commemorative forms were intended to condense the (positive) moral lessons learned from the past and tie up loose ends so that the present could move on along its steady path of progress (Savage 1999). Because monuments and memorials of this era were intended to be celebratory and to inculcate a unified sense of a great history, difficult or controversial subjects were avoided. As Renan (1882) reminds us, forgetting is "a crucial factor in the creation of the nation," which was a future-looking enterprise.

The totalitarian regimes of the twentieth century used similar hegemonic and monolithic memorial forms to utilize the past for their present and future purposes: imposing figures, grand architectural arches and pillars, and portraits of the heroes of the ideological movement. Communism, especially, created thousands of monuments to itself as an ideology, while at the same time erasing and rewriting the past according to its present needs. And central to both fascism and communism was the attempt to erase even the memory of their victims, so as to leave no trace. The totalitarian ideologies of the twentieth century manipulated the past and memorial forms to such a degree that, upon their fall, old commemorative forms could no longer legitimately be used by governments and regimes that wished to enter the liberal democratic political sphere (Young 2005). Faith in modernity and the march of progress was irreversibly shaken, and traditional commemorative forms were found to be no longer adequate for addressing the negative past with the requisite political regret.

The forms in which memory is embodied are thus very important in shaping collective memory and its meaning. Robin Wagner-Pacifici has written extensively on the cultural forms of collective memory, arguing that "meaning emerges and is sustained through the dynamic interaction between the content of historical events and the forms of collective memory available to those intent on their preservation and public inscription" (1996, 301). Thus while the past is an existential reality, cultural and collective meaning are made of past events through their embodiment in cultural forms. However, some events challenge "the adequacy of the available forms to the specific contents of historical events" (1996, 305). These "limit cases" necessitate new cultural forms better able to remember complicated pasts. One such event is the Holocaust, as we shall see in the next chapter; another example is the Vietnam War. Wagner-Pacifici's work on form and genre is excellently illustrated in her study with Barry Schwartz on the Vietnam Veterans Memorial, a war memorial that presents a "genre problem" in that it must commemorate a war the United States did not win (1991). And yet Maya Lin's memorial rises to the challenge and is a paradigm of a new commemorative form: it remembers the past with ambivalence, allowing for multiple interpretations and alternative versions of the past, and it encourages interaction and participation with the memorial and with memory. The Vietnam Veterans Memorial is viewed by many as one of the first examples of the shift in memorialization that occurred in the second half of the twentieth century, emerging with the politics of regret (Young 2005). Following it, a whole new set of practices and principles for memorializing have developed that go beyond the Vietnam Memorial's ambivalence and doubt and instead actively seek to use the past to promote human rights, democracy, reconciliation, and peace.

Around the world, especially in countries and societies emerging from conflict, memorials are increasingly used in tandem with other transitional justice mechanisms like truth commissions, trials, and reparations and are a central mechanism for dealing with past violence, human rights abuses, and atrocities (Bickford and Sodaro 2010). They are forms of symbolic reparation that can be used in situations where more robust transitional justice measures are not possible. They are also symbols erected by governments and other groups to acknowledge victimization and past wrongs. Rooted in the assumption that remembering the past is healing, they demonstrate regret for the negative and atrocious past, but they also promise a better future contingent on learning the lessons of the past; they attempt to be Levy and Sznaider's memory imperative built in stone. And they are efforts at attaining legitimation, internationally and internally. Though there are many examples around the world, memorial museums are among the most prominent of these new commemorative forms working to build peace and democratic culture.

MEMORIAL MUSEUMS AS A NEW COMMEMORATIVE FORM

Memorial museums embody this new ethos for dealing with the past. The very concept of memorial museum implies that a memorial alone cannot fully address the past, and so the museum form is utilized. While memorials can create solemn spaces for remembrance (such as the Vietnam Veterans Memorial); active sites for participatory memory (such as the Monument to Fascism in Hamburg, Germany, which invited visitors to write messages on it as it slowly disappeared into the ground [Sturken 1997; Young 2005]); or challenging spaces that are open to interpretation or reflection (such as the Memorial to the Murdered Jews of Europe in Berlin [e.g., Dekel 2013]), museums have the force of history on their side. Not only are they able to collect and display the physical remnants of the past, preserving it for posterity, but they can also tell the story of the past, imparting knowledge and understanding. Though they use the material culture of the past, memorial museums are most often not located on the sites of atrocity. The memorial museums that are constructed on the historic sites of atrocity—like the House of Terror and the 9/11 Museum, in this book—go beyond mere preservation of the site as evidence of what happened. Instead, through built-out spaces and sophisticated architectural and exhibition designs, they attempt to be more universal spaces in which the broader implications and reverberations of the past can be explored. They are thus not simply historic sites, museums, or memorials, but memorial museums.

That they are museums is important to the work they do and their privileged status in society. In addition to being spaces for education and preservation, museums play a number of other important roles in society. They are spaces in which the "ritual of citizenship" is played out, and individuals learn what it means to belong to a group or nation (Duncan 1991). They are "exhibitionary complexes" in which society learns self-regulation and discipline (Bennett 1999). They are vital public spaces for the building and fostering of identities of communities and nations (Karp 1992). And perhaps most importantly, museums have a "legitimizing function" (Huyssen 1995, 16). They are imbued with authority and widely considered to be trustworthy sources for information.[6] Memorial museums are so popular because they capitalize on all these functions of museums.

However, part of what separates them from history museums of the nineteenth century that served similar functions is that they provide a new kind of interactive engagement with the past that constitutes a whole new category of "experiential" museum.[7] Museums today are changing. In order to appeal to our media-saturated society, especially young generations, the museum itself has become a form of mass media, geared toward a society that is increasingly looking for what Andreas Huyssen calls "emphatic experiences [and] instant illumination" (1995, 14). Experiential museums are focused more on teaching and creating an experience for the visitor than they are on the traditional museological functions of collecting and displaying. Rather than simply telling the story of the past, memorial and other experiential museums seek to make the visitor "experience" it. Driven by a narrative or a concept, such as the story of the Holocaust or the concept of human rights, experiential museums use multimedia and interactive displays to draw the visitor into the story that they are telling, making the visitor play an active role and identify with the story's characters. The stories they tell are more important than the objects contained and displayed by the museums, though artifacts and other material remains and reproductions are essential to infusing the story with both authenticity and emotional impact.

There are a number of common exhibitionary strategies and tropes that memorial museums use to create this interactive, experiential engagement with the past. They almost always use a controlled circulation path, meaning the visitor is deposited at the beginning and led through the exhibition so that it unfolds according to the exhibition designer's intent; often along this path there are few or discreet chances to exit. The story of the past as told in these museums generally proceeds chronologically, using text, photographs, artifacts, and documentary footage to chronicle the history in a richly detailed way that tells an apparently complete story for visitors who might not know it. Most memorial museums include interactive elements, like touch screens and headphones or parabolic speakers,[8] that let the visitor create her own experience, within a carefully scripted narrative. Echoing today's distrust of traditional memorial forms and historical narratives, memorial museums seek to create a more subjective and individualized experience for their visitors.

In addition to the history that is told through text, photos, and artifacts, memorial museums use other, more experiential techniques to make the past more visceral and present; memorial museums rely on affect and emotion to reach their visitors. Lighting and architecture create spaces of claustrophobia and exposure, and haunting ambiance and sound effects—music, testimony, historical speeches, and political rallies—help round out the "experience" of the past. Spaces are reconstructed, like the cattle cars, concentration camps, and ghettos of the Holocaust or the torture cells used for political prisoners by the communist secret police or the military junta, and visitors are encouraged to enter these spaces to feel for themselves the victims' suffering. And to further encourage identification and empathy, an emphasis throughout the exhibits is placed on individual victims and survivors: photographs; names; personal effects like clothing, shoes, identity cards, and other belongings; and video and audio testimony from survivors help make the individual victims real and present to visitors, making the entire experience more visceral and immediate. One of the most distinguishing features of memorial museums is that they are very much victim-oriented institutions that seek to put the individual at the center of memory of the negative past, reflecting victims' privileged position in today's politics of regret. Memorial museums also share a set of common memorial elements like eternal flames, walls of names, and memorial sculptures and other works of art that ensure that their commemorative functions are fulfilled. All these elements together make the memorial museum a new cultural form with a novel set of functions: it is intended to give the visitor an intense, affective, and emotional experience that will help her identify and empathize with the victims in a way that will morally educate her to work to prevent future violence, repression, and hatred. And all these common tropes—found in memorial museums across the globe—reflect the ways in which "forms, and practices of memory" circulate and "travel . . . across social, linguistic and political borders" (Erll 2011, 11).

In this way, memorial museums attempt to create what Alison Landsberg termed "prosthetic memory" in the visitor: a "personal, deeply felt memory of a past event through which he or she did not live" (2004, 2). Going further than history museums that impart knowledge about the past, memorial museums use experiential techniques and affect to make visitors feel that they have had a personal experience of the past that will shape their present moral sensibility. This prosthetic memory, because it places the individual in the proverbial shoes of the other who has experienced the traumatic event, creates empathy in the visitor. For Landsberg, this prosthetic memory "has the ability to shape that person's subjectivity and politics" based on empathy and understanding of others and so holds promise for a new form of ethical political engagement (2004, 2). In this, they represent radical departures from more traditional museums or memorials and are very much a product of the technology and media age in which we live. They are forms of mass culture intended to create prosthetic memory in their visitors that will ethically alter the individual to internalize the moral messages of the museum.

Memorial museums, as if highlighting the limitations of more traditional modes of remembering, thus fulfill a wide variety of commemorative functions. They are at once massive archives of historical knowledge, housing artifacts, documents, photographs, and film footage; memorial spaces devoted to the memory of the victims; emotional journeys designed to experientially re-create the past for the visitor and leave them with a prosthetic memory; and educational institutions that seek to teach the visitor about the past in order to instill in her the moral imperative of "never again." Most have broad mandates that go well beyond their exhibitions, and they seek to play active roles in their local, national, and global communities. They collect and archive survivor testimony and support new scholarship and research. They hold teacher trainings and conferences intended to disseminate knowledge and understanding about the past. They work with governments and NGOs to educate about the past and prevent future violence and atrocity. And they attract millions of visitors each year, making them increasingly visible and important cultural centers in the places in which they are built. Because of the broad scope of memorial museums' functions, they aim to attract broad and diverse publics and become spaces for public debate and discussion about the past, the present, and the future. In the words of Silke de Arnold-Simine, the (memorial) museum has become something of a "panacea" that "promises to offer democratic and inclusive approaches to difficult pasts, to preserve the collective memory of a generation of first-hand witnesses, to channel public debates and to regenerate urban and rural areas" (2013, 8).

We can surmise that from the rate at which they are being reproduced around the globe, memorial museums are believed to be highly effective in fulfilling these functions and coming to terms with a difficult past. They can be sophisticated and elaborate national initiatives, such as the US Holocaust Memorial Museum (USHMM) in Washington, DC, or small, local projects, such as the District Six Museum in Cape Town, South Africa, which commemorates the forced removal of thousands from their homes in the District Six neighborhood of Cape Town. They have proliferated in Eastern and Central Europe to commemorate the victims of fascism and communism; there are museums in the Baltic countries, Poland, Hungary, Czech

Republic, former East Germany, and Georgia and plans for new museums throughout the region. They have transformed former sites of detention from Phnom Penh, Cambodia, to Rosario, Argentina, into sites of memory and learning. Memorial museums remember genocide in Rwanda and Armenia, nuclear destruction by the United States in Japan, and the poison gassing of the Kurds by Saddam Hussein in Halabja, Kurdistan. They are literally emerging all over the world, and their proliferation around the globe implies that any country emerging from a difficult past needs such a mechanism to address the past if it wishes to be a legitimate political player in the international (Western, liberal democratic) scene.

CONCLUSION

Out of the detritus of the violent twentieth century have emerged a new set of memorials that regretfully acknowledge what is negative and abhorrent in the past. Memorial museums in particular attempt to burden their visitors with responsibility—if not for the past, then for the future—and empathy for their fellow human beings. They are attempts to make up for the grave errors of the past in the only way possible: they are Arendtian "promises" to the future made by societies to guarantee that never again will such violence and atrocity be allowed. As Hannah Arendt describes it, the promise is a form of social contract that allows us to live together in the world (1958, 244). We cannot take back actions previously committed, but we can promise not to do harm again in the future. Thus the nations and groups that build memorial museums seek to demonstrate to the rest of the world and to their own populations their commitment to a different future. While they cannot undo what has been done "out of the 'darkness of the human heart'" (Arendt 1958, 244), memorial museums can attempt to create a new contract with their people, with humanity, and with future generations that such acts will not be allowed in the future. They are intended to be a sort of "prosthetic conscience" for all of society. This is a very large commitment on the part of these museums and reflects and supports the claim that political legitimation increasingly relies on coming to terms with the past. The nations and groups that build these promises to the future are demonstrating to the international community their present and future adherence to international standards, increasingly universal norms of human rights, and democratic values.

What does this tell us, then, about our relationship to the past that we believe the construction of a memorial museum can serve as a promise that violence will not be allowed in the future? One thing it demonstrates is that—contrary to Halbwachs—the creators of these museums embrace the notion that the past does exist and can teach us something. The presumption is that by uncovering, displaying, and telling the "truth" about what happened in the past, something will be learned in the present that will shape a better future. But the museums are created in and by the present, often with deeply political motives that shape the past as they tell it and so belie this notion of the existential truth of the past.

This reveals a fundamental tension in our present relationship to the past and in much of the recent literature about memory: on the one hand, we have a postmodern skepticism of those modern concepts that let society down in the violent twentieth century. Modern beliefs about progress, the objectivity of history, and even truth have been shaken by the failure of modernity and its dark ideologies, leading us to this regretful relationship to the past from which memorial museums emerge. Where once the (glorious) future was the social and political way of ordering and orienting the world and the past was simply tradition that was incorporated into everyday life, today the future is uncertain and the past becomes the primary field for enacting and ordering politics and life. Memorial museums, then, are central to this ordering of our world vis-à-vis the past.

On the other hand, however, the active efforts of memorial museums and other commemorative and transitional justice mechanisms to learn the lessons of the past in order to shape the present and future demonstrate that we continue to hold onto the very modern notion that progress is possible. In the words of Levy and Sznaider, contemporary mechanisms for dealing with the past seek to "continue the project of modernity by retaining some of its normative quests for a better and a just life" (2010, 7). The idea that learning the lessons of the past will help us avoid the same mistakes in the future is one of the foundational principles behind the creation of memorial museums, but ironically it is rooted in modernity's optimistic belief that through knowledge and education, society's ills can be ameliorated, prevented, and ultimately eradicated.[9] Thus these postmodern museums are built upon modern assumptions about the preventability of social evils that continue to order our present relationship to the past.

A closer examination of memorial museums—why and how they are conceived and created, how they exhibit and narrate the past, and what roles they play or attempt to play in their societies—sheds light on this fundamental tension within memory studies and practice of how and whether the "truth" of the past is accessible and useful to us today. It reveals the potential and limits of some of our present presumptions regarding the past. Violence, atrocity, and genocide continue to rage around the world, despite robust efforts at remembering. Thus we need to understand not only what is behind this urgent need to remember but especially the limits of memory's ability to aid in the prevention of violence, promotion of democracy, and promise of peace.

2 · THE UNITED STATES HOLOCAUST MEMORIAL MUSEUM

The Creation of a "Living Memorial"

The US Holocaust Memorial Museum (USHMM) was dedicated by President Clinton in 1993 as a new kind of museum and memorial—one that would go beyond preserving the past and remembering the victims, instead working as a "living memorial" intended to "stimulate leaders and citizens to confront hatred, prevent genocide, promote human dignity, and strengthen democracy" (Clinton 1993). Clinton spoke of it as "an enduring tribute to democracy," from which we could "learn the lessons [of the Holocaust] and transmit those lessons from generation to generation," by seeking to "find in our diversity our common humanity" (1993). Harvey Meyerhoff, chairman of the US Holocaust Memorial Council, spoke of the museum's ability to demonstrate the "awful consequences of bigotry, oppression, hatred and intolerance." The museum was there, he said, to teach the American people "about the responsibilities that each of us has as citizens of a democratic society," those responsibilities that would ensure "liberty and justice for all" (Meyerhoff 1993).

The museum had been first conceived fifteen years earlier, in 1978, when an anxious President Carter, worried about alienating the important community of Jewish voters, formed a presidential commission to recommend an appropriate American memorial to the victims of the Holocaust. The idea of an American memorial to the Holocaust was controversial from the start. However, Carter's commission believed that "Americans have a distinct responsibility to remember the Holocaust," not only because the US army had liberated many camps, but also because America had stood by passively for years while the Nazis annihilated the European Jews: America, as a leader of the free world, must remember her indifference and work to prevent any such tragedy from happening again.[1]

The commission also believed that a mere monument or memorial would not accomplish this goal. The commission's report says, "While a monument alone may commemorate the victims, no structure can fully reveal the process that culminated in extermination; nor can it document the awesome dimensions of the crime or analyze its causes and implications." Rather, they wanted to create a "living memorial" that could serve as "a moral compass to keep America on course" (Bloomfield, qtd. in Linenthal 1995, 65). And so this memorial was intended not only to honor and remember the victims but also to create a lasting, permanent record of the past that could stand up to any future attempts at historical revisionism, to educate the public about the causes and implications of the Holocaust, as well as to morally educate its audience to work to prevent such atrocity from happening again in the future.

The idea of a "living" memorial that would harness the memory of the past in a way that would shape the future was quite a new proposal, and the breadth of these goals that the commission set for the memorial necessitated an entirely new form of memorialization; one that not only would work within today's "regretful" politics and incorporate responsibility, regret, and empathy but would also actively work to build a better future. A memorial alone was deemed insufficient to accomplish the commemorative and educative goals of the commission, and so, after fifteen long years of discussions, debates, and planning, the USHMM opened as a very new kind of institution.

In this chapter, I examine the USHMM as an exemplar of a new cultural form of commemoration that marks a peak in efforts to find new ways to memorialize and educate about past atrocity, especially the Holocaust. First, I briefly outline early approaches to Holocaust memorialization, including the sites of destruction themselves and Yad Vashem in Israel. I then focus on the conception and development of the USHMM, which sheds light on why this new form emerged and what exactly it is intended to do, as well as the particular politics that shaped the museum. Finally, I examine the USHMM's exhibitions and strategies to understand how, as a memorial museum, it seeks to use the memory of the Holocaust to prevent future violence and build a better, more democratic future. However, as Jennifer Hansen-Glucklich reminds us, a Holocaust museum like the USHMM "reveals the national Holocaust ideology of its context, including the way that the Holocaust is framed within the country's 'civil religion'" (2014, 23). Like the other memorial museums examined in this book, the USHMM reveals much more about America's attitude toward its past—and especially its present—than it does about the historical event that it recounts.

THE HOLOCAUST'S CHALLENGE TO MEMORIALIZATION: TO COMMEMORATE AND PRESERVE

From the moment the Nazi labor, concentration, and death camps were liberated, the challenge of memorializing the millions of victims of the Holocaust arose. The earliest Holocaust memorials were makeshift markers erected in the camps and on the sites of massacres and battles by the prisoners and survivors who wished to remember those who had perished and by the American, Soviet, and British soldiers who liberated the camps and wished to remember their comrades who were killed in the brutal war (Young 1993, 49). These wooden obelisks, stone markers, and handmade plaques were the first efforts to remember the victims before the Holocaust became known as the Holocaust and well before its impact would be fully felt. These were memorials in honor of those who had died; their purpose was not unlike a headstone in a cemetery, though they were intended to remember multitudes.

Together with this impulse to remember was an impulse to preserve and to document evidence of the atrocities. Even before the end of World War II, in November 1944, Majdanek, a Nazi concentration camp outside of Lublin, Poland, was turned into a memorial and museum. The purpose then, which holds today, was to "cultivate the memory and promote historical education . . . particularly by means of *commemorating* the victims, *preserving* the relics and *documenting* the history of the concentration camp at Majdanek and the death camp in Bełżec" (my emphasis, Majdanek). Just one year later, in 1945, the Polish Committee of National Liberation granted the same status to Stutthof, the first Nazi camp created in Poland,

and to Auschwitz-Birkenau (Young 1993, 120). In Germany as well, those camps that were not turned into refugee camps or prisons were left as they were found for the purpose of preservation and education about the incomprehensible: American soldiers led memorial tours through Buchenwald; in Dachau, they put up an exhibit of graphic photographs from the camp (Young 1993, 75). As the American soldiers photographed and recorded what they found to rally Americans around their just cause,[2] so too the impulse immediately following the end of the war seemed to be to preserve the camps as evidence of the crimes committed and justification for the brutal end to a terrible war.

This double impulse to commemorate as well as preserve and document the truth of what happened has endured through the decades of debate and discussion about how to memorialize the Holocaust and is evident in examples from the sites of destruction themselves and those far removed. The drive behind the desire to commemorate is clear. For all of their existence, humans have found ways to remember and honor those who have died. However, the need to balance commemoration with efforts to preserve and document what happened with the urgency and fervor with which it has been done is new. As the world struggled to make sense of the incredible atrocity that was the Holocaust, material evidence that documented the scale of the Nazi destruction—like the barracks where prisoners were inhumanely confined; the remains of the crematoria the Nazis had tried to destroy; the shoes, eyeglasses, hairbrushes, suitcases, clothing, and other personal effects stolen from the victims; and the piles upon piles of hair shaved from the victims' heads—took on an importance not seen in prior efforts at commemorating war (or other) dead. In this way, sites and their material remains were mobilized to tell certain stories and provide evidence of particular crimes. Thus the persistent moral obligation to remember the dead met with what Jeffrey Blustein deems remembrance's "duty of justice" to preserve the past in the effort to shape the present and future (2015, 75).

Throughout Europe, these sites of destruction were variously preserved and interpreted in ways that would tell particular narratives of victimization, persecution, and resistance according to present needs and politics. In Germany, initially many of the memorials erected were to celebrate and commemorate those who had resisted Nazi policies and rule. In the death and concentration camps that were turned into sites of memory and education in Poland—Auschwitz being most notable—the narrative was of Polish suffering under fascist rule until the fall of communism in 1989; framed by the communist leadership, with an emphasis on the victimization of Polish citizens, the story of the Jewish genocide went untold for decades. In a very different context, the Anne Frank House in Amsterdam, which opened to the public in 1960, told stories of the horrors of occupation and the universal suffering under Nazi rule as embodied by the iconic Anne Frank—a not-very-Jewish German-Dutch "everyteenager" who has become a "primary symbol of identification with the victims of the Holocaust" (Stier 2015, 101). And so it is no surprise that in other places deeply affected by the Holocaust and World War II, notably Palestine, though far removed from the sites of destruction, particular narratives were gaining traction and needed a home in which to be told.

From 1942, when the first reports of the mass killings in Europe made their way to Palestine, until the end of the war in 1945, in what would soon become Israel, a number of more ambitious programs of remembrance and documentation were proposed. Over the course of these three years, Mordechai Shenhavi, who had grown up in Eastern Europe and Russia before emigrating to Palestine in 1920, conceived, reconceived, and fought for a "national project" that would both commemorate the suffering and loss of the Jews of the Diaspora as well as firmly root memorialization of the Holocaust in the Zionist vision of redemption and rebirth (Brog 2002, 305). It would take several years to clarify his proposal and make it public, including gaining an understanding of what exactly was being commemorated, but in 1945 Shenhavi submitted a proposal to the Jewish National Fund in Palestine for the "Yad Vashem Foundation in Memory of Europe's Lost Jews: An Outline of a Plan for the Commemoration of the Diaspora" (Young 1993, 244).

More than just a memorial site, Yad Vashem was proposed to be a multidimensional remembrance and documentation site, and the first proposal already contained many of the elements that we continue to see in Holocaust and other memorial museums around the world: a hall of remembrance, a collection of names of those who perished, a research center, conference facilities, a museum, and of course, a memorial (Brog 2002, 324). Further, it was proposed to be far from the sites of destruction, built in what was Palestine to remember Europe's Jews, and envisioned as an integral part of the Zionist political goals: Yad Vashem "shall have two goals: a) everlasting historical documentation and b) a political and legal aim. . . . Its political value lies in the tangible basis that it will create for our demands: Look what they did to us" (Goldberg, qtd. in Brog 2002, 324–25).

It would take more than a decade before Yad Vashem would be built, and it continues to develop;[3] by the time it opened in 1953, it was no longer in Palestine but in Israel, adding another dimension to the memory work it was intended to do. In Israel memory of the Holocaust has a special meaning; as the state itself was born from the ashes of the Holocaust, so the memory of the Holocaust is present in every threat to Israel and her people as well as in every celebration of having a homeland at long last. The narrative of the Holocaust that Yad Vashem tells is one that is completely intertwined with the story of Israel, with a dual focus on both victimization and heroism and resistance (Cole 2000). Just as the earliest Holocaust memorials at the sites of destruction told the story of each country's or people's suffering, it inscribes "its visitors into a collective and national narrative" (Hansen-Glucklich 2014, 138).

In many senses, Yad Vashem is the first example of the memorial museum as a new form of commemoration. Much more than a memorial or a museum, its multidimensionality is evidence of a new approach to remembering and dealing with the negative past coming out of the pervasive political regret of the day. Remembering is no longer simply about the victims, though this is central; today, remembering past violence strives to activate that memory to build a community around democratic ideals that run counter to the persecutions and oppressions of the past, with the goal of preventing future violence and victimization.

THE HOLOCAUST IN AMERICAN LIFE

Just as the various political, social, and national contexts of Europe or Israel determined how the Holocaust was remembered, Holocaust memory in America has its own particular genealogy and emphasis. Unlike countries that experienced the Holocaust directly like Nazi-occupied Europe, and unlike Israel, which in many senses owes its existence to the Holocaust, the United States has no special, direct relationship to the Holocaust. With the exception of its role as bystander and later as liberator, the United States is far removed from the sites of the atrocities. And despite the fact that many Jewish survivors made their homes in the United States after the war, the Jewish American community makes up less than 3 percent of the population. Nevertheless, the Holocaust has found a place at the center of American consciousness, and memory of the Holocaust has experienced a tremendous boom in America in the past few decades. The opening of the USHMM in 1993 was something of a peak in this frenzy of memorialization, though memorials and museums continue to be erected throughout the country and the Holocaust shows no sign of budging from its central position in American memory and perceptions of the twentieth century.

Most of the American Jewish historiography of the postwar period focuses on an overwhelming silence vis-à-vis what would become known as the Holocaust; scholars have asserted that the American Jewish population engaged in a "conspiracy of silence" (Sorin 1997, 217) in which the Holocaust was "barely remembered [and] rarely mentioned" (Jick 1981, 308–9). Eager to forget the horrors of what had happened and to start a new life, the story goes, American Jews sought assimilation and the American Dream. This unwillingness to remember the Holocaust is argued to have been broken at last in the 1960s and 1970s by a series of events, including the publication of Raul Hilberg's *The Destruction of the European Jews* (1961), the capture of Adolf Eichmann in 1961 and his subsequent trial and execution in Jerusalem, Israel's Six-Day War in 1967 that has been argued to have "awakened dormant memories of the Holocaust" (Linenthal 1995, 9), the Yom Kippur War of 1973, and popular culture events such as the nine-and-a-half-hour NBC miniseries *Holocaust*, which aired in the United States in 1978, reaching an audience of more than one hundred million.

As entrenched as this narrative of an awakening of Holocaust awareness in the United States is, recent work by Hasia Diner (2009) has compellingly argued otherwise. In her book *We Remember with Reverence and Love: American Jews and the Myth of Silence after the Holocaust, 1945–1962*, Diner argues that American Jews had fully incorporated memory of the Holocaust into their collective lives and experiences well before the 1960s and 1970s. Though there was not yet an agreed upon name for the event—it was referred to variously as "the catastrophe," "the six million,"[4] or the "Hitler Holocaust," among others (Diner 2009, 21)—or set of practices and modes for memorializing the victims, Diner argues that Holocaust remembrance was very much part of Jewish life. Diner argues that in the 1960s and 1970s, when events like those outlined above encroached on Jewish—and American—life, the Holocaust began to take a more central place in not just Jewish communities but American society as well, and new modes of remembrance emerged. Thus when President Carter announced plans to create a US Commission on the Holocaust in 1978, this marked a shift in Holocaust remembrance in the United States from the "earlier disorganized, scattered and spontaneous" memorials of American Jewish communities to a new model of Holocaust commemoration distinguished by its "prominence, mammoth funding, and colossal size" (Diner 2009, 17). Though there are clear disagreements in historiographical analysis of the Holocaust's place in American Jewish life in the immediate postwar period, what cannot be denied is that by the end of the 1970s, the Holocaust had become a central part of American historical consciousness.

WHY A HOLOCAUST MUSEUM?

In 1978, at a ceremony celebrating Israel's thirtieth anniversary, President Jimmy Carter announced plans to set up a President's Commission that would make recommendations for the creation of a national memorial to the "six million who were killed in the Holocaust" (Novick 1999, 216). As is often the case with Holocaust memorials, especially in the United States, this was a political decision, prompted by Carter's increasing troubles with the Jewish community for his perceived lack of support for Israel. The president's alienation of the Jewish community through his sale of arms to Saudi Arabia and his support for the "legitimate rights of the Palestinian people" had the potential to be disastrous in his efforts for reelection; to placate the important Jewish community of voters, Jewish White House staff members suggested that the president propose a national memorial, as his "relations with the Jewish community need[ed] every boost possible" (Novick 1999, 217). So, out of political motivations, and with a keen eye to the Jewish response, the President's Commission was born to recommend an appropriate national memorial to the victims of the Holocaust.

It is important to note that from the start it was a Holocaust memorial that was proposed, not a museum or monument celebrating Jewish culture and history. A century ago, political placating would have likely taken the form of a celebratory monument, but with the rise of political regret and reparations politics, a memorial to the genocide of the Jewish people was deemed appropriate and effective. Further, the decision to build a Holocaust memorial in the nation's capital points toward the centrality of the

Holocaust as a reference to past violence that instills a moral obligation to remember. To justify a Holocaust memorial in the nation's capital, the museum would have to convey a more universal message than the destruction of European Jewry. Indeed, the construction of the USHMM suggests that Levy and Sznaider were correct in arguing that the Holocaust has created a "memory imperative" that shapes how individuals, groups, and societies around the world remember their own pasts and those of others. But what Levy and Sznaider overlook in their optimistic account of a cosmopolitan memory imperative is that memory is always political and can be easily co-opted by the nation-state to promote national political agendas.

The formation of the President's Commission thus marked not only the institutionalization of Holocaust memory in America but also its politicization in the form of a governmentally appointed body that would determine the shape of American memory of the Holocaust. The selection of Elie Wiesel as chairman of the commission perhaps determined, more than any other single factor, the shape that memory would take. Wiesel, a survivor, writer, and extremely important figure in the creation of America's reading of the Holocaust,[5] believed that the Holocaust is a "sacred mystery" that can only be understood by those who were there (Novick 1999, 211). Wiesel was also one of the most outspoken proponents of the uniqueness of the Holocaust.[6] Had another prominent American Jewish figure—like Simon Wiesenthal—been appointed, the museum might have looked much different.

Upon its formation, the President's Commission began to search for the best way to memorialize the event that many, especially Wiesel, believed to be unapproachable. In its research on Holocaust memorialization, the commission solicited advice from numerous groups, such as survivors and civic organizations and Polish American, Armenian, African American, and American Indian groups. Several members traveled to Europe and Israel to understand how the Holocaust was remembered and memorialized abroad, a pattern we will see replicated in each of the other museums in this book. Immediately, however, the question of the uniqueness of the Jewish Holocaust versus inclusion of other victims arose, and what was intended as a political gesture by President Carter to placate an important constituency turned into a fifteen-year struggle over the meaning of the Holocaust, ownership of the Holocaust, and the place of the Holocaust in American life.

The answer to the question of why a Holocaust museum, then, can be quite simple: it was an effort to bolster the support of the important and influential Jewish community in America. However, a national memorial to the victims of the Holocaust is one thing; a $168-million, state-of-the-art museum cum memorial that has attracted more than forty million visitors since its opening, steps from the National Mall, is quite another. How precisely Carter's political strategy turned into such a massive undertaking and resulted in such an elaborate institution is the next part of this chapter. Certainly the selection of Wiesel as chairman was one important decision that shaped the entire process of the creation of the museum. Though the White House would argue for inclusion over uniqueness, the museum is ultimately intended to remember "the six million Jews and millions of non-Jews who were murdered by the Nazis" (Weinberg, qtd. in Berenbaum 1993, xiv), and this politics of uniqueness would plague the process of its development. The museum's creation would also be challenged by the tension inherent in representing that which Wiesel and many others believed could not be represented. Each step of the way, the decisions made to address these and other problems shaped the way the Holocaust is remembered by and represented in the USHMM, and—as the USHMM serves as a model for memorial museums around the world—these decisions have helped produce the present form of memorial museums.

THE STRUGGLE TO CREATE AN AMERICAN HOLOCAUST MUSEUM

The decision to establish a national Holocaust memorial in Washington, DC, provoked a wide response from those groups who felt they had been victimized and should be represented in the museum. In order to convince the public that such a memorial deserved a place in the center of the nation's capital, amid the symbols of national pride and triumph, an emphasis in the museum had to be placed on American ideals such as pluralism, immigration, liberty, and tolerance. Thus members of Armenian, Romany, Polish, Ukrainian, Russian, and other groups who had been victimized felt that it was their right as American citizens to have their experience acknowledged in what would be one of the most prestigious Holocaust memorials in the world.

The demand by groups for recognition of their victimization is something new that, as we have seen, accompanied and even spurred the rise of political regret and its focus on coming to terms with the past. Victimhood attained a privileged status as previously marginalized groups sought recognition, and in doing so, they brought the negative past to the forefront of historical consciousness. As is well illustrated by the case of the USHMM, Olick and Coughlin argue that "memory and regret are not the result of the integration of the collectivity but of the impossibility of this in an age of competing claims, multiple histories, and plural perceptions" (2003, 56). The Holocaust, and in particular its commemoration in an American context, could be seen as what Levy and Sznaider describe as a "universal 'container' for memories of myriad victims" (2006, 195). However, this new opening up of the claims of memory to such a diversity of groups vying for recognition of victimization does not at all mean that memory is no longer a political tool that is wielded by the state; rather, it often makes memory an even more diffuse political strategy, and it leaves the past wide open as a battlefield for current political battles.

Because "memorials and museums represent public statements about what the past has been, and how the present should acknowledge it" (Hodgkin and Radstone 2003, 12), the stakes attached to recognition of victimization in the museum are clearly very high. The argument over inclusion is, indeed, over ownership of Holocaust memory. American national memory is made up of a plurality of narratives of those many groups who have made their homes in America. At the same time, to counter the assimilation that is inevitable in America, group identity reinforcements are necessary. The Holocaust, being viewed as a pivotal moment in American history, is therefore an important memory to "own."

In the beginning, it was primarily Polish American and Ukrainian American communities who fought hardest for representation on the Museum Council. Both argued that their people had been slated for extermination and should take their rightful place next to their Jewish counterparts on the council and in the museum itself. This presented a significant problem, though; despite the fact that many Poles and Ukrainians suffered at the hands of the Nazis, many looked the other way, and still others took active part in the murder of their Jewish neighbors. Though the Jewish council members were willing to "share" Holocaust memory to some degree, to sit on the council with members from nations that were perceived to have been complicit in Nazi crimes was seen as "disturbing, if not offensive"

(Berenbaum, qtd. in Linenthal 1995, 41). Nevertheless, the White House, in order to avoid "open controversy with concerned ethnic groups and their advocates in the Congress," remained firm on the issue of inclusion, expanding the council in the attempt to please everyone (Linenthal 1995, 43).[7]

It was not only reluctance to sit on the council with members of groups that had possibly persecuted Jews that worried Jewish council members but also suspicion of the motives behind their desire for representation on the council and involvement in the planning of the memorial. They feared the Americanization of the Holocaust and its politicization and eventual degradation. The sacred event that Wiesel saw as impossible to ever truly understand was falling into the realm of political maneuverings and seemed now to belong to any group that wished to lay claim to it. Many Jewish council members felt that they were losing their hold on the memorial that was supposed to honor the six million, especially as Romany and Armenian groups entered the struggle for inclusion in the museum's narrative. As one member Hyman Bookbinder warned, "Careful as we may be . . . the very inclusion of non-Jewish victims will be interpreted by the average viewer as meaning there were Jewish and non-Jewish victims of the Holocaust" (qtd. in Linenthal 1995, 54).

In the attempt to synthesize the arguments for and against the uniqueness of the victims, Michael Berenbaum, then project director of the USHMM, proposed that only through inclusion and comparison is it possible to truly see the uniqueness of the Jewish Holocaust. He claims that inclusion "deepens our moral sensitivity while sharpening our perception" and that "comparisons do not innately obscure the uniqueness of the Holocaust—they clarify it" (1989, 96). Instead of viewing inclusion as "submersion" of the Jewish experience, seeing the Holocaust from a universal perspective would carry its message beyond Elie Wiesel's sacred mystery, to all of humanity. Still a proponent of uniqueness, Berenbaum attempted to mollify both sides, and this was ultimately the approach that was adopted by the museum. Essentially Berenbaum proposed a hierarchy of victims, with Jews at the center and other victim groups radiating out.

In addition to struggles for inclusion, which, for the most part, were decided in favor of the Holocaust's uniqueness, there were other struggles and questions about how to represent the event that many believe is unrepresentable that helped shape the institution that is the USHMM today. Wiesel's idea was for the museum to express the impossibility of understanding the Holocaust: a place where "the sacred mystery that was the Holocaust would stamp itself on individual psyches, and visitors would, ideally, emerge with a renewed appreciation of its mystery" (Linenthal 1995, 122). Wiesel thus believed that the prosaic matters that were in fact an essential part of the planning would contaminate the sacredness of the event, but the museum's planners had to address these issues. Museum professionals were necessarily called in to actually make the museum work, but most survivors did not believe that they could ever understand the Holocaust enough to be entrusted with bringing their stories to the public (Linenthal 1995, 127). Thus several teams of museum professionals presented numerous plans for the museum in the nine years following its conception, all of which were rejected.

However, while survivors were worried that their stories could never be represented by those who were not there, it was understood by all that the purpose of the museum was to bring the story of the Holocaust to generations of (mostly) Americans who were not there and couldn't possibly understand; the museum would need to present the Holocaust as what James Young refers to as a "vicarious past" (2000). The museum *had* to tell the story of the Holocaust and *had* to render it comprehensible. Hence Jeshajahu Weinberg, the creator of the Museum of the Jewish Diaspora in Tel Aviv, was brought into the project, introducing the "conceptual" or "story-telling approach" that would most successfully blend a chronological, narrative approach with elements of Wiesel's mystery (Linenthal 1995, 128). Under Weinberg's leadership, in 1989 an exhibition team led by Michael Berenbaum was able to put together a story line for the permanent exhibit that was unanimously approved by the Council, and work was able to commence. Though numerous questions would continue to arise, such as how graphic the exhibit should be and how best to convey the horror of the Holocaust without putting off visitors, the major hurdles had been overcome.

The actual construction of the museum was perhaps the simplest part of its coming into being. Congress passed a bill allocating a plot of federal land on the National Mall, and James Ingo Freed's impressive design worked within the requirements for federal buildings located on the Mall. Although it is a federal institution, the museum was funded through private donations, which would have been a problem but for the outpouring of generosity of the American Jewish community. The museum was funded by the contributions of more than two hundred thousand private donators, mostly from the Jewish community. It was also these private membership contributions combined with federal funding that kept the museum's programs and operations running, though today the federal government has for the most part taken over operating costs. The importance of the museum to the American Jewish community is evidenced by the extraordinary amount of money that has been privately poured into it.

Though wildly successful today, there were many steps along the way when it looked as if the museum would never be realized. With each dilemma that arose, the project became more complicated. To address the difficult issues that surfaced throughout the fifteen years of the museum's development—questions of inclusion and representability, of necessity and sacredness, and of who the proper stewards of such an undertaking should be—the museum's council had to come up with ways to include other victims without dejudaizing the Holocaust, balance mystery with comprehensibility, and negotiate the tensions between museum professionals and Holocaust survivors. Throughout years of compromise and collaboration between a plurality of actors with divergent memories and agendas, the project grew, and today the USHMM is one of the largest Holocaust research, education, and memorial centers in the world. And because of these particularities of the context of its creation, the project evolved into the first self-conscious *memorial museum*, which has firmly planted itself at the center of American Holocaust consciousness and memory, telling a particularly American version of the Holocaust.

THE USHMM: AN AMERICAN HOLOCAUST

The USHMM is unlike any other museum, monument, or memorial on the National Mall. In the midst of Washington's bland, neoclassical landscape of democracy and freedom, James Ingo Freed's building stands as a symbol of mankind's ultimate inhumanity. Though throughout the facade, it maintains the requisite limestone of the surrounding architecture, beyond that facade, the building conveys the "essence" of the Holocaust. Freed traveled to a number of Holocaust sites for inspiration and created a building meant to be a "resonator of memory" (USHMM). Brick and steel in the construction are reminiscent of the barracks of Auschwitz and a critique of the modern, industrial society that enabled the Holocaust to occur; other elements such as disconcerting and disproportionate dimensions, simulated watchtowers and ruptures, and alternating stark emptiness and claustrophobic closeness take the visitor from the heart of the free world into its antithesis. It is what Hansen-Glucklich refers to as an "architecture of experience, as it seeks to lead visitors into a vicarious encounter with the sites and spaces of the Holocaust" (2014, 158). Yet despite its deeply disturbing subject matter, since its dedication in 1993 "as a physical container to preserve the memory of the Holocaust for all Americans" (Linenthal 1995, 1), the USHMM continues to be one of the most popular tourist destinations in Washington, DC.[8]

History and memory of the Holocaust are such sensitive subjects to navigate, particularly in an American setting, that the museum has had to transcend the usual role of museum as collector and displayer of historical artifacts. As Leon Wieseltier (1993) pointed out, the very name—memorial museum—presents a paradox that is emblematic of the institution's many duties. Memorials are the embodiment of memory, while museums are traditionally viewed as houses of history—fact-driven, objective, and empirical. Thus this museum attempts to be a space in which "the vividness of recollection joins the sturdiness of research" (Wieseltier 1993, 19). History is a corrective to memory's fallibility, and memory is often believed to be a therapeutic alternative to history's objectivity and scientific claims, and the museum attempts to embody the best of each.

Contending with issues of memory and history, any museum must carefully negotiate the "post-modern dilemma" of today's museums, described by Iwona Irwin-Zarecka as "the need for the museum not to claim authority on historical truth, all the while constructing legible exhibits about the past" (1994, 102). As a national memorial, the museum strove for an "objective" telling of the story of the Holocaust, presenting "all that happened, the way it happened, without embellishment, without emotion, without distortions" (Linenthal 1995, 111). This, however, is easier said than done. The museum is meant to serve as a living memorial, composed of different and dynamic forms of remembrance and education, which are intended to resolve some of the difficulties arising in Holocaust memorialization. Thus the USHMM has a permanent exhibit, rotating temporary exhibits, a Committee on Conscience, a Holocaust learning center, a library and archive, a Center for Advanced Holocaust Studies, and full programs of conferences, functions, lectures, and days of remembrance.

While the other parts of the institution, such as the rotating exhibits and learning centers, are there to flesh out the experience and story of the Holocaust, the permanent exhibit is there to tell the story, and in this

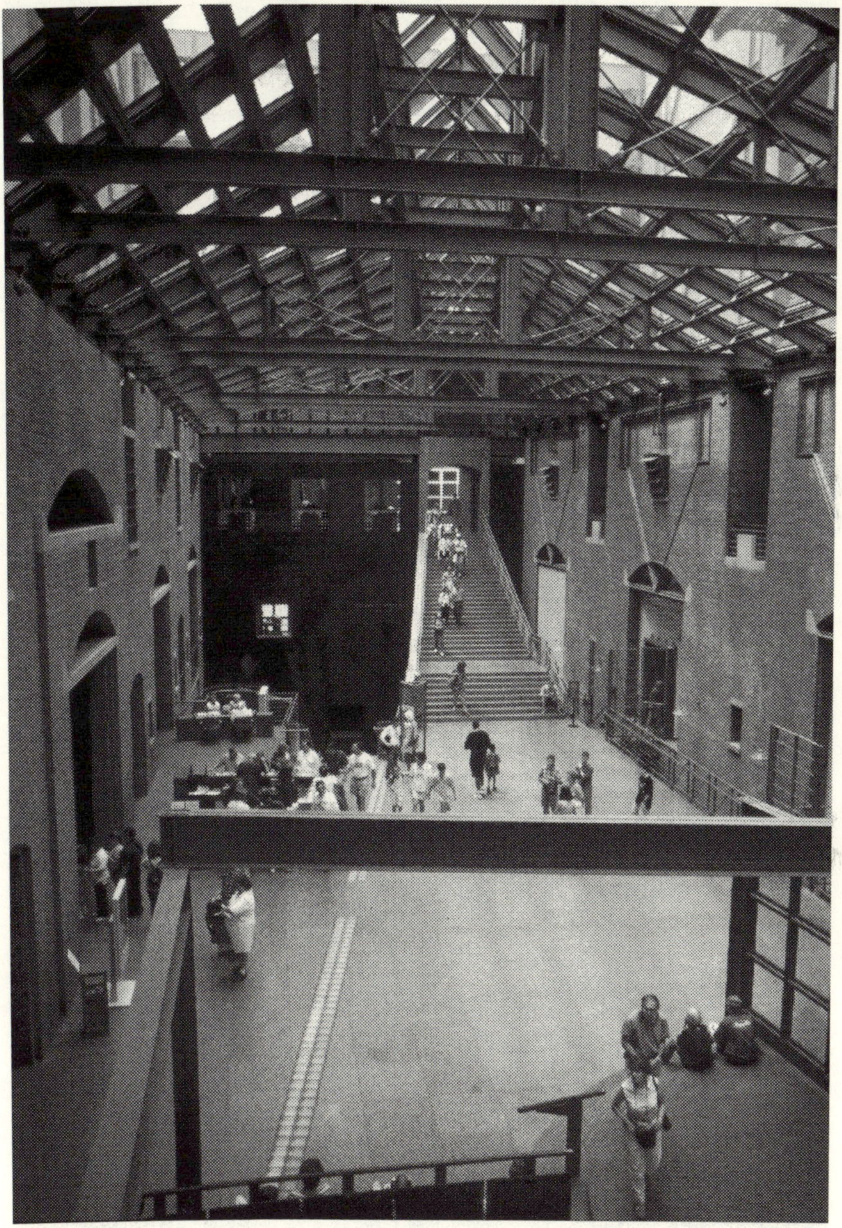

FIGURE 1. Visitors in the Hall of Witness at the US Holocaust Memorial Museum. Photo by Max Reid, US Holocaust Memorial Museum.

it departs from traditional conceptions of museums. Traditional history museums revolve around their collections, displaying, cataloguing, and educating through artifacts. The USHMM, though it has the world's largest collection of Holocaust artifacts, does not take its point of departure from the collection; former director Jeshajahu Weinberg instead argues that "its point of departure is the story line of Holocaust history"; it is "an attempt at visual historiography . . . a narrative museum" (1994). But it is more than that and is best described as an "experiential" museum. Traditional museums are repositories for artifacts to be studied and displayed in the effort to impart an understanding of history, science, or art; this museum, however, is first and foremost telling a story, and its collection is only important to the extent that it advances the narrative. In this it lays the groundwork for a new kind of experiential, memorial museum that seeks to do something dramatically new.

In combining historical storytelling with experiential memory, the USHMM seeks an emotional response from its visitors, not mere intellectual impact—it is meant to upset and disturb. It is a plot-driven narrative, which induces identification with the "hero" (victims, survivors, and liberators) and the development of a "negative attitude towards the villain" (Weinberg 1994). Aside from the fact that the subject of the Holocaust is highly emotional, even for those visitors who have no direct connection to or memory of it, "the emotional involvement of the visitor has great cognitive importance. It facilitates the internalization of the moral lessons embedded in the story" (Weinberg 1994). The permanent exhibit is designed to tell the story of the Holocaust "from a specific point of view, to evoke specific responses and instill specific ideas for today's world and for future generations" (USHMM Design Concept Proposal 1986).

The museum also differs from those Holocaust memorials and museums that are constructed on the sites of the atrocities, such as Auschwitz-Birkenau or Majdanek. Place and memory are intimately connected and the places themselves often speak of the tragedy that occurred there. Though of course texts are necessary to explain and contextualize those artifacts and buildings that remain in situ, the story is primarily told through the place itself. The USHMM, however, is far removed from the "topography of terror" and so must tell its own story. As is evident even from approaching the imposing facade of Freed's building, the Holocaust as told by this museum is a meticulously constructed story and memory of something that occurred far away and long ago.

In the attempt to simulate the authenticity of place, the museum did actually transplant a railroad car, bunks from Auschwitz, trees, stones, and many other artifacts from their original sites; it has also re-created things that couldn't be removed from their sites, such as the Auschwitz entry gate and the Warsaw Ghetto wall. These artifacts and reproductions create the scenic backdrop for the telling of the Holocaust story and are as carefully designed as any Hollywood set. In addition to authentic artifacts and re-creations, the exhibit relies heavily on texts, photos, and documentary and audio footage, all of which are submitted to various forms of interpretation. The permanent exhibit is the result of a major collaboration between historians, documentary filmmakers, exhibition designers, and other museum professionals; their collective contributions to its design and implementation are further testimony to its departure from traditional museums. The result is an exhibition that is carefully constructed and presented: the design team strategically made "choices of which aspects of that chronological history . . . define the emotional effect on the visitor's memory of the experience" (USHMM Design Concept Proposal 1986).

In order to tell its story, the permanent exhibit, *The Holocaust*, uses a controlled circulation path that covers three floors of the museum building and presents a mostly chronological, narrative history using more than nine hundred artifacts, seventy video monitors, and four theaters playing historic film footage and testimonies. There are three chapters composing the exhibition: "Nazi Assault," "Final Solution," and "Last Chapter." The exhibition begins with an elevator ride to the fourth floor, during which the visitor hears a US serviceman describe in horror what his battalion had just encountered: "A big prison of some kind, and there are people running all over. Sick, dying, starved people" (qtd. in Cole 2000, 152). The elevator doors open onto a gruesome image of American soldiers staring in disbelief at a pit of charred corpses. Thus the museum begins with the United States' liberation of the camps in Germany, orienting the visitor to the American telling of the story; it becomes clear that the story in the USHMM is one of not just victims and perpetrators but also liberators.

After this unusual orientation, upon turning a corner, the visitor is swept back through time to a very brief presentation of Jewish life in prewar Europe, orienting the visitor to the American telling of a Jewish story. Serene images of the Jewish Diaspora merely set the stage for the "Nazi Assault," which chronicles, step-by-step and in a linear, chronological framework, the rise of Hitler, National Socialism, and anti-Semitism starting in 1933.

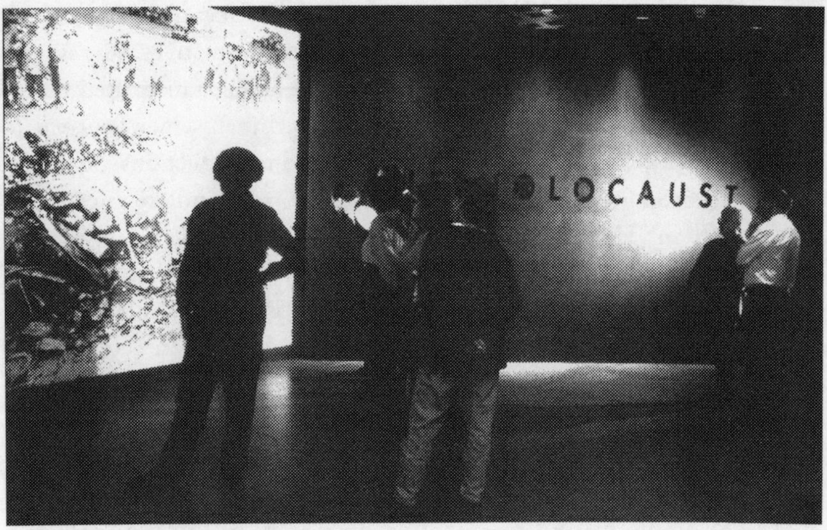

FIGURE 2. Visitors view the liberation mural on the fourth floor of the permanent exhibition in the US Holocaust Memorial Museum.
US Holocaust Memorial Museum.

This confusing chronology in the start of the exhibit—beginning with the liberation, then sweeping the visitor back in time only to start the story in 1933—points toward a tension that all memorial museums face: determining the temporal context of the story they are telling. While technically World War II did start in 1933, Armenians, for example, argued that the Armenian genocide should be included in the story as a precedent (Linenthal 1995). And it could be argued that World War I or the rise of anti-Semitism in Europe in the decades before World War II should really be the start of a story that is well contextualized historically. However, because of the politics behind the creation of the museum—a story that had to be nominally inclusive, though focused on the Jewish experience; one that had to be comprehensible to an audience with no prior historical knowledge; and one that must focus on American ideals and values—the story that the museum's temporal framing begins in 1933 with the rise of Nazis to power and ends with emigration, framing the story in terms that will resonate with an American audience.

"Nazi Assault" is the most text-heavy of the chapters: dense with photos, documentary footage, and artifacts, it creates the feeling that the visitor is witness to the "objective" voice of history. Documents, photos, and charts follow the rise of anti-Semitism and intolerance and the withdrawal of Jewish civil and fundamental rights. To the sound of Nazis goose-stepping in the background and heiling Hitler, the visitor reads about race science, book burnings, anti-Semitic propaganda, the 1933 boycott of Jewish shops, and the growing terror as the Nazis launched their attack on the Jews of Germany and Austria. A corner of the exhibit gives a glimpse of other victims—Roma, Jehovah's Witnesses, and Communists—but bringing the visitor back to the central, Jewish narrative, "Nazi Assault" culminates with the Kristallnacht pogroms of 1938. The visitor also has the first of two encounters—the second will come on the descent to the final chapter—with the USHMM's Tower of Faces exhibit, a stunning three-story tower of photographs from the Eishyshok Shtetl in what is today Lithuania. The approximately one thousand photographs of daily life in the village, which was wiped out by the Einsatzgruppe in 1941, help give a sense of the individual identities of some of the six million whose lives are remembered in the museum and, as we shall see, establishes a key trope used by memorial museums—photographs of individuals—that is meant to help restore humanity and individual identity to the victims and inspire empathy and affect in visitors. Having foreshadowed the destruction that is to come, the narrative is suspended while the visitor descends to the third floor.

"Final Solution" takes the visitor out of the role of witness to history and places her in the role of victim. No longer strictly chronological, the exhibition path leads the disconcerted visitor into a reconstruction of *l'univers concentrationnaire*. Though there are a few discreet early exits, the visitor sees no way out, as she is taken from the ghettos of occupied Poland, through "transport" in a railroad car, arriving in Auschwitz itself. Walking under the steel "Arbeit Macht Frei" entry gate, the visitor/victim ends up in a prisoners' barracks—a simulation of that camp, which is emblematic of the depths of evil. After being led through the barracks, past images of medical experiments, forced labor, and inhuman living conditions, one finally escapes the camp, but only after passing a small scale model depicting the murder of the victims in the gas chambers and crematoria.

Testimonies from Auschwitz survivors play in the background, and thousands of artifacts including toothbrushes, kitchen gadgets, suitcases, and piles of shoes—an intended allusion to Auschwitz—provide the emotional and physical evidence for the horrors of the camps and demonstrate not only the magnitude of the lives lost but also the individuality and humanity of the victims. Before leaving "Final Solution," one must pass one last panel,

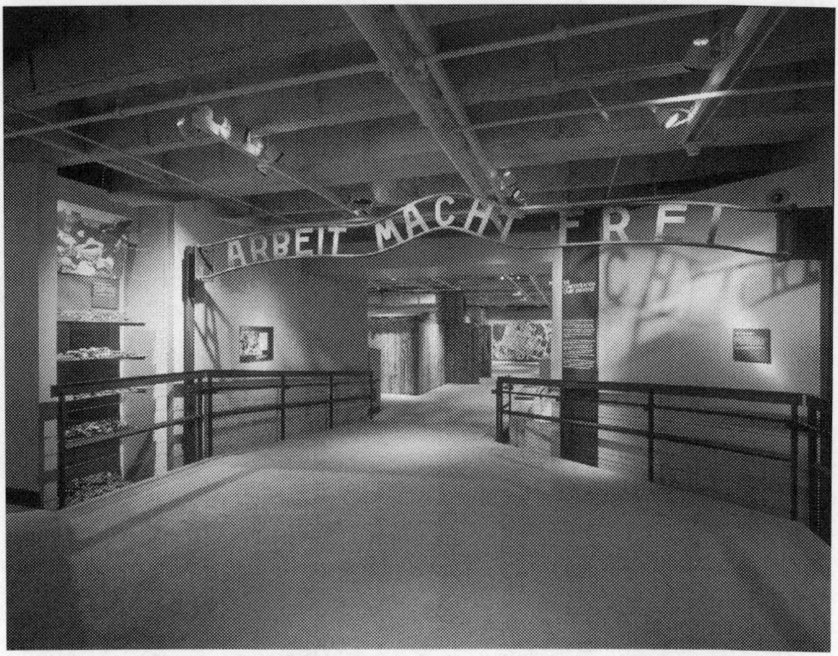

FIGURE 3. View of a casting taken of the gate to the main camp at Auschwitz with the sign "Arbeit Macht Frei" (Work Makes One Free) that is displayed on the third floor of the permanent exhibition in the US Holocaust Memorial Museum. US Holocaust Memorial Museum.

asking "Why Wasn't Auschwitz Bombed?" Puzzling over the indifference of the US government, the visitor is relieved to descend once more, this time into the "Last Chapter." The second and final floor is devoted to the defeat of the Germans, resistance and rescue, and the redemption of the victims. Displays on the rescue of European Jews, footage of the Nuremberg Trials, images of Jewish immigration to the United States, and a triumphant display on the founding of Israel allow the visitor to leave on a cautiously positive note. While the horror is overwhelming, democracy and liberty have prevailed in the end, and the visitor leaves the exhibition confident that the whole Holocaust story has been told and that good has triumphed over evil.

The permanent exhibition is a multimedia Holocaust experience. It simulates for the visitor the experience of the Holocaust in a way that appeals to today's world of media inundation; the exhibition uses film, television, and audio effects, complete with scenery and props, to facilitate the telling of one of history's most horrific stories. Scripted and designed, it is as if one has walked onto a Hollywood set and been thrown into the role of victim. This Holocaust simulation is part of Weinberg's "visual historiography," which intends to tell the story in a way that maximizes the emotional response of the visitor and so must engage the visitor in ways that other history museums do not. For those who were not there (most of the visitors), the exhibition attempts to render the Holocaust comprehensible: "If visitors could take the same journey [as the victims], they would understand the story because they will have experienced the story" (Berenbaum, qtd. in Linenthal 1995, 170). It is this Holocaust experience that provides a basis for understanding and remembering the Holocaust for all those young visitors who have no direct experience with it; and through the museum, in part, a national memory of the Holocaust is proliferated through American culture.

Deepening the "Holocaust experience" and aimed particularly at young visitors is the other permanent exhibit, "Remember the Children: Daniel's Story." Echoing a visit to the Anne Frank House, this exhibit takes visitors through the World War II experience of a young German Jewish boy Daniel who, with his family, is swept up in the horrors of the Holocaust. Drawn from stories of children's experiences in Germany, the Łódź Ghetto and Auschwitz, with Daniel's (fictional) diary providing the narrative, the exhibit takes visitors from Daniel's carefree childhood filled with laughter and love to his mounting fear as the Nazis came to power and enforced increasing restrictions on the Jewish population. Daniel's world becomes smaller and more precarious as he is prohibited from going to school, his family's synagogue is burned down, and he is forced to wear a yellow star; finally his family is deported to a ghetto and then a concentration camp. While Daniel survives, he never sees his mother and sister again. The exhibit presents visitors with spaces where they can touch, listen, and learn in an experiential and interactive way: they are invited into Daniel's world—a world that cannot help but resonate with young visitors for whom the Holocaust is far removed. Its vivid evocation of a "typical" childhood that was ripped apart by Nazi terror is a powerful lesson in the dangers of hatred and intolerance, and the exhibit implores its visitors to read Daniel's diary, visit his house, and remember his story. In this way, the exhibit asks visitors to take some responsibility for the fate of Daniel and the millions of other children swept up in the Holocaust.

This transfer of memory is precisely what Alison Landsberg (2004) means by "prosthetic memory," which is acquired in experiential spaces like the USHMM by visitors who have no actual memory of the Holocaust, but who internalize the experience, memory, and message of the museum. However, while Landsberg finds prosthetic memory to be liberatory in that it removes claims of ownership from any traumatic memory and instead opens up the past to different communities and groups, it is also clear from the USHMM that the particular experience and memory provided for the visitor is highly mediated with very specific goals in mind. Further, this prosthetic memory, as mediated and porous as it is, can replace the need to work harder at an understanding of the Holocaust. Iwona Irwin-Zarecka argues that museums like the USHMM, with its "attractive packaging of the past" and carefully constructed narrative, can allow us "to claim we have gained understanding without having to work at it" (1994, 108). The Holocaust in the museum is packaged like a Hollywood movie—scripted, well-designed, and widely accessible—intending its visitors/audience to have a specific reaction and thus carry away with them a specific Holocaust memory.

And it is a uniquely American telling of the Holocaust. The USHMM frames its narrative according to American ideals, set in sharp contrast to the Nazi's horrific policies. Upon entering the exhibition, the first sounds and images that greet the visitor are the American liberators of the camps. The irony, of course, is that the Soviet army was the first to liberate Nazi camps, in particular those that were most notorious, like Auschwitz, in Poland; those that the US army liberated were in the west and mostly held non-Jewish political prisoners. Nevertheless, in beginning the exhibit with the US liberation of Ohrdruf, the visitor realizes that this is an American telling of the story and that, despite America's faults and failures during the war, the United States was ultimately a liberator. The final chapter of the exhibition brings the visitor back from the horrors of the ghettos and concentration camps of Europe to the liberation, the founding of Israel, and immigration to America. Thus American ideals of liberty and immigration frame the story, and the view of the United States as watchdog and savior is maintained throughout the story. As Tim Cole argues, the permanent exhibit's narrative is one of "redemptive closure offered by liberation and post-war emigration from the scene of the murders" that is meant to "reaffirm in those who visit a commitment to American values" (2000, 153–54). Politically, to build the museum on the mall in Washington, DC, it was necessary for the museum to represent an American telling of the Holocaust that emphasizes American ideals and values. Through its carefully constructed telling of the story of the Holocaust, the USHMM "defines what it means to be American by graphically illustrating what it means not to be American" (Young 1993, 337).

MOBILIZING HOLOCAUST MEMORY

From the start, it was not enough for the USHMM to be an American museum educating about and remembering the Holocaust. In order to justify its position in the heart of the nation's capital and its existence so far from the site of the events (not to mention the fact that when it was built there was no national museum to remember the horrors of America's own past, such as the destruction of the Native Americans or foundation upon the institution of slavery[9]), it had to have a broader mission. And as we can see in the examples of the earliest memorials in Europe as the war came to an end, and Yad Vashem's dual political and commemorative purpose, Holocaust memory is not simply about the past but very much created by and for the present and future. After all, the USHMM claims to be "a living memorial to the Holocaust," intended to "inspire citizens and leaders worldwide to confront hatred, promote human dignity, and prevent genocide" (USHMM "About").

This presumption that a visit to an experiential museum will lead to moral transformation that will contribute to the prevention of future violence means that the USHMM, and all memorial museums that have moral education as their purpose, must determine how to transform the experience of the museum into sustained action beyond the duration of the visit. Thus another element of memorial museums' work that sets them apart from more traditional museums or memorials is a commitment to public and educational programs that will make them active centers of memory and education for their communities in the hope of enacting change. The USHMM has perhaps the most robust set of public programming of any memorial museum; intended for its local community, the nation, and the world, the USHMM's programs have the goal of transforming memory of the Holocaust into an active commitment on the part of individuals, educators, leaders, and policy makers to prevent genocide, intolerance, and atrocity.

The arm of the museum aimed at turning history's lessons into the present and future struggle against genocide and other atrocities is the Simon-Skjodt Center for the Prevention of Genocide, under the purview of

Committee on Conscience, which was founded in 1995 as a watchdog group intended to "alert the national conscience, influence policy makers, and stimulate worldwide action to confront and work to halt acts of genocide or related crimes against humanity" (USHMM "Confront Genocide"). In addition to many public programs related to genocide and human rights, the Committee on Conscience and Simon-Skjodt Center produce educational films, hold teacher trainings, curate temporary exhibits, produce policy papers, hold conferences, conduct research, and assess risks of genocide in places like Myanmar and Central African Republic. For example, at the moment, they have the small exhibition "Genocide: The Threat Continues," which examines genocidal policies and the targeting of populations by the Islamic State and the Assad regime in Syria.

While this exhibit brings the work of the Simon-Skjodt Center to the museum's visitors who may otherwise leave the permanent exhibition grateful that freedom and tolerance have triumphed, the museum also attempts to reach those around the country and world who cannot visit the museum itself. It has a very sophisticated website with interactive components related to the permanent and temporary exhibitions, a vast archive of photographs, podcasts of museum events, videos about the museum and the Holocaust, ongoing blogs on present and past topics related to genocide, and resources for stopping or preventing genocide. The museum's website itself is intended to be a center for Holocaust and genocide education and research and is constantly updated with news about the museum, Holocaust research and remembrance, genocide and genocidal situations around the world, and commentary on political issues and events. It is a clearinghouse of Holocaust and genocide information, commentary, and news and is the most dynamic and accessible part of the museum; with the world as its audience, the site had more than 18.5 million visits last year (USHMM "Press Kit" 2016).

The museum also sends traveling exhibitions and events around the country and world (more than three hundred presentations of nine exhibitions since its opening) and has strong partnerships with many other Holocaust museums around the world. In this way, it shares not only its content, especially in the steady stream of loans and exchanges of collections, but also its museological practices; its influence can be seen in Holocaust and other museums, from Houston to Cape Town as well as in the other museums analyzed in this book.

CONCLUSION

According to Michael Berenbaum, the story of the Holocaust as told in the USHMM must "resonate not only with a survivor in New York and his children in Houston or San Francisco, but with a black leader from Atlanta, a Midwestern farmer, or a northeastern industrialist. Millions of Americans make pilgrimages to Washington; the Holocaust Museum must take them back in time, transport them to another continent, and inform their current reality. The Americanization of the Holocaust is an honorable task provided that the story is faithful to the historical event" (qtd. in Young 1993, 337). In order to build an American memorial to the Holocaust on the National Mall, the Holocaust had to be fit into American history and ideals and the current American reality. Thus the museum works to Americanize the Holocaust and make it comprehensible to every American, ensuring that the event enters and remains in the American collective consciousness.

The process of creating the USHMM was fraught with controversy, and along the way decisions were made to ensure that the museum's story of the Holocaust would resonate with its visitors. Thus inclusion was nominally chosen for political purposes, but the museum maintains a strict hierarchy of victims that places Jewish victims firmly in the center of the American telling. The museum also had to make sure that the Holocaust would remain accessible to American generations who are further and further removed from the event; thus, the museum seeks to tell the full story of the Holocaust in as detailed and comprehensible a way as possible so that future generations of Americans come to understand this ultimate example of humankind's inhumanity. But lest the horror of the Holocaust alienate American visitors, American values, such as democracy, liberty, plurality, and immigration, prevail. The ultimate tale of oppression, inhumanity, racism, genocide, and hatred is thus mobilized in the USHMM to reinforce the opposite values—freedom, democracy, plurality, protection, and tolerance. The USHMM works to create for Americans a shared understanding of a past that was not ours, but has become central to the ways in which we imagine America and our duties as American citizens.

In an effort to keep the museum and the memory of the Holocaust relevant to its many visitors for whom the Holocaust is and will be far removed, the USHMM developed new, experiential, and affective exhibitionary strategies and an unparalleled level of public programming in the attempt to bring the lessons of the Holocaust into the twenty-first century. These programs actively seek to turn the Holocaust's lessons into lessons about present and future genocide and atrocity and seek to do so for generations to come, and the USHMM is unquestionably a leader in its attempt to translate the lessons of history into action. It has also been, from the start, a self-reflexive institution, very aware that it is doing something that has not been done before. We can see within the USHMM some of the tropes that emerged with the very first memorials in Europe and in the initial proposals and ultimate realization of Yad Vashem, but the USHMM has institutionalized the memorial museum form in a way that others seek to emulate.[10] Around the world, it is considered a model to those looking for ways to memorialize and educate about genocide and atrocity, and it serves as such, though sometimes indirectly, for the other museums that I visit in this book.

Clearly, the USHMM comes out of today's politics of regret and the urgent need to remember the negative past. The fact that the museum was built as a solution to Carter's political problem evidences just how powerful regret as a political tool is today; it is very revealing that a museum celebrating Jewish American heritage and culture was not proposed and a Holocaust memorial was. And the museum seeks to embody the memory imperative of Levy and Sznaider that posits Holocaust memory as a universal lesson that will ultimately benefit us all; the museum is America's (and the world's) "prosthetic conscience." However, what these theories of the transformative power of memory overlook, but that is obvious in a close examination and reading of the museum, is that it is a highly political institution that tells us much more about American politics in the present than about the Holocaust or even about the memory of the Holocaust. The universal lesson of the Holocaust is actually, in the USHMM, a lesson in what it means to be an American (Cole 2000; Young 1993). Though the museum suggests that this means standing up for freedom, tolerance, and rights, being American has often meant something quite different throughout history, including since the museum's creation.[11] This is particularly worrying in the political and social climate in the United States at the time that this book is being written. Donald Trump rode a wave of xenophobia, racism, and sexism into power and is, with the support of a considerable portion of the population, creating exclusionary and discriminatory policies, such as his "immigration [Muslim] ban" of January 2017. In this climate, there is an even greater chance that Holocaust memory as represented in the museum will serve as a screen, allowing Americans to feel "self-righteous" (Cole 2000, 158), while masking the intolerance, racism, and hatred, including anti-Semitism, that is circulating in American society. Hate crimes are spiking in the United States since the election of Trump, including many instances targeting Jewish populations. While the museum has forcefully spoken out against the rise of white nationalism and neo-Nazi ideology and parallels have been drawn between some of the contemporary political rhetoric and that of the Nazis (USHMM "Museum Condemns White Nationalist Conference Rhetoric" 2016), there is still the risk that, as Tim Cole reminds us, it will be "so much easier to look at someone else's racism, intolerance, dictatorship and persecution in the past, than to confront the racism, intolerance, dictatorship and persecution in . . . our own present" (2000, 158).

While the USHMM serves as a model for the tropes, exhibition and narrative strategies, and experiential and educational techniques that other memorial museums utilize, it also reminds us that each memorial museum is born of a particular political context and what they might have in common—beyond their eternal flames, narrative structures, or "experience" of genocide and terror that they provide for visitors—is their deeply political role in the societies that have born them. Once memory is taken from the realm of the individual and presented in an institutional framework, it becomes inherently and indisputably political; memorial museums, as containers for education and memory about past violence and genocide—some of the most politically sensitive moments of any history—are thus deeply political institutions and must be read and understood as such.

3 • THE HOUSE OF TERROR

"The Only One of Its Kind"

The Terrorhaza, or House of Terror, opened in 2002 in what was once an apartment building on one of Budapest's most beautiful avenues. Its location, 60 Andrassy Boulevard, is loaded with meaning and memory: the building was taken over in 1944 by the Arrow Cross, Hungary's National Socialist movement, which deemed it the "House of Loyalty" and used it as its headquarters and prison; after 1945, the Hungarian communist secret police took over the building and used it until 1963. The renovated building now houses the ultramodern museum meant to tell the story of these two regimes of terror and to serve as "a monument to the memory of those held captive, tortured and killed in this building" (Terrorhaza). The past it remembers is difficult indeed—a complicated past of collaboration and complicity, suffering and terror under two of the twentieth century's worst totalitarian regimes.

The House of Terror was conceived by Viktor Orbán, head of the right-wing Fidesz Party, and paid for using government money[1] in the midst of the bitter 2002 election campaign against the Socialist Party, the successor to the Hungarian Communist Party. Orbán, who in 2010 again became prime minister when Fidesz regained control in the Hungarian Parliament, which it retained in the 2014 election, is a highly controversial figure. His detractors argued in 2002 and continue to argue today that the museum was and is a political device employed by him to vilify the Communist Party and—by association—all left-of-center politicians and politics in Hungary today. The nearly twenty-million-dollar museum opened in February 2002, just two months before Orbán lost the election, to a crowd of thirty thousand Orbán supporters. As Orbán's government approaches the opening of their highly controversial House of Fates Holocaust museum and with the wave of right-wing populism sweeping Europe and deepening in Hungary, the politics behind the House of Terror are again in the spotlight, highlighting the ways in which Orbán and Fidesz use the past and its memory for political purposes.

Like other memorial museums, the House of Terror has an ambitious and complicated mission. It seeks not only to remember the victims of the two totalitarian regimes—the fascist Nazis and Arrow Cross and the Soviet and Hungarian communists—but also to serve as a space of history and learning, with its central task being to morally educate its visitors to reject totalitarian and dictatorial ideologies in the future. By injecting its exhibitions and portrayal of the past with a powerful moral message about the evils of totalitarianism, the House of Terror positions itself as something of a "moral compass," like the US Holocaust Memorial Museum (USHMM), against which contemporary Hungarian society can measure itself. However, its political provenance and unbalanced representation of twentieth-century Hungarian history (of more than a dozen rooms, only two are devoted to fascism, the Holocaust, and the Arrow Cross) threaten to undermine its moral message and instead have made it a highly controversial museum and memorial. The politics surrounding the House of Terror, in particular, and Hungarian memory of the recent past, more generally, are complex and emotionally charged.

Hungary had an extremely difficult twentieth century. It started the century as part of the Austro-Hungarian Empire, controlling a large expanse of territory stretching from Russia to the Mediterranean and enjoying semiautonomous rule and booming economic growth. However, World War I shattered all that; Austria-Hungary took the side of Germany and suffered serious losses, and ultimately the union of Austria-Hungary was dissolved. In the 1920 Treaty of Trianon, Hungary lost three-quarters of its territory, almost 70 percent of its population, and more than three million ethnic Hungarians, who were living outside of Hungary's borders. This was a devastating loss and a national trauma that continues to haunt Hungary ninety years later (Jordan 2010). Following World War I and Trianon, Hungary searched for a way to regain its territory and rebuild its economy and again looked toward Germany.

With the outbreak of World War II, right-wing politics had already taken hold in Hungary under the leadership of Miklós Horthy, in large part a response to the fear of communism sparked by the short-lived revolution of communist Béla Kun in 1919. When World War II broke out, Hungary again joined the losing side, fighting with Nazi Germany and suffering crippling losses. In 1944, Germany lost patience with Hungary's reluctance to toe the fascist party line in regard to its Jewish population and invaded and occupied the country, ushering into power the brutal Hungarian fascist Arrow Cross Party under the leadership of Ferenc Szálasi. Over the short span of several months, approximately four hundred thousand Hungarian Jews were deported to death camps in Poland, and the country was devastated by the war. Hungary surrendered unconditionally in 1945 and was promptly occupied by the Soviet Union. Under a new totalitarian regime, Hungary went through the same repression and terror of the other countries of the Eastern Bloc, enjoying a momentary glimpse of freedom in the 1956 uprising, only to see the Iron Curtain again descend. It was not until 1989 that Hungary again tasted independence, but it has since struggled with how to remember and come to terms with its difficult past.

Pierre Nora has written about the "recovery of memory" that occurred with the fall of communism in 1989; this recovery released a flood of memories not only from the communist period but from the preceding fascist period as well, complicating memory in the postcommunist world and presenting challenges to the representation of the past in public memorial initiatives, especially memorial museums. Nora's "recovery of memory" also echoes the theories of Olick and others that see a breakdown in hegemonic collective memories in the late twentieth century and a move toward inclusive, discursive, regretful memory. Using Nora's notion of the "recovery of memory" as a point of departure for the particular Hungarian case, in this chapter, I analyze the exhibition narrative and strategies employed by the House of Terror in light of Hungary's postcommunist political and social context. An analysis of the House of Terror, one of the most prominent but also problematic memorial museums in postcommunist Eastern Europe, reveals the often-conflicting legacies and memories of fascism and communism found in other memorial initiatives throughout the region. Similar tensions are evident in memorial museums from former East Berlin to the Baltic countries,[2] indicating the difficulty of representing and remembering the tumultuous twentieth century in this part of the world. However, while the particularities of repression and persecution under two of the twentieth century's worst totalitarian regimes are unique to the former Eastern Bloc, the chosen tools for memorializing this past, specifically memorial museums, are not. Throughout the former communist world, memorial museums abound; the House of Terror is one of many, but it puts the issues related to the dueling memories of fascism and communism into very sharp focus and is therefore an excellent lens through which to examine the complexity of memory and memorialization in this part of the world.

1989 AND THE RECOVERY OF MEMORY

> The struggle of man against power is the struggle of memory against forgetting.
>
> —Milan Kundera (1978)

Even before the collapse of communism in 1989, a new emphasis on memory, with a focus on coming to terms with past violence and atrocity, had been trickling into consciousness, shaping today's pervasive politics of regret. While World War I presented its own challenge to remembering and commemorating the past, resulting in new priorities and forms of commemoration (Winter 1995), the Holocaust presented an entirely new set of challenges and necessitated a new vocabulary (crimes against humanity, genocide) and a new system of international justice (exemplified by the Nuremberg trials), as well as new forms of commemoration. And while memory of the Holocaust tells us much about the emergence of the memorial museum, understanding what Nora terms the "recovery of memory," which occurred with the fall of communism in 1989 and the subsequent toppling of dictatorships and democratization around the globe, can further help us understand what is at stake in the practice and study of memory today, as well as the new solutions, like memorial museums, that have emerged to deal with the past.

While in the nineteenth century the nation-state was the dominant producer and caretaker of memory and history, using the past to unite a people around a common identity and set of political objectives, the totalitarian regimes of the twentieth century sought an even greater hegemonic control over the past in the service of their ideological goals. For the many dictatorial regimes of the twentieth century, including not only fascism and communism but also apartheid in South Africa and the military dictatorships of Latin America, it was in their greatest interest to suppress the diverse, plural memories of oppressed populations and instead manipulate history and rewrite the past to suit their present political needs. Especially under regimes like those in communist Central and Eastern Europe and the Soviet Union, history and memory were imposed top-down by the state. This allowed the state to reduce the official and dominant versions of the past to those events and persons that supported the goals of the regimes. One striking example of this is communist regimes' portrayal of World War II as the triumph of communism over fascism—one that completely obscured memory of the Holocaust and the persecution and murder of Jews or other nonpolitical groups.[3] Memory and the past became tools of oppression; following Orwell, the communist regimes firmly believed that "he who controls the past controls the future. He who controls the present controls the past" (1949, 34).

Accordingly, regaining "control" of memory was central to the struggle against communism and for the future, and Nora's recovery of memory has its roots in the collapse of various hegemonic ideologies throughout the twentieth century. With the fall of fascism and the breakdown of trust in modernity caused by World War II, one hegemonic history was shattered and, along with it, some of the faith in the nation-state and nationalism as ruling principles of modernity and progress. Throughout the Cold War, remaining repressive ideologies and hegemonies were questioned and dismantled, especially in the domestic revolutions of the 1960s: the feminist, student, and civil rights movements further diversified the voices of individuals and groups claiming the past and its memory. And with the end of the Cold War, yet another "subterranean stream" of history that had long been repressed and silenced by the dominant narrative entered global consciousness (Arendt 1973 [1951], ix).

Nora describes this as an "ideological decolonization [that] helped reunite these liberated peoples with traditional, long-term memories confiscated, destroyed or manipulated by those regimes" (2002, 5). In addition to the release of longer-term, "traditional," and national memories that had been suppressed by communist regimes throughout the region, there was the recovery of memories of the horrors of World War II and the Holocaust as well as the liberation of more recent memories of the suffering of individuals and groups at the hands of the Soviet-controlled communist governments. Memories of suffering under communism were the most recent and acute of those memories suddenly allowed to have public life, and it was the communist regime that transitional governments were most zealously trying to put behind them. In many senses, then, the recent past of communist dictatorship loomed largest in the sphere of collective memory and became important political capital for new regimes trying to move forward.

However, as Tony Judt writes, "the real problem was the temptation to overcome the memory of communism by inverting it" (2005, 824). Thus while the mostly peaceful revolutions of 1989 cleared the way for the development of open, democratic societies, on pace with the development of individualism, constitutionalism, and liberalism were nationalism, xenophobia, and ethnic tensions. The breakup of the former Yugoslavia is the most dramatic case but certainly not the only one. The rise of nationalism and the ethnicization of politics are not surprising following the fall of a repressive regime, especially in the former Communist Bloc, whose nations had been buffeted about throughout the late nineteenth and twentieth centuries, changing hands, borders, and alliances at a dizzying rate and having barely tasted sovereignty. Without communist or fascist ideology to provide meaning and structure society, the countries of the former Eastern Bloc emerged from the ashes of communism with their national belonging as the most cohesive and prevalent identity to cling to. After a century of occupation, persecution, and domination, many postcommunist countries embraced nationalism as a central pillar of their newly formed political autonomy.

With this renewed sense of national belonging and an emergent national identity centered on the newly independent nation-state, ethnicity and other forms of difference surfaced. The flood of memories and alternative histories that accompanied the liberation of society came as something of a shock: "The fall of communism destroyed this shroud of sameness, and the world was caught napping by an outburst of the many unanticipated differences concealed beneath it" (Havel, qtd. in Tismaneanu 1998, 39). Ethnic, religious, and other identities that had been repressed were suddenly freed, making the world a new place full of difference and numerous "others" with alternative—and sometimes competing—versions of the past and present, as well as differing views of the future. In other words, following the fall of communism, there was "too much memory, too many pasts on which people can draw, usually as a weapon against the past of someone else" (Judt 1992, 99). Hence throughout the region—and especially in Hungary—together with the constitution of liberal democracy, we have seen the rise of right-wing parties and nationalistic ideologies, as well as a proliferation of memorial museums of national suffering created to portray the newly liberated nation as an innocent victim of the terror of totalitarian—namely, *communist*—rule.

POSTCOMMUNIST POLITICS IN HUNGARY

Hungary has been especially susceptible to the rise of nationalism and extreme right-wing politics resulting from nostalgia for the communist past and insecurity in the present and about the future. While it is beyond the scope of this chapter to provide a thorough analysis of Hungarian postcommunist politics, I would like to offer a few conclusions about the particularity of the Hungarian transition that help illuminate the political uses of the past in the House of Terror.

The communist experience in Hungary following the suppressed 1956 revolt was arguably different from that of its neighbors. The relatively open and comfortable so-called goulash communism of János Kádár's regime meant that many Hungarians enjoyed not only relative wealth but also greater freedom compared to more severe neighboring regimes. However, the economic compromises of the Kádár regime to keep the people relatively content paved the way for a host of economic challenges: inflation, debt, and deficits immediately threatened the economic stability of the country throughout the period of transition to democracy and a market economy (Bohle and Greskovits 2009, 54). For many, the fall of communism most obviously brought an end to personal economic stability, not necessarily the long-desired freedom and openness that other countries experienced.

Additionally, as János Kis argued shortly after Hungary's first democratic election (1991), the nature of Hungary's transition as negotiated by the communist elites and dissident intellectuals, instead of resulting from a larger civil society movement, left much of the Hungarian public feeling disenfranchised and disconnected from Hungary's new democracy. Unlike the large Solidarity movement in Poland, for example, the Hungarian people had not been very active in the struggle for political change, and so their stakes in the new political system were not as high; according to Kis, this made it much more difficult for them to accept the sacrifices necessitated by the transition to democracy and a free market.[4] Because "the overwhelming majority of Hungarians [could] detect little or no change in their lives" (Kis 1991, 5), the perceived success of the postcommunist leadership was largely based on the economic situation of the Hungarian people, which was often not better but worse than under communism.

This link between political leadership and the economic situation "on the ground" took new form after the economic crisis of 2008. Hungary was one of the worst-hit EU nations in the economic crisis of 2008—its economy shrank by 7 percent—and it is still reeling from the effects. Viktor Orbán's Fidesz Party was reelected in 2010 and has since moved further and further to the right. Orbán has shocked Europe with his open promotion of what he calls "illiberal democracy" and his party's deeply troubling antidemocratic laws regulating the media and freedom of religion. Most recently, Hungary erected a razor-wire wall to keep migrants out, revealing an increasingly xenophobic, populist stance that is gaining traction throughout Europe and the United States. With Donald Trump (whom Orbán no doubt sees as an ally) assuming the presidency of the United States, Fidesz has stated that any civil society group funded by George Soros should be "swept out" of Hungary, including – and perhaps especially – Budapest's well-regarded Central European University (Than 2017). According to Freedom House, Hungary has been downgraded in the last few years of Orbán's rule from a free, consolidated democratic regime to "semi-consolidated" (Freedom House 2016). And it is in this climate that the far right-wing Jobbik Party has gained in popularity and influence. Though Orbán vowed to rein in the anti-Semitic, anti-Roma ultranationalistic party, Fidesz has in fact been more and more openly supporting Jobbik's positions and capitalizing on its exploitation of the memory of a once great and powerful "Hungary for Hungarians" to consolidate its political power.

The political, economic, and social upheavals of Hungary following 1989, like many of its neighboring former Soviet satellite states, have bred a powerful combination of nationalism and nostalgia for the simpler and stabler communist past, both of which are evident in the House of Terror. In addition, politicians and political parties in Hungary have evoked memory of the recent and more distant past to further their political agenda. This political use of the past is starkly evident in the House of Terror, which both plays to the nationalist rhetoric of the Hungarian right and touches on the nostalgia for the "good old days"; what is lacking, though, is any sort of critical or engaged examination of the more distant past of Nazi occupation and the short but brutal Arrow Cross regime. Though it is meant to be a memorial museum to the two totalitarian regimes that controlled Hungary for much of the twentieth century, it remembers only the horrors of communism and underscores Hungary's sharp jolt toward the right.

HISTORY, MEMORY, AND POLITICS OF THE HOUSE OF TERROR

Already in 1997, József Szájer, a leader of the then-out-of-power Fidesz Party, had the idea to turn the building at 60 Andrassy into a museum of communism. The seed was thus planted, and when Fidesz gained power in 1998, with Orbán as prime minister, the project began to take shape. In 2000, the beautiful building at 60 Andrassy was purchased by the Public Foundation for the Research of Central and East European History and Society, a government-sponsored foundation under the directorship of Maria Schmidt, a historian by training who was one of Orbán's closest political advisors and has been director of the museum since its inception.

According to Schmidt (personal communication), the primary impetus behind the creation of the House of Terror was the question of what to do with the many perpetrators of crimes committed under the communist regime. Hungary has had an uneasy relationship with transitional justice, swinging back and forth between calls for opening the secret police files, criminal prosecution, and lustration (the purging of former communist officials from government) on the one hand and closing the door on the past on the other. However, most proposals for any form of "transitional justice" were at the root primarily political posturing, meaning none were ever taken very seriously by the Hungarian people, and little in the way of transitional justice ever came to fruition (Kiss 2006). In the early nineties, the Hungarian parliament created a law that would allow perpetrators from the communist leadership to be tried for those crimes committed during the darkest days of Hungarian communism, especially those immediately following the suppressed 1956 uprising. However, the Hungarian Supreme Court overturned the law as unconstitutional and not fitting the criteria of rule of law (Kiss 2006, 932), essentially placing the "rule of law over justice" (M. Schmidt, personal communication). This was not at all uncommon in the region; many countries throughout Central and Eastern Europe struggling with coming to terms with the past and its perpetrators rejected the notion of criminal trials as impractical, divisive, and expensive: the perpetrators seemed too old and too numerous and the peace and democracy too tenuous to be threatened by lengthy criminal trials (Rosenberg 1995). Rather, an uneasy amnesty was settled upon, and the gaze of the former Eastern Bloc and Hungary was toward the future.

However, this was a deeply unsatisfying resolution to many people, especially Schmidt and her colleagues in the Fidesz Party, which has moved steadily to the right after 1989 in the effort to wrest power from the Socialist Party, which has been seen as the remnants of the old, communist regime. Firmly believing that without justice in the form of holding perpetrators responsible Hungary would not be able to move forward, plans for a museum to expose the truth about the communist past were drawn up in the effort to come to terms with Hungary's recent history. The museum, then, was conceived in large part to be a public forum for holding the perpetrators of communist crimes accountable—if not judicially then morally. Like the USHMM, truth-telling about the past was central to its mission, though in this case, a part of that mission was publicly exposing the crimes of individuals still alive and active in Hungarian political and cultural life. By extension, however—because the building itself had been used by both the communist regime and the preceding fascist regime and because of the striking similarity of repression under these two totalitarians—the museum was also created to remember Hungary's more distant past of suffering under German Nazi occupation.

Further, it was not enough for the museum to serve as a space for those who had experienced communism (and fascism) to come to terms with the past and find some sort of reparation in the public exposure of their victimizers. Rather, echoing similar initiatives around the world—like the USHMM—the creators of the House of Terror wanted to create a museum for the younger generations. For those who did not live through communism or are not old enough to remember, the House of Terror is intended to portray such a picture of Hungary's past under communism (and fascism) as to make today's youth appreciate that they do not live under dictatorship. As many have noted, in the years following the fall of communism, it was difficult to have a positive relationship to democracy (Kis 1991); things had not gotten especially better for the many people who found themselves worse off economically, still politically disenfranchised, and longing for the stability of socialism. For this reason, it was deemed important to create a museum to show the "reality" of life under dictatorship. By demonstrating how terrible it was, the House of Terror is intended to teach young generations the advantages of democracy over dictatorship—no matter how much effort is required to make democracy work and despite the fraying Hungarian democracy today.

In order for the museum to effectively tell the story of totalitarianism in Hungary for the young generations, the museum's creators believed that it needed to first "reach the heart" of its visitors before reaching their minds (M. Schmidt, personal communication). Like the USHMM's intention to give the visitor an emotional "Holocaust experience" that augments the intellectual content of the exhibit, the House of Terror is intended to provoke an emotional reaction first and foremost, with an intellectual response following. It also, for Schmidt, had to be a museum in which her daughter (fifteen when the museum opened and born just one year before the collapse of communism) would not be bored. Having visited similar memorial museums in Germany, the Baltic countries, France, and the United Kingdom, Schmidt and her team envisioned something that would be even more interactive, technological, and engaging than what they'd seen. Hence the museum is a dramatic, experiential, and haunting encounter for the visitor, with numerous audio, visual, and interactive components that attempt to engage the visitor and seek to provoke an emotional, guttural response to the horrors of totalitarianism. Design and special effects like lighting, music, and atmospheric scenery are the most immediately striking characteristics of the House of Terror—and it surpasses the USHMM and most other memorial museums in its use of these dramatic elements. It is clear this sort of interactive theatricality was central to its mission to reach the hearts and minds of young people who might not have direct experience of life (and terror) under totalitarianism.[5]

INSIDE THE HOUSE OF TERROR

The dramatic and emotional experience of the House of Terror begins before one even enters the building. Architecture plays varyingly important roles in memorial museums but is never simply an afterthought; although the House of Terror is actually a site of historic significance to the story it tells, the architecture of the original building has been altered enough to make striking what is otherwise only an especially lovely building on an avenue of beautiful buildings.

The graceful nineteenth-century facade is completely dominated by the striking black "blade walls" that separate it from the building next to it and warn the visitor of what is inside: jutting from the roof is a stark black overhang

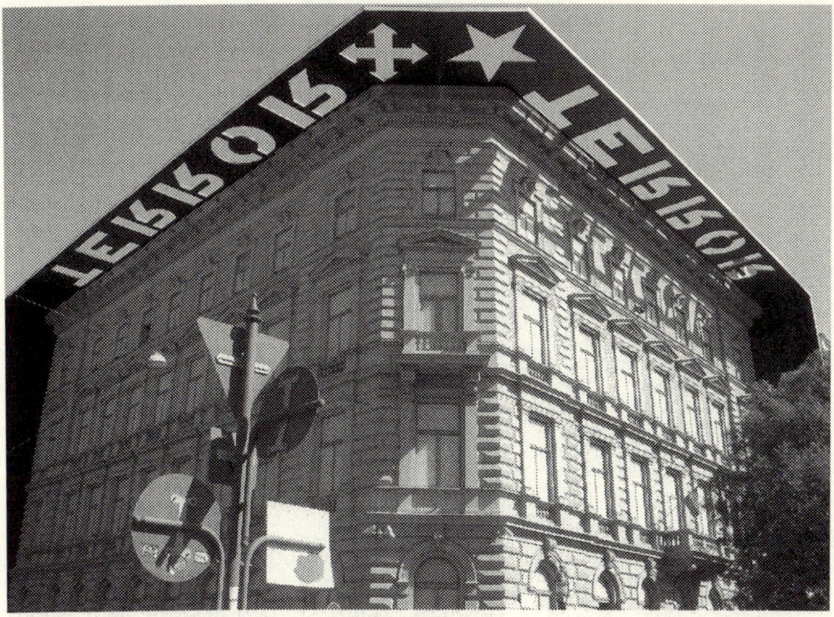

FIGURE 4. House of Terror exterior.
Photo by Amy Sodaro.

with the word *TERROR* spelled backward, the communist five-pointed star, and the Arrow Cross symbol cut out of it to let the sun shine through to spell out the terror of the two regimes that awaits inside. It is claimed that at precisely noon, the sun shines so that the *TERROR* shadow fills the sidewalk below (Rev 2008, 64); but at any time of day, it is obvious what lies inside the museum. Designed by award-winning architect and scenic designer Attila Ferenczfy-Kovács, who also designed the museum's interior, the striking facade not only spells out the museum's dominant theme; it is also prelude to the dramatic experience that lies within. It was also a fierce point of controversy, as Andrassy Boulevard is a UNESCO World Heritage site and such a dramatic change to the facade was arguably not to be permitted.[6]

Greeted by *TERROR*, the experiential rendering of the past begins before even gaining entrance to the museum: the museum's entrance is small and cramped, meaning that visitors often must stand in long lines to buy tickets, calling to mind the bread lines that dominate popular imaginaries of life under communism. It also echoes the lengthy security lines at the USHMM and the 9/11 Museum, and the experience at these museums of mild violation as one is asked to remove watches, belts, and jewelry and walk through a metal detector. The lines and obstacles to get into these museums speak at once to their popularity, the sensitive nature of what lies inside, and the overall experience of visiting the violence of the past. Once inside the House of Terror, the visitor is greeted by an ominous and foreboding soundtrack[7] that will haunt her throughout the entire museum. Rising up over the music, on television screens lining the entry, a sobbing victim of communism asks "Why?," seeking to understand the senselessness of the terror one is about to witness. Like the facade and lines to get in, these dramatic elements set up the entire experience for the visitor, which is as carefully narrated, framed, and rendered, as the glaring, cut-out word *TERROR* is angled for the proper effect.

Past the ticket counter is a courtyard, which must have once been beautiful but is now dominated by a massive Soviet tank sitting in a pool of oil against a towering wall of photographs of victims, underlining the magnitude of victimization that one is about to witness (though it is not clear if these are victims of communism or fascism or both). The tank clearly symbolizes the Soviet occupiers, who in 1945 promptly took over the graceful but menacing building and planted themselves, unwanted and unwelcome, into Hungarian society. Already well-oriented toward the narrative the museum will tell, then, the visitor is directed to an elevator to the third floor where the journey through the two totalitarian regimes begins with "Double Occupation." The name of the room articulates the museum's overarching message and indicates that Hungarians were victims, first pawns of the Germans and then the Soviets. Dramatically arranged with a wall splitting the room into fascist and communist occupations, what is immediately striking—and what will remain true throughout the rest of the museum—is the sacrifice of information and documentation in the form of text, labels, photographs, and documents to dramatic renderings and artistic and imaginative scenes that blur concrete, historical data with symbolism that leaves much room for the imagination. In "Double Occupation," the wall has screens playing documentary film footage, but there are no signs (in Hungarian or English) to tell the visitor what she is seeing; rather the effect of the bold wall, splitting the room (and symbolically splitting the spoils of Hungary in the twentieth century) seems intended to convey all that needs to be conveyed. Each room is dominated by a quote on the wall, which is intended to "say it all" (A. Mathe, personal communication)—in the case of "Double Occupation," the quote is "Last night I dreamt the Germans left

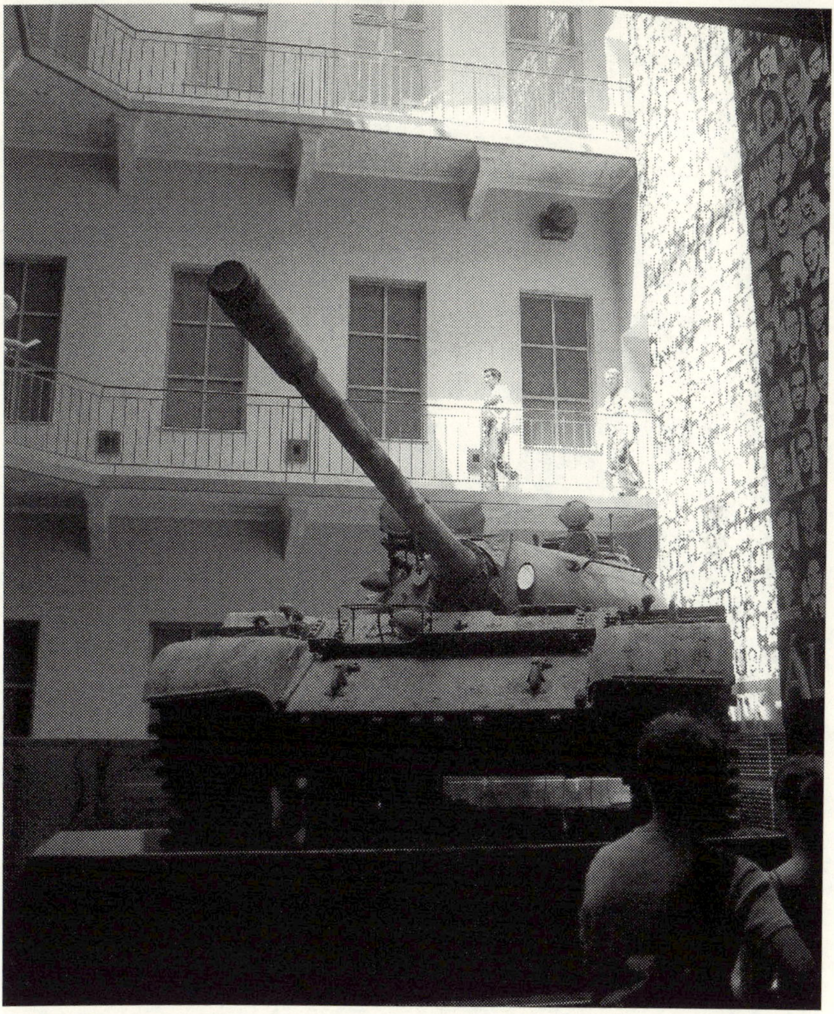

FIGURE 5. House of Terror Courtyard with Soviet tank and wall of victim photos. Photo by Amy Sodaro.

and no one stepped into their shoes," from Imre Kovács—and make up for the lack of other text and information; however the quotes are in Hungarian, and there is no translation. An information sheet accompanies each room, for those willing to seek the information out, but otherwise the museum is striking in its lack of textual information, especially for the non-Hungarian visitor. While it is not necessarily unusual for a Hungarian museum not to have

English or other translations, the fact that the museum intends to be—and is—one of the most popular and visited tourist sites for non-Hungarian visitors to Budapest, the lack of translation is somewhat surprising.

The next two rooms, "Hall of the Arrow Cross" and "Arrow Cross," constitute the extent of the museum's representation of fascist occupation by Germany, the Holocaust, and Hungary's Arrow Cross movement. Through the vilification of Hungary's fascist leader, Ferenc Szálasi, some of the horrors of the Holocaust and the destruction of Hungarian Jewry are touched upon, though with scant reference to the homegrown anti-Semitism that brought the Hungarian fascist Arrow Cross movement (and the Germans) to power. The "Hall of the Arrow Cross" is dripping with symbolism and arranged as a kind of "last supper of hatred" (A. Mathe, personal communication). A fascist dinner party convenes in the center of the room, with china inlaid with the Arrow Cross symbol and a ghostly leader standing at the head of the table (Szálasi?); behind him, a blurry projection on the wall makes no sense to the visitor, until it's explained that this represents the Danube, where many Jews from Budapest met their end at the hands of the Arrow Cross. Alternating Nazi and Arrow Cross uniforms hung on the walls remind one that it was the German infiltration of Hungarian politics that led to the Holocaust's devastation in Hungary and underlines the museum's message of victimization at the hands of the occupying regimes. It is also in this room that the House of Terror's indifference to authenticity first becomes apparent, though not necessarily on first glance; the uniforms and Arrow Cross plates on display are not actual artifacts, but reproductions, like much of the museum, with no labels indicating their provenance. As the layers of symbolism and dramatic interpretation—impenetrable without a Hungarian guide and preferably one who is very knowledgeable about the museum—become apparent in the museum, the departure from traditional museological principles becomes ever more striking. And yet the lack of information is surprisingly effective: the experience is one of affect and emotion, and there is little space for critical thought or historical comprehension.

Following these two small rooms that are the museum's sole focus on fascism, the visitor is taken to the "Gulag" in the far reaches of Siberia, where lighted cones with artifacts from the labor camps rise up out of a floor map of the dreaded archipelago; from here the visitor enters a small antechamber, "Changing Clothes," which shifts the focus of the exhibit to the heart of the museum's message. In "Changing Clothes," members of the Arrow Cross

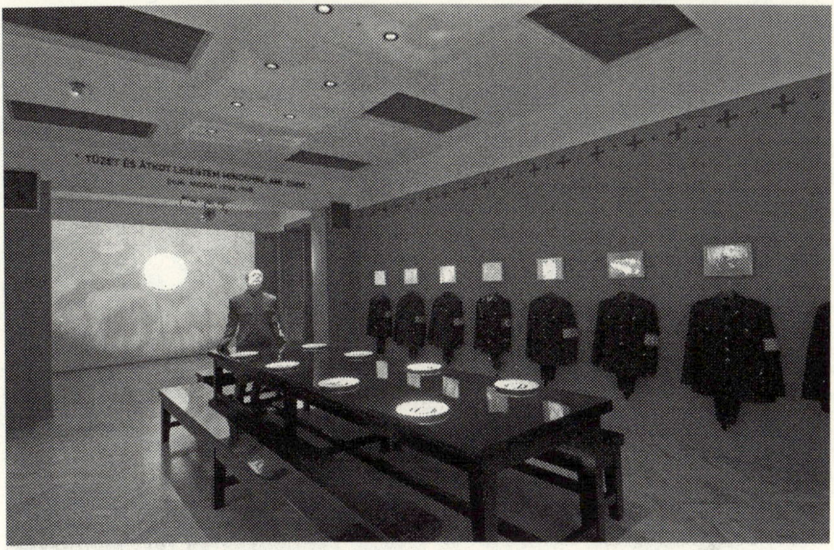

FIGURE 6. Arrow Cross Assembly Hall exhibit on Hungarian Fascist Party collaboration with Nazis.
Photo by http://thomasmayerarchive.com.

are depicted as switching sides after the war and joining the communists; while their uniforms and politics may have changed, this small minority of "bad" Hungarians shifted sides to remain in their role as tormentor of innocent Hungary. The implication—in light of the full museum experience—is that these former fascists-turned-communists learned from the Nazis how to be especially evil, which was a skill that they would develop to its greatest potential under the Soviet occupation. From here, the visitor is immersed in the terror of the communist occupation of Hungary.

Beginning with Hungary's darkest period of communism, the exhibit takes the visitor through "The Fifties"; the front of this room has red-curtained poll booths, which ironically reference at once the "perfect democracy" that communism purported to be (A. Mathe, personal communication) and the rigged election of 1947 and which allow visitors a moment to sit down and listen, on the period-style phones that are placed throughout the museum, to archival speeches from the era.[8] Behind the facade, though, the visitor finds the "reality" of life under communism in the shape of surveillance devices, blaring propaganda speeches, and the proscriptive Socialist Realist paintings of the period. This depiction of "Life under Communism" reminds the visitor that communist principles and ideals permeated every aspect of life, even the most private corners of existence and gives her an opportunity to "experience" totalitarianism. However, lest one sense any complicity of the Hungarian population in the everyday life under communism, the next two rooms, "Soviet Advisors" and "Resistance," emphasize the foreign nature of the communist regime and the effort to resist the totalitarian occupation, at all levels of Hungarian society. This society-wide resistance to communism is symbolized by the three desks on display moving from simple and poor to scholarly and intellectual to elegantly aristocratic. According to researcher Aron Mathe (personal communication), the reconstructed props and heavy symbolism like the three "resistance" desks, would be immediately understood by all Hungarian visitors who lived through the Stalinist period, though this might remain obscure to the casual international visitor.

From here, the horrors of communism persist, with "Resettlement and Deportation" depicted by a veiled Black Maria; the ominous black automobile—recognizable to even those with no direct experience of communism—evoking the heart-pounding knock on the door in the middle of the night that came with the car. From here, the visitor moves on to "The Torture Chamber," on the wall of which hang ominous (imagined?) instruments of torture; without explication, the visitor is left to imagine what sorts of torture innocent victims were subject to. Two rooms on the "Hungarian Political Police" deliberately name and display photographs of members of the higher echelons, and the room entitled "Justice" depicts the staged nature of the communist show trials, complete with audience seating, a tiny room cut into the wall for the "prompt" to whisper forgotten lines to the actors, and a stage, all of which are papered with bureaucratic dossiers and documents related to trials, indictments, sentences, appeals, and investigations.

Tucked between these rooms that are meant to depict the brutality and arbitrary terror of communism are several rooms devoted to everyday life under the regime that are humorous, ironic, and even nostalgic. A room devoted to Hungarian peasants is a maze of one-kilogram blocks of lard, complete with a papier-mâché pig, intended to stir up memories of the 1969 satiric Hungarian film *The Witness* and evoke humor and irony in visitors for whom one kilogram of lard was precious under communist rationing. There are two rooms devoted to propaganda, which alternatively depict the vibrant colors of propagandistic posters and advertisements and drab black-and-white photographs of the reality of everyday life; however, the empty food tins, old radios, newspaper cutouts, round, vinyl settee, and fake plant hold a poignant nostalgia for what was. Another room, completely aluminum with eerie blue lighting pokes fun at the "Hungarian silver" made from the bauxite mines of Hungary, again using kitsch to almost fondly recall life under communism. These rooms remind even the inexperienced visitor that life under communism was not so completely pervaded by the terror depicted in the preceding rooms and that "normal" life went on; however, the seemingly perfunctory nature of these moments of levity in what is otherwise a house of terror gives reason for skepticism that the museum is telling a balanced story of life under communism.

Departing again from nostalgia, the exhibition moves on to a dramatic, dark, and uncanny cave-like room with a lighted cross cut out in the floor and a disembodied priest at its head. Though there is no text to explain the room, the visitor knows that it refers to communism's war on religion in Hungary. Dark, brooding music plays in the background under speakers recalling the blaring propaganda of the period, and small cut-out lighted shelves in the walls hold diminutive religious artifacts. Videos show footage of the arrest and persecution of various members of the clergy; however, again, all is in Hungarian, and other than soaking up the atmosphere and affect, the non-Hungarian visitor is a bit lost to historical understanding and is simply swept up in emotion.

Nearing the end of the exhibit, the visitor finds herself in an elevator descending painfully slowly to the (completely reconstructed) torture cells in the basement, while a former execution assistant describes the process of hanging political victims. Trapped in the enclosed and claustrophobic space, the visitor cannot help but imagine that this is how the victims felt as they were caught in the nightmare of detention and torture. In the basement, this affective experience continues, as visitors are encouraged to enter the torture cells, which have been re-created, as no records remain of what the cellar of 60 Andrassy actually held. There are cells too narrow to sit down in or too low to stand up and cells that forced the visitor to imagine standing in icy water for hours on end or to sit in complete darkness. There are small cells in which prisoners would have lived, arranged thematically with photographs of famous dissidents, clergy, antifascist activists, and others who may or may not have been imprisoned in 60 Andrassy. And there is the execution cell in which a gallows is erected, though if you do your research, you learn that no executions took place in this house of terror.[9] Nevertheless, the visitor is invited to identify with the victims of communist oppression and step into their proverbial shoes for a few moments in order to comprehend communism's terrors more completely.

The torture and "execution" cells open onto a moment of short-lived triumph, with the "Hall of the 1956 Revolution," where a haunting empty coat of one of the victims of the Soviet crackdown hangs from the ceiling and a bicycle damaged by a shell rests on a low wall of screens that bisects the room and shows footage from the brief uprising and brutal suppression. This is followed by an evocative memorial, "The Hall of Tears," that is dedicated to "those who were executed for *political* reasons between 1945–1967" (my emphasis). The names of these victims are inscribed in light on the room's four walls, and in the center, a graveyard of wobbly, tall crosses, each affixed with a flashlight, memorialize these victims.[10] At last, emerging from the horrors of the Soviet totalitarianism, the final room, "Farewell," bids farewell to the Soviet occupiers, assuring the visitor that they are gone forever and that Hungary has been justly—and finally—liberated. The visitor is brought to the edge of the abyss and then led out of the torture chamber and into liberty. Passing a wall of photos of the perpetrators,[11] the visitor is reminded that liberty has prevailed and that those who committed such atrocities will not escape (moral) judgment.[12]

OUTSIDE THE HOUSE OF TERROR

While the public and educational programming of the House of Terror is nowhere near as robust as the USHMM's, like other memorial museums, the House of Terror sees itself at the intellectual center of discussions and issues related to memory and history of the recent past. The administrative offices' walls are hung with dozens of posters advertising conferences, temporary exhibitions, book launches, and lectures hosted by the museum—implied testament to its central place in Budapest's intellectual life. The website lists dozens of colleagues, associates, and scholars from around the world who are associated with the museum; at once a seeming attempt to legitimate it within the international academic community while remaining vague enough so that their connections to the museum are not quite clear.[13] Despite the controversy surrounding the museum—especially its unbalanced depiction of fascism and communism and its deeply political provenance—the museum and its director maintain that it is at the center of Budapest and Hungary's intellectual life and that it leads the contemporary dialogue about Hungary's past.[14]

In addition to hosting temporary exhibitions and scholarly events, the educational outreach of the museum, though minimal, is growing. There are the requisite school visits and occasional trips by staff to schools (mostly on important dates and anniversaries), but for a museum aimed at youth and the younger generations, there is not much public educational programming. A recent project, funded by the EU, with secondary schools throughout Hungary, had students collecting oral histories from family members and acquaintances. The video testimonies gathered by the students are being archived in the museum. Schmidt and her colleagues are determined to continue to develop and implement additional educational programs, as well, though it seems that much of their energy is being poured into the House of Fates, a sister museum that is poised to open this year and devoted to remembering and educating about the Holocaust.

In addition to serving as a model for the new Holocaust museum, the House of Terror is also a model for other similar museums in Central and Eastern Europe. Schmidt describes a loose network of similar institutions that collaborate with each other and look to each other for inspiration and ideas about how best to try to represent and come to terms with the past. In addition to working with occupation museums in Riga, Latvia, and Tallinn, Estonia, Schmidt was involved in the creation of the Warsaw Uprising Museum in Poland[15] and has consulted on similar initiatives in Bucharest, Romania, and Kiev, Ukraine. She and her team of designers also completed a museum that is strikingly similar aesthetically in the southern Hungarian town of Hódmezővásárhely.[16] Their sleek, interactive, technologically sophisticated model utilizes dramatic—and often suggestive and symbolic rather than realistic—renderings of the past that rely on lighting, sound effects, and props in a way more reminiscent of stage scenery than museum displays; yet it seems to be increasingly reproduced throughout the region. And these institutions seem much more intent on conveying emotional impact than historical understanding.

MEMORY, HISTORY, AND AUTHENTICITY IN THE HOUSE OF TERROR

As director Maria Schmidt avers, the purpose of the House of Terror is to help Hungary come to terms with its past in order to enter a new era of freedom and democracy, though ironically, as has been noted, under Orbán Hungary has been slipping away from democracy toward authoritarianism. This needs to begin, for her and the creators of the museum, with holding the (communist) perpetrators accountable and teaching the younger generations the dangers of totalitarianism. As with all memorial museums, this intention is noble. However, the ways in which these goals play out in the House of Terror are troubling.

The House of Terror describes its exhibition as follows: "The exhibition is structured within a framework: that frame is provided by the rooms called 'Double Occupation' and 'Farewell'. The frame-like structure indicates that the Nazi occupation of the country on March 19, 1944 enabled the introduction of an autocracy modeled on foreign examples, while the Russian withdrawal, which ended on June 19, 1991 guaranteed—and made irreversible—the independent, national, democratic evolution of the new Hungarian Republic" (Terrorhaza "Permanent Exhibition"). The purpose of the museum is thus to depict the terror of foreign occupation and to juxtapose it against Hungarian independence, nationalism, and democracy. It is a museum for the newly independent Hungary to celebrate her independence, and the narrative it tells is intended to bolster Hungarian nationalism in the present and future. Istvan Rev, a historian and political scientist at Central European University, summarizes the story of the museum: "After the long decades of degeneration—starting with the German occupation on 19 March 1944 and terminating with the humiliating retreat of the Soviet troops on 19 June 1991—the new era has begun. The leader [Orbán] and his native people . . . have finally found each other, and are ready to embark on a smooth road leading to the future" (2008, 72).

Issues of past collaboration are lightly touched upon—and cannot be avoided when dealing with the Arrow Cross and communism—but ultimately in the museum's portrayal, virtually all (true) Hungarians were innocent victims of German and Soviet occupiers. And now that Hungary is liberated and reunited, the future is at last in the hands of "real" Hungarians. This sort of nationalistic narrative is understandable in these countries that emerged from nearly a century of occupation, and as Tony Judt points out, it is very prevalent throughout the region (2005). However, the nationalistic, though implicit, effort to define *real* Hungarians and put the future in their hands is dangerous in countries like Hungary, where exclusion of minorities (Roma and Jews especially, but also, more recently, migrants from the Middle East) is central to the politics of the far right and Orbán's own party platform. One sure lesson that emerged from World War II and European fascism is the danger of nationalistic, exclusive ideologies; this lesson seems to be missing from the House of Terror.

However, equally troubling, and the subject of much of the controversy surrounding the museum and the highly political context of its creation, is the utterly imbalanced representation of fascism and the Holocaust versus communism; unfortunately, like the nationalistic tenor of the exhibition, this imbalance reveals much about Hungarian politics and society today. Though it is meant to be a museum focused on the terror of both regimes, in the terrible building that was used first by one and then the other, just two rooms are devoted to the Arrow Cross, Holocaust, and German Nazi occupation of Hungary; and these rooms emphasize German control over Hungary's actions and allude to how short-lived fascism in Hungary was, while barely touching on Hungarian complicity. Nowhere is it clearly stated just how devastating the Hungarian Holocaust was (75 percent of the Jewish population was killed), nor is the homegrown build-up of anti-Semitism in Hungary that paved the way for the Holocaust addressed. In the most biting interpretation of this dramatic imbalance, Rev argues that the House of Terror indicates that it was the Jews who were responsible for the decades-long communist rule, their intention being to "take revenge for the Arrow Cross rule and to punish all of Hungary for what had been done to them (by the German Nazis)" (2008, 65).

The House of Terror purports to use the authenticity of space—of this terrible, beautiful building on Andrassy Avenue that for much of the twentieth century was a symbol of supreme repression, fear, and totalitarianism—to tell the evils of *both* totalitarian regimes: "The site was intended to provide authority for the historical events being described" (Rev 2008, 61). It is troubling not only because it does an extremely uneven job of telling these historical events, and in doing so exposes its deeply political roots and objectives, but also because it sleekly packages "history"—exemplifying Irwin-Zarecka's critique of contemporary museums' "attractive packaging of the past"—with so little regard for authenticity and actual history that it compromises the power of place that it attempts to harness. It differs from the USHMM, the Kigali center, the Museum of Memory and Human Rights, and many other memorial museums around the world that are not on the actual site of the terrible events that they commemorate, often because a neutral site enables the museums to promote a more universal message. The House of Terror, on the other hand, attempts to use the site-specificity of 60 Andrassy to tell its story of horror, but in its flagrant use of reproduction, guesswork, artistry, and emphasis on symbolism at the expense of actuality, it is more of a communist crimes theme park than museum, aimed more at affect than education: as Sara Jones writes, "The visitor experience of the House of Terror is not based on the 'auratic' nature of the artefacts themselves, but on the stimulation of the senses" (2011, 103).

In each part of the exhibit, it is dramatically evident that the building renovation and exhibitions were designed by an architect who has primarily worked in scenic design for theatre, opera, and film. The theatricality of the museum design is stunning and clearly meant to evoke a specific response in visitors: revulsion at the cruelty of the communist regime. As Rev writes, "The House of Terror and the story it tells were presented as the embodiment of concrete, tangible, historically situated horror, as the only conceivable story to tell. Yet the concrete details of the terror it was meant to evoke was merely fictional" (2008, 61). While memorial museums in general have departed from the traditional museological focus on collecting and displaying with the intent to provide a richer, more emotional, and more affective experience for the visitor, the lack of authenticity[17] in the House of Terror marks a new era of experiential exhibition strategies.

Like other memorial museums, the House of Terror is intended to tell the truth about what happened under the communist totalitarian regime (and to a far lesser degree, under fascism); however, if the museum itself is so careless with truth, in the form of the many reconstructions, reproductions, and re-creations that do not explicitly state their provenance, and offers so little in the way of explanatory text about the artifacts, film footage, and other objects and documents on display, what are we to make of its claims of authenticity and the idea that it is telling the truth about the past? While we know that the building itself is dripping with history and memory, what is authentic and could reveal something "true" about what happened there has been stripped away and covered by elaborate paint, images, wallpaper, and silver leaf and no longer can "speak" for itself. And knowing the political origins of the museum and the present politics being enacted in Hungary and in the museum, we must wonder about what words are being put in 60 Andrassy's mouth.

Rather, the House of Terror seems to support the Halbwachsian notion that the past does not exist as an existential reality but is always a reconstruction in and by the present. In this particular museum this is quite literal; the actual building has been reconstructed to tell a particular narrative of the past. While perhaps often we think of this reconstruction as more metaphorical, the House of Terror is a useful reminder of just how good the present is at reproducing the past for its own needs. In the words of historian Zsolt K. Horvath, it is not so much a historical museum as a "memorial representation with a teleological function, whose main purpose is the affirmation and confirmation of a political identity" (2007, 270).

CONCLUSION

The House of Terror, like most memorial museums, is intended to induce moral reflection on the past, in addition to telling and teaching twentieth-century Hungarian history. This is evident in its intent not only to reveal the "truth" about communism in Hungary, and so hold perpetrators accountable on a moral level, but also to use the memory of the past in a way that will morally educate Hungarians (and visitors) about the evil of totalitarianism so that they will more readily embrace democracy. However, the overt politics behind the museum, the scant and imbalanced nature of its narrative, and the artificiality of its exhibitions seriously undermine its role as a moral authority. Yet the drama of the visitor experience and the forceful story that the museum tells make it extremely compelling, especially for a visitor without much background knowledge, or one whose opinions are reinforced by the House of Terror's message. A rave review of the museum in a *New York Times* travel blog post calls it "a brilliant amalgam of history museum, performance art and touching architectural memorial" (2008), and the visitor book is filled with comments about the power of the museum and invocations of the ethic of "never again." It seems that the trust that people place in museums as spaces of truth and authenticity, coupled with the emotional impact of the House of Terror's story, is indeed convincing and having the desired effect. However, in a country like Hungary that has struggled since

1989 with right-wing extremism, ethnic tension, and economic hardship, perhaps a prominent public memory institution should be striving for more subtlety, inclusivity, and openness to diversity and plurality.

In many ways, like the communist regimes that gripped Hungary and the Eastern Bloc for much of the twentieth century, the House of Terror tells a hegemonic version of the past that leaves no space for the flood of alternative narratives and "recovery of memory" that emerged after 1989. On the contrary, it minimizes the experience of the Holocaust and Hungary's own dangerous brush with fascism, and it shapes the past and its memory in the service of present day (Fidesz) politics. Though, as I have argued, in much of the literature on memory today and in the realization of many contemporary "regretful" memory projects, there appears to be a move toward a more self-reflexive and introspective approach, with careful attention to inclusivity, pluralism, and even-handedness (Bickford and Sodaro 2010). This is not evident in the House of Terror. Rather, it is often one-sided and brash in its representation of the past, and its creators too easily disregard legitimate criticism and the potential for democratic debate and dialogue that nuanced discussions of the past and its representation could provoke. For a museum intended to portray the benefits of democracy over dictatorship, it seems dangerously authoritarian in its execution, undermining the important moral role in Hungarian society that has been set for it. Hungary's past is filled with enough divisiveness, ideology, and violence; a better moral lesson might be derived from an examination of the politics that divide Hungarian society today and how these politics are using—and abusing—the memory of the past.

Criticism of the museum points toward a broader criticism of Orbán, Schmidt, and the Fidesz Party—namely, that they are actively revising history in a way that abdicates Hungary of any responsibility for the destruction of its Jewish population. Further, that they are doing this from a right-wing, exclusionary stance that seeks to silence Jewish and other voices and to take back Hungary for Hungarians. To counter this criticism, the Fidesz government deemed 2014 a year of Holocaust commemoration, with various events, tributes, and ceremonies as well as the construction of a memorial[18] and, the crowning project, the House of Fates museum. The House of Fates, as the name might suggest, is already highly controversial. The brainchild of Maria Schmidt and fellow revisionist historian Szabolcs Szita, the non-Jewish man Orbán made head of Budapest's Holocaust Memorial Center after removing its leader, it is located well outside of the city center in the abandoned Józsefváros Railway Station. While the Jewish community in Budapest would have rather seen the 7 million forints put toward its construction used to enhance the already existent Holocaust Memorial Center, the government went ahead with its plans. The House of Fates—a "love story" to the Jewish people, in the words of Schmidt (Hungarian Spectator, "House of Fates")—is intended to mirror the House of Terror's exhibitionary and narrative strategies to tell the story of the Holocaust, though Budapest's Jewish community—and good portions of the international Jewish community as well—have distanced themselves from the project and it remains to be seen where the ill-*fated* project will go.

Like the USHMM, the House of Terror (and perhaps someday the House of Fates) is one of the city's most popular tourist attractions and so has become central to national (and international) perceptions about the past it is depicting. It is striking in its use of new, interactive museological strategies and bold exhibition design that are aimed at a younger generation of museum-goers, and like the USHMM, it is more concerned with telling an emotionally moving story of the past than with simply documenting and collecting. Both museums attempt to bring the visitor back in time to "experience" the past in a way that will create a new "prosthetic memory" that will ultimately change their moral and political outlook in the present; in the USHMM, the goal is to embrace American ideals of tolerance, pluralism, and democracy, and in the House of Terror, it is to embrace democracy over dictatorship, though what comes through the exhibition is an even more simplistic—and less universal—message that (communist) totalitarianism is evil.

The institutions are also similar in that their conception, design, and representation of the past are rooted in a particular political context and each has a distinct political agenda. The House of Terror is much more blatant and its politics much more problematic than those of the USHMM, and so it has rightly been the more controversial of the two; nevertheless, the explicit politicization of the past as portrayed in the House of Terror helps illuminate the highly political nature of memorial museums as public, national institutions of memory even when their politics are more understated. The House of Terror tells us much more about present Hungarian politics than Hungary's past under fascist or communist occupation, and in this it tells us much about memorial museums themselves and the roles that they play in the societies that create them.

4 • THE KIGALI GENOCIDE MEMORIAL CENTRE

Building a "Lasting Peace"

In April 2004, the Kigali Genocide Memorial Centre was dedicated to commemorate the tenth anniversary of the Rwandan genocide. Perched on a hill overlooking the city of Kigali, the center houses a museum with three permanent exhibitions, memorial gardens, the Genocide Archive of Rwanda, and mass graves holding the remains of more than 250,000 genocide victims who were killed in and around the city of Kigali. While the museum is built on a neutral site, chosen for its striking location and its convenience to the capital city rather than its meaning to genocide memory, the Kigali Centre strives to be the center of Rwandan national genocide remembrance. In this country that is not only still deeply wounded by the devastation of the genocide but also furiously putting the past behind it in a flurry of development, the Kigali Centre seeks to be both a solemn, enduring site of commemoration for survivors and families and an active partner in Rwanda's postgenocide development.

In April 1994, ethnic tensions in Rwanda between the Hutu majority and the Tutsi minority erupted in an extremely lethal genocide that, over approximately a hundred days, left between five hundred thousand and one million Tutsi and moderate Hutu dead. What initially emerged as a primarily socioeconomic distinction between Tutsi as herder and Hutu as farmer was hardened into real ethnic difference under colonization first by Germany and then by Belgium (Des Forges 1999). Rwanda's colonizers found a population that was easily divided along lines that followed the prominent racial theories of the day and installed the Tutsi, who were thought to be more aristocratic and closely related to Europeans, into power over the Hutu.[1] For years the Tutsi ruled the Hutu majority and were privileged by their white benefactors, while resentment among the Hutu simmered.

Ethnic tensions erupted with the Hutu "social revolution" in 1959, and in 1962 Rwanda became independent. Hutus swept into power with the backing of the majority of the Rwandan population and their Belgian colonizers, but with their rise to power, the "ethnic" distinction hardened as the Hutu sought to make up for decades of repression under the Tutsi leaders and limited the opportunities for Tutsi to hold positions of power. Periodic violence marked the second half of the twentieth century; pogroms against Tutsi broke out every few years and an estimated seven hundred thousand Tutsi fled the country between 1959 and 1994, becoming exiles in neighboring Tanzania, Uganda, and Congo (then Zaire). A group of Tutsi rebels living in Uganda, the Rwandese Patriotic Front (RPF), invaded the country in 1990 in a bold and militaristic demand for the right of return and political, social, and economic equality for all the exiled Tutsi. A civil war broke out, which gave the Hutu government the opportunity to start a sweeping propaganda campaign intended to convince the population that their Tutsi friends and neighbors were a threat to their existence. After four years of careful planning, the Hutu extremists found the excuse to commence genocide against the Tutsi when the Hutu president's plane was shot down over Kigali under mysterious circumstances on April 6, 1994.[2] For three months, Hutus—extremists and others—hacked their friends and neighbors to death with machetes and the international community did nothing; the genocide ended in July when the RPF took control of the country, and its commander at the time, Paul Kagame, has been the leader of Rwanda since. The extremely bloody genocide has left Rwanda a terrible legacy that the country is still struggling to come to terms with today.

The Kigali Centre is a central part of the effort to come to terms with the genocide. It was created under the leadership of a British antigenocide organization, the Aegis Trust, at the behest of a Rwandan government that was deeply uncertain about how best to memorialize and come to terms with the genocide. Inspired by the UK Beth Shalom Holocaust Centre, which was inspired by Yad Vashem and is today called the National Holocaust Centre and Museum, the Kigali Centre signifies the transnationalism of the memorial museum form and its spread to diverse cultures and contexts around the world. For the Kigali Centre is unlike many other memorials in Rwanda, which remain raw sites of massacre and murder, where the gruesome evidence of the genocide is displayed, such as bones and bodies, and which serve as spaces of mourning and remembrance for their local communities. Rather, the Kigali Centre—like the memorial museums analyzed in this book and others around the world—actively engages and utilizes memory of the genocide to educate visitors to prevent future genocide, and it ultimately seeks to do this on a national, regional, and international stage.

If indeed, as I have argued, political legitimacy today relies on coming to terms with the past and memorial museums are one of the essential mechanisms for legitimating nations or groups in the eyes of the international community, it is clear why Rwanda would desire and need a memorial museum just ten years after the genocide. It also helps clarify why Rwandans looked to the West to find a commemorative form that would not only remember the genocide but also educate present and future generations and legitimate its nascent democracy within today's politics of regret. However, as I have also argued and as is clearly evident from the US Holocaust Memorial Museum (USHMM) and the House of Terror, politics are an essential factor in the creation of memorial museums; despite its transnational roots, the particular local and national politics of the Kigali Centre cannot be ignored. The Kigali Centre is under the purview of the Rwandan government's National Commission for the Fight against Genocide (CNLG) and is operated by the Aegis Trust, which raises funds for operations and essentially runs the center on behalf of the Rwandan government. It is built on government land, and this public-private partnership means that the government has a strong say in how the Kigali Centre remembers the genocide. In Rwanda, the political use of memory of the genocide has the potential to be very troubling, as many would argue that the current Rwandan government—a dictatorship, by many accounts, with an extremely weak human and civil rights record (Reyntjens 2011)—does not deserve the international political legitimacy that a memorial museum can help to bestow on a regime.

The Kigali Centre seeks to negotiate the difficulty of genocide remembrance in a country in which perpetrators continue to live next door to survivors, justice and reparation have been agonizingly slow, the divisions in society that caused the genocide have not been addressed but simply forced out of sight, and the all-Tutsi government rules with an iron fist to maintain not only the precarious peace but also Kagame's political power. This political and social context of genocide remembrance in Rwanda compromises the Kigali Centre's ambitious goals of fostering tolerance and reconciliation and working to prevent genocide. Rather, genocide memory in the Kigali Centre, as one of the "official" sites of genocide remembrance, is deeply political and represents the ways in which memory is exploited by the current regime to legitimate its antidemocratic policies and advance its political agenda at the expense of the victims and survivors.

AFTER THE GENOCIDE

While Rwanda still calls to mind images of unspeakable violence and destruction, more than twenty years later that genocidal violence is hardly visible, especially in Kigali. As the Rwandan government works to turn the country around, the fast pace of development means that new buildings, roads, and commercial complexes have obliterated many massacre sites and conceal the devastation of what happened relatively recently (Meierhenrich 2009; 2010). Rwanda today is widely considered to be one of the cleanest, safest, most orderly, and least corrupt nations in Africa. In its zealous effort to leave the past behind and look toward the future under the guise of "national unity,"[3] the government has officially "abolished" ethnicity in Rwanda, claiming that there are no Hutus and Tutsis, only Rwandans. This belies the truth of Rwanda's precarious situation and masks what is often an authoritarian, exclusively Tutsi, and fundamentally undemocratic government (Reyntjens 2004). And while the Rwandan government and many in the international community laud the "peaceful" coexistence of former perpetrators and survivors that one sees throughout the country, this coexistence is often borne simply out of sheer economic and geographic necessity, as survival depends on it. Underneath Rwanda's "national unity" simmer divisions and fear much like those erupted in 1994 (Buckley-Zistel 2006; Rettig 2008; Thomson 2011).

Immediately after the genocide, Rwanda experienced massive displacement and chaos. Up to two million Hutus fled the country fearing revenge, most settling in refugee camps in the Democratic Republic of Congo (DRC); many others were slaughtered by the RPF as they took the country and stopped the genocide. More than one million Rwandans were internally displaced; and more than half a million Tutsis who left the country between 1959 and 1994 returned, called back by the victorious RPF government

(Reyntjens 2004). While trouble brewed in the DRC as the Rwandan *interahamwe*[4] terrorized the population and thousands of Hutu refugees died in the abhorrent camp conditions, the new Rwandan government set about trying to rebuild a country that was literally in ruins.

Foreign aid poured in, "driven by an acute guilt syndrome after the genocide," and the West stood firmly behind the victorious RPF and its American-trained leader, Paul Kagame (Reyntjens 2004, 179). Meanwhile, over the last twenty years, the Tutsi government has consolidated power—a fact that became strikingly obvious in August 2010, when Kagame won his second seven-year term with 93 percent of the vote and subsequently changed the constitution to allow him to run for a third seven-year term, which he won with over 98 percent of the vote in August 2017, indicating that he is indeed becoming simply another African strongman. His inner circle has shrunk as former allies and cabinet members-turned-dissidents have fled the country, some meeting suspicious deaths or assassination attempts abroad while Rwanda denies any involvement.[5] Those who are brave enough to oppose Kagame in Rwanda meet similar violent fates or are imprisoned (Reyntjens 2011).

Ending up on Kagame's bad side is not difficult; since 1994, in the name of unity and reconciliation, the government has forbidden mention of ethnicity and continues to accuse anyone who opposes or questions their policies of genocide ideology—a very serious accusation. Any questioning of the official story of the 1994 genocide of almost one million Tutsi is deemed genocide denial, a serious crime in Rwanda. Increasingly, any action or speech against the government, especially mention of the RPF's human rights abuses,[6] is deemed "divisionism" and subject to punishment. While the international community pours money and aid into "donor darling" Rwanda to support the government's ambitious development plans,[7] human and civil rights have come under increased pressure in the purported fight against divisionism and genocide ideology (Reyntjens 2011). There is reason to worry that Rwanda "is experiencing not democracy and reconciliation but dictatorship and exclusion" and that it is strikingly similar politically and socially to pregenocide Rwanda (Reyntjens 2004, 177).

Scholars have noted that the ethnic tensions that are meant to be dissolved by the government's official policy of unity are actually heightened and exacerbated without an outlet for open discussion about ethnic fissures in Rwanda (Buckley-Zistel 2006; Rettig 2008). Many Tutsis only support the government because they are terrified of another genocide, and many

Hutus deeply resent the government and RPF for their seizure of political control and failure to acknowledge their own human rights abuses; yet neither group can freely speak about their fears (Thomson 2011; Buckley-Zistel 2006). Further, there is the concern that "to stress the absence of ethnic identities has become a means of masking the monopoly by Tutsi of military and political power" and has allowed for the "Tutsization" of the country's positions of power (Bradol and Guibert, qtd. in Reyntjens 2004, 187). In other words, the government is, in many ways, a "dictatorship in the guise of democracy" but is supported and encouraged by much of the international community as a democratic regime (Reyntjens 2004, 177).

In addition to the troubling antidemocratic tendencies of the Tutsi government, the problem of justice in postgenocide Rwanda has further strained ethnic tensions. With more than one hundred thousand individuals accused of crimes related to genocide, the International Criminal Tribunal for Rwanda (ICTR) and Rwanda's broken judicial system could not possibly hope to bring them all to a fair trial. To attempt to overcome this problem, in 2002 the Rwandan government decided that the vast majority of those accused would be tried in local or provincial *gacaca*.[8] The *gacaca* operated until May 2012, and more than 1.2 million cases were tried in more than twelve thousand community-based *gacaca*.

Gacaca were traditionally used to resolve disputes at the local level and were intended to mete out restorative, not punitive, justice (Rettig 2008). However, the genocide *gacaca*, in addition to judging guilt and sentencing the accused, were also intended to gather evidence of what happened and to provide a platform for survivors to tell their stories and for the accused to defend themselves. Because the entire community was supposed to be involved—to tell their sides of the story and to accuse or defend—many saw *gacaca* as a tool for reconciliation and truth-telling in addition to delivering justice. However, the process was laden with problems, in particular resistance to participation by individuals and communities (Rettig 2008; Buckley-Zistel 2006; Thomson 2011), and outsiders and Rwandans are increasingly skeptical that they were able to contribute to reconciliation *or* justice. Many Rwandans increasingly believed that *gacaca* did not uncover the truth and maybe even caused further rifts; there have been claims of "punishment" being dealt to neighbors who denounce neighbors and stories of individuals using the genocide *gacaca* to get back at others for offenses predating the genocide (Waldorf 2006; Rettig 2008). However, the government claims that the *gacaca* were a resounding success and point to them as further evidence that Rwanda has put the genocide behind it; in the words of Kagame at the closing ceremony, the *gacaca* "challenged every Rwandan into introspection and soul-searching that resulted in truth-telling, national healing, reconciliation and justice. And it worked because Rwandans largely believed in it" (2012).

It is in this complicated environment that the Kigali Genocide Memorial Centre was conceived to give voice and acknowledgment to the victims and survivors, to educate future generations against the divisions that sparked the genocide, to preserve the truth of what happened, and to foster reconciliation, forgiveness, and democratic culture. However, as memory of the genocide is often wielded by the government to enforce dictatorial policies and many Rwandans feel that national unity is a myth, the Kigali Centre, as Rwanda's national memorial, is often compromised in its efforts.

THE KIGALI GENOCIDE MEMORIAL CENTRE

While across the country, the sites of massacres and death were preserved as simple and often crude memorials, with bones or even bodies displayed, often in situ,[9] in Kigali mayor Theoneste Mutsindashyaka had plans for something different: a national site of genocide remembrance. The Kigali City Council donated the Gisozi site, which has no particular importance vis-à-vis the genocide. This dramatically distinguishes the Gisozi memorial from the other memorial sites in Rwanda, yet calls to mind many Holocaust and other memorial museums around the world, including Yad Vashem, the USHMM, or the UK Holocaust Center. The mayor and Ministry of Culture immediately set about trying to determine what kind of memorial would be appropriate and set their gazes toward the West and to other commemorative precedents—namely, the Holocaust. As they began to conceptualize a Rwandan memorial, they visited Yad Vashem, several Holocaust sites in Europe, and the UHSMM, all of which they considered too large, elaborate, and expensive for Kigali. They also visited the Beth Shalom Holocaust Centre in the United Kingdom and there found a much better approximation of what they were looking for.

The Beth Shalom Holocaust Centre was created by brothers James and Stephen Smith who, moved by a visit to Yad Vashem, decided that the United Kingdom needed a similar site of remembrance. They created the center in the mid-1990s to be a place for survivors to tell their stories and for young generations to learn the history of the Holocaust and the dangers of racism and intolerance that led to the genocide. However, as they were completing the center in the mid-1990s, the genocides in Rwanda and Bosnia were raging, and they had to ask themselves what use a Holocaust center is if it's not actually working to prevent genocide. The brothers set about trying to find a way to use the memory of the Holocaust in a way to more actively prevent genocide and laid the foundation to create the Aegis Trust, a genocide-prevention organization.

In 2000–2001, the Smith brothers and Aegis Trust first visited Rwanda and, in tandem with the Rwandan Ministry of Youth, Sport, and Culture, traveled the country to speak with survivors, visit the sites of the genocide, and initiate collaborations between the Beth Shalom Holocaust Centre or UK Holocaust Centre and Rwandan survivor organizations and government ministries. They were not new to working in Africa and had contributed to the development of the Cape Town Holocaust Centre, which opened in 1999 as the first Holocaust museum in Africa and which has the distinct goal of connecting the racism and intolerance of the Holocaust to South Africa's experience of apartheid.[10] At the Cape Town Holocaust Center, in 2000–2001, they had helped design a traveling exhibit on the Rwandan genocide, called "100 Nights." Their familiarity with the Rwandan genocide and its remembrance, their experience with the Cape Town Holocaust Centre, and the small scale and focus on survivors of the UK Holocaust Centre, made the Smith brothers and Aegis Trust a natural choice to lead the development of a Rwandan genocide memorial in the eyes of the mayor of Kigali and the Minister of Culture.

Concerned that it was too early to create a memorial and that the memories of the genocide were just too raw, as well as deeply ambivalent about the idea of a Western organization coming into Rwanda and imposing ideas about how to memorialize Rwanda's tragedy, the Smith brothers first turned down the request to design the national memorial. At the same time, from their experiences with survivors in Rwanda, they knew that there was a deep frustration among survivors that they were not being acknowledged and that with this sort of "double abandonment," violence would inevitably recur (James Smith, personal communication; see also Buckley-Zistel 2006; Meirhenrich 2009). Convinced that memorials serve as an important form of symbolic reparation—cheaper and more accessible, memorials can be a form of acknowledgment of survivors that is more effective than other transitional justice mechanisms like the ICTR, from which many Rwandans are completely divorced—like the other memory entrepreneurs in this book, the Smiths also believe strongly that memorials can help heal a community as well as educate in the effort to prevent genocide in the future. Wishing to do something for the survivors that would have a meaningful and lasting impact and remind them that the "world remembers," James and Stephen Smith agreed to hold discussions with the mayor about the memorial.

Mayor Mutsindashyaka described his plan for the memorial: a darkened crypt filled with bones; in the darkness, a soundtrack of screaming, pleading, and machetes falling on their targets that would make the visitor experience that horror of those hundred days. Worried that this was not the proper form of reparation and acknowledgment that the survivors needed, and that it would inadequately educate younger generations about the genocide, the Smith brothers agreed to take control of the project. As part of the agreement, the city of Kigali donated the land and would pay for the maintenance of the building, but Aegis would be responsible for raising money for the museum and education center, as well as the costs of operating the center. With the tenth anniversary fast approaching, throughout 2002–3, the brothers worked to compile a team of experts, survivors, and other stakeholders while also looking to raise money to ensure that the project could move forward in a timely manner.

Money began to trickle in, with the first donation coming from Bill Clinton's foundation, but it was not until December 2003, just four months before the planned anniversary celebration, that enough funds were secured to complete the project.[11] Working day and night, the Smith brothers and a team of fifty workers completed the museum building; installed the exhibition panels, which had been constructed in the United Kingdom; finished the first of the mass graves, burying remains of individuals that had been killed in the city of Kigali; drafted an exhibition narrative written by a Rwandan and translated into Kinyarwanda, English, and French; and planted the memorial rose gardens, finishing the museum and complex in time for a ceremonial opening in April.[12]

The Rwandan government's look toward the West and, in particular, Holocaust memorialization for commemorative inspiration as well as the rush to complete the memorial point toward the transnational nature of the memorial museum form and the international normative demand for regimes transitioning from violence to democracy to demonstrate that they are actively confronting their past violence.

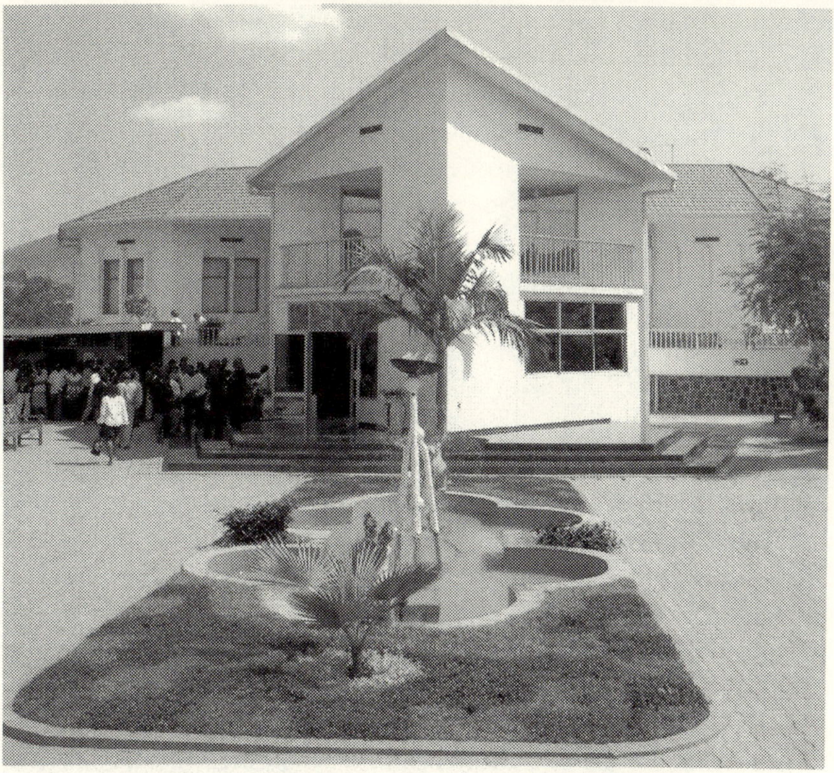

FIGURE 7. Kigali Genocide Memorial Centre exterior.
Photo by Amy Sodaro.

THE PERMANENT EXHIBIT

The permanent exhibition of the Kigali Centre is housed in a modern-looking yet nondescript building and composed of three parts: "Wasted Lives," which examines genocide around the world; "Genocide," which tells the story of the Rwandan genocide; and "Our Future Lost," a memorial to the children killed in the genocide. The museum experience is bookended by two films, both of which feature survivors' testimony about the genocide and the centrality of the Kigali Centre in their lives and memories today. The purpose of the permanent exhibitions is to tell the story of the Rwandan genocide and place it within the broader history of genocide. This contextualization is intended to aid the visitor in understanding how the genocide could have happened and how its legacy shapes Rwanda today and "to teach visitors about what we can do to prevent future genocides" (Kigali Genocide Memorial "Our Mission" 2017).

The first part of the exhibition, "Wasted Lives," contextualizes genocide internationally and historically through a chronological description of the major genocides of the twentieth century, including the genocide of the Hereros in today's Namibia, the Armenian genocide in 1915, the Holocaust, the Cambodian genocide, and genocide in former Yugoslavia. Beginning with the UN definition of genocide, the exhibit attempts to distill the elements that these genocides have in common and to detail the background and history of each. Through the use of text, photographs, and film, the exhibit takes the visitor through the violent twentieth century.

The exhibit is only three small rooms and so cannot address the complexity of each genocide. However, certain themes are emphasized to connect these genocides to what happened in Rwanda, such as the fact that genocide is not the result of a spontaneous hatred but relies on planned and sustained processes of dehumanization, and it reminds the visitor that genocide destroys many more lives than those who are murdered. In addition to giving the history and background, in the description of each genocide, particular attention is paid to the victims, the survivors, and questions of genocide denial.

Because of the amount of information meant to be conveyed in such a limited space, the exhibit has the feel of a miscellany of details about each genocide, and it is not always clear why certain elements, such as the excavations at Treblinka death camp, for example, receive the space and attention they do. In other cases, the basic facts of the genocide remain foggy, such as the section on Cambodia, which never really clarifies who was killing whom and why. Nevertheless, the point of the exhibit is to demonstrate the waste and horror of genocide, which cannot help but come across as the visitor begins to add the numbers of lives lost in the twentieth century. It also reminds the visitor that genocide is not unique to Africa or the "ancient tribal hatreds" in Rwanda, as the international community might like to think (Des Forges 1999), but has occurred in the most advanced counties in the West and results from planned and meticulous policy decisions. The exhibit ends rather uncertainly, however, reflecting on whether genocide can be prevented; pessimistically, it seems to conclude that by the time you can identify genocide as such, it's too late.

This effort on the part of a national memorial museum to contextualize the Rwandan genocide within the multiple genocides of the extremely violent twentieth century is novel; such comparisons are usually resisted or, if incorporated into a museum exhibition, perfunctory.[13] In Rwanda it points toward not only the growing influence of the field of genocide studies on how genocide is rendered in public fora and media but also an opening of memory that might best be described using Michael Rothberg's concept of multidirectional memory, or memory as "subject to ongoing negotiation, cross-referencing, and borrowing; as productive and not privative" (2009, 3). In other words, the Kigali Centre's deliberate comparison of the genocide in Rwanda with the Holocaust and other twentieth century genocide implies at least a truce in the "competition of victims" that seemed to dominate late-twentieth-century memory of trauma and atrocity and situates the Rwandan genocide within historical context and in comparison to others, with the Holocaust at the center of the comparison. On the other hand, in Western commemoration of genocide and trauma, Holocaust victims tend to be privileged and at the top of the "hierarchy"—we have seen such discussion play out in the debate over inclusion in the USHMM—and this comparison in Rwanda could be viewed as an acknowledgment of the hierarchy and its maintenance.

After the historical contextualization of "Wasted Lives," the visitor is led to the heart of the permanent exhibit: "Genocide." "Genocide" radiates out from a memorial rotunda, at the center of which is a sculpture by Rwandan artist Laurent Hategekimana that consists of six figures, carved by local craftspeople out of local wood, depicting the three elements of the genocide and the permanent exhibition: "Before," "During," and "After." A stained glass installation "Window of Hope" shines light into the rotunda; designed by Ardyn Halter, son of a survivor of Auschwitz, this other memorial element underlines the museum's deep connections to memorialization and memory of the Holocaust and its effort to place the Rwandan genocide in a continuum of genocide spanning the twentieth century.

Like "Wasted Lives" and following the curatorial and exhibition strategies of memorial museums around the world, "Genocide" uses a combination of text, photographs, film, artifacts, and recorded survivor testimony to tell a narrative history of what happened. It also follows a controlled path that leads the visitor chronologically through the buildup to and aftermath of the genocide. "Before" starts with the history of Rwanda before colonization and depicts a harmonious Rwanda of one people peacefully coexisting. In video footage of traditional Rwandan ceremonies, the exhibit narrative describes a land of eighteen tribes, peacefully intermingled and intermarried, living as one people. The language is that of unity: "We held elections," "We did not choose to be colonized" and the point is clear that the white colonizers destroyed this harmony. Under colonization, first at the hands of Germany, then after World War I, Belgium, race science and ethnic classifications enforced by identity cards were introduced into Rwandan society, beginning the dangerous division of the Rwandan people. Following the current government's explanation of the genocide, the museum's narrative emphasizes that ethnic division and strife were imposed top-down by the colonists (Reyntjens 2004). The implication is that ethnic division in Rwanda was as foreign as the European colonizers, and so, following this reasoning, Kagame, in abolishing ethnic division in Rwanda today, has returned the country to its more pure, harmonious, and wholesome precolonial state; though of course it's not possible to "abolish" this kind of entrenched ethnic division.

Placing the blame for the genocide on colonization again calls to mind the notion of multidirectional memory at the heart of which is Rothberg's argument that the interaction between historical memories, especially those of the Holocaust and of colonization, opens a fruitful and productive space for the recognition of diverse, multicultural memories. In fact, he goes further to argue that Holocaust memory emerged and consolidated during the apex of decolonization and so is deeply infused with anti- and postcolonial rhetoric and understanding (2009, 7). Decolonization, according to Rothberg, allowed memory of the Holocaust to be articulated in a way that it had not been before. This means that while we often view the Holocaust and its memory as at the center of not only memory studies as an academic discipline but also a global political, cultural, and social discourse on memory, it in itself is already in dialogue with alternative memories of colonization, racism, and oppression, and in fact, Holocaust memory allows for the articulation of other memories. Thus not only does the museum utilize the many museological tropes of Holocaust remembrance and display, but the Kigali Centre also directly places the Holocaust as a precedent to what happened in Rwanda, drawing a clear line of comparison between the two genocides. By framing the Rwandan genocide within the context of colonization, the museum implies that the ethnic hatred that led to genocide in Rwanda can be traced directly to the German and Belgian colonial policies. While this suggests precisely the multidirectional, traveling, transcultural movement of memory and its forms that have moved to the forefront of memory studies' theorizing today, as we shall see in the Kigali Centre, there is a political purpose to this historical comparison and contextualization that reinforces the goals and ideologies of Kagame's regime.

The exhibit goes on to describe Rwanda's independence of 1959 and the further divisions in society that it wrought. Tracing the rise of genocide ideology in Rwanda postindependence, the exhibit brings the visitor to what it calls the "Path to the Final Solution," drawing explicit parallels to the Holocaust and reminding the visitor of the museum's provenance out of the (Western) tradition of Holocaust memorialization. Here, the exhibit tells of the seven hundred thousand Tutsis exiled from Rwanda between 1959 and 1973; the periodic massacres of those remaining; the RPF's heroic struggle for rule of law and equality; the rise of propaganda like the Ten Hutu Commandments, including such dictates as number four: "Every Hutu should know that every Tutsi is dishonest in business," and number eight: "The Hutu should stop having mercy on the Tutsi"; and the incipient use of radio to spread hatred. "Path to the Final Solution" tells the tale of genocide carefully planned and methodically executed, stressing that "death lists had been pre-prepared [*sic*] in advance" and that genocide had been brewing since before Rwanda gained independence. "Before" brings the visitor to that April night when the president's plane exploded over Kigali, and exiting the first part of the exhibit, the visitor finds herself reading Romeo Dallaire's desperate cables to the UN, before entering the horror of the hundred days.

"During the Genocide" seems to heed most closely to Mayor Mutsindashyaka's initial idea for the memorial of the dark labyrinth of terror, and attempts to convey the absolute horror of the genocide. Terrifying testimony from victims plays in the background, and video screens vividly depict the violence and brutality, panning from shots of bodies lying in the roads or waterways to machete wounds and injuries, to burned villages, churches, and schools. There are display cases filled with machetes, the traditional farming implements still used today, which take on a new meaning when one tries to imagine them cutting down hundreds of thousands of people. There are panels describing the horrors inflicted on women and children and the torture of many Tutsi and moderate Hutu victims before their slaughter; and there is a wall of panels describing some of the most chilling massacres that occurred in the churches of Rwanda where the victims congregated, seeking cover in the house of God, and where—in some cases—their priests and fellow parishioners helped murder them. Ultimately, "During the Genocide" seeks to demonstrate to the visitor the

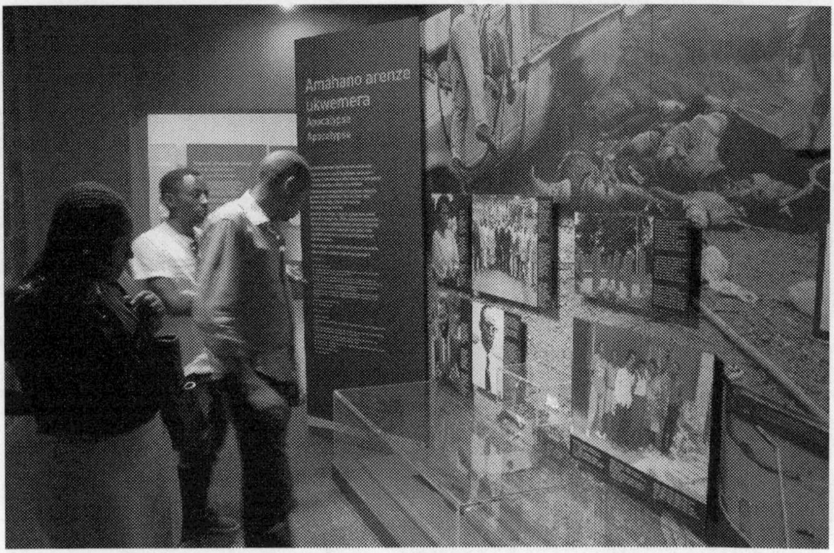

FIGURE 8. Detail of Kigali Genocide Memorial Centre exhibit on Rwandan genocide.
ZUMA Press, Inc. / Alamy Stock Photo.

extreme violence of the genocide in a deeply emotional and affective way: a million lives lost and scores or even hundreds of thousands wounded physically and psychologically in ways that will haunt them forever; children orphaned; women, children, and the elderly murdered; and the entire infrastructure of Rwanda plunged into a nightmarish chaos.

Leaving this part of the exhibit, the visitor encounters three large panels about resistance to the genocide, using text and photographs to describe the story of a school and church where the Tutsis fought their killers with sticks and stones until finally they were overcome, and another focused on individuals who helped Tutsi and moderate Hutus escape the *genocidaires*. Finally, the visitor comes to three small panels on the silence of the international community throughout the genocide. Subtle and without the indignity and outrage one might expect, the panels neutrally describe the way the world watched the genocide and did nothing.

It is at this point that one realizes that throughout this part of the exhibition, despite the horrors depicted, the graphic details, and the incomprehensible numbers, very little blame has been ascribed at all. Not only are the roles of the international community and the church minimized in the permanent exhibit, but any real collective blame is missing. Of course the exhibition tells of the *interahamwe,* the Hutu militias that prepared for the genocide for months leading up to it, and it names and describes, including photographs, some of the individual leaders of the genocide, notably Colonel Bagasora, the head of the army; Hassan Ngeze, the journalist who published the Hutu Ten Commandments; and the directors of Radio Mille Collines, which incited the genocide in its hateful and dehumanizing anti-Tutsi propaganda.[14] But on the whole, there is a noticeable lack of blame ascribed to the Hutus—even extremists—or anyone else of Rwanda. Rather, the exhibit depicts a collective victimization of a Rwandan people that were torn apart by colonial forces. This is deliberate; in the effort to make sure that the museum does not threaten the fragile peace and tenuous unity among the Rwandan population, the agency behind the genocide was taken out of the hands of human perpetrators and instead "genocide ideology" is to blame. However, as is very evident today, this concept of genocide ideology can be very easily manipulated for political ends; Kagame often gets rid of his enemies and detractors by accusing them of genocide ideology and any questioning of his policies and government can be deemed genocide ideology. Both in the museum and outside it, in removing human agency and instead blaming genocide on an abstract and malleable concept of ideology, almost anyone who says the wrong thing could potentially be deemed a *genocidaire.*

"After" takes the visitor through the chaos and upheaval immediately following the genocide as millions of refugees fled out of and into the country, plagued by guilt, fear, and confusion. It describes the refugee camps in Congo, where international aid was finally delivered—to those who had perpetrated the genocide—and which quickly became hotbeds for the dissemination of Hutu power ideology as well as deadly diseases like cholera. It also, through heart-wrenching testimony, tells of the survivors' search for their families and their attempts to rebuild their lives when literally everything had been taken from them. It tells of the multitudes of children orphaned by the genocide and of the long term consequences, such as the alarming rates of HIV/AIDS in the many thousands of women who were raped. It describes the efforts to enact justice through the ICTR and the *gacaca,* while highlighting the impossibility of justice ever being fully meted out, and the irony that prisoners in Arusha awaiting trial have access to AIDS medication, while the women in Rwanda do not. A *gacaca* plays on video—the prisoner uncomfortable in his pink uniform, pleading his side of the story while members of the community speak up with their sides of the story or sit under the trees, fanning themselves in boredom; the looping footage of this one instance underlines the magnitude of the project. What "After" pointedly does not tell is the massive human rights abuses committed by the RPF under the leadership of Kagame or the ongoing conflict in DRC that has been perpetuated in large part by the Rwandan government through the exploitation of genocide remembrance.

"After the Genocide" ends with a few panels on the need to confront and remember the past, which seem to read as a justification for the memorial center's existence. It reminds the visitor that though it is painful, it is impossible to forget and necessary to remember the victims as redemption and the events as a warning to the future. It also stresses the center's priority on education as the way forward and underlines the notion that this is a site of education in addition to commemoration. These self-reflexive panels demonstrate the Kigali Centre's strict adherence to the international norms and assumptions about the ethical duty to remember: the expressivist ethical imperative that remembering is the correct thing to do and the consequentialist view that memory will help prevent future violence. Thus both the form of memory traveled across national and social borders, from the United States and Europe to Rwanda, and also the ethics of memory, reflecting a global set of expectations and best practices vis-à-vis past political violence.

With this, the visitor leaves the interpretive parts of the exhibit and enters the dimly lit and eerie memorial rooms. The first has a large screen showing survivor testimony, and the walls are covered in photographs. There are family photos, ID cards, candid snapshots—thousands of them. This room echoes the USHMM's Tower of Faces, and like that and other walls of photographs that are present in each museum described in this book, this common memorial museum trope is intended to restore individuality, humanity, and vitality to those who were killed. In the Kigali Centre, the photos are loosely clipped to wires and are often taken by visitors who know the individual or who are reminded by the photo of a lost loved one. As in other memorial museums, the photographs in the Kigali Centre are evidence of what happened and an effort to restore humanity to those who were killed; yet unlike the photos from the Nazi concentration camps or the Cambodian detention center, Tuol Sleng, which seem distant due to their black-and-white, grainy quality, these photos are in color and feel immediate.

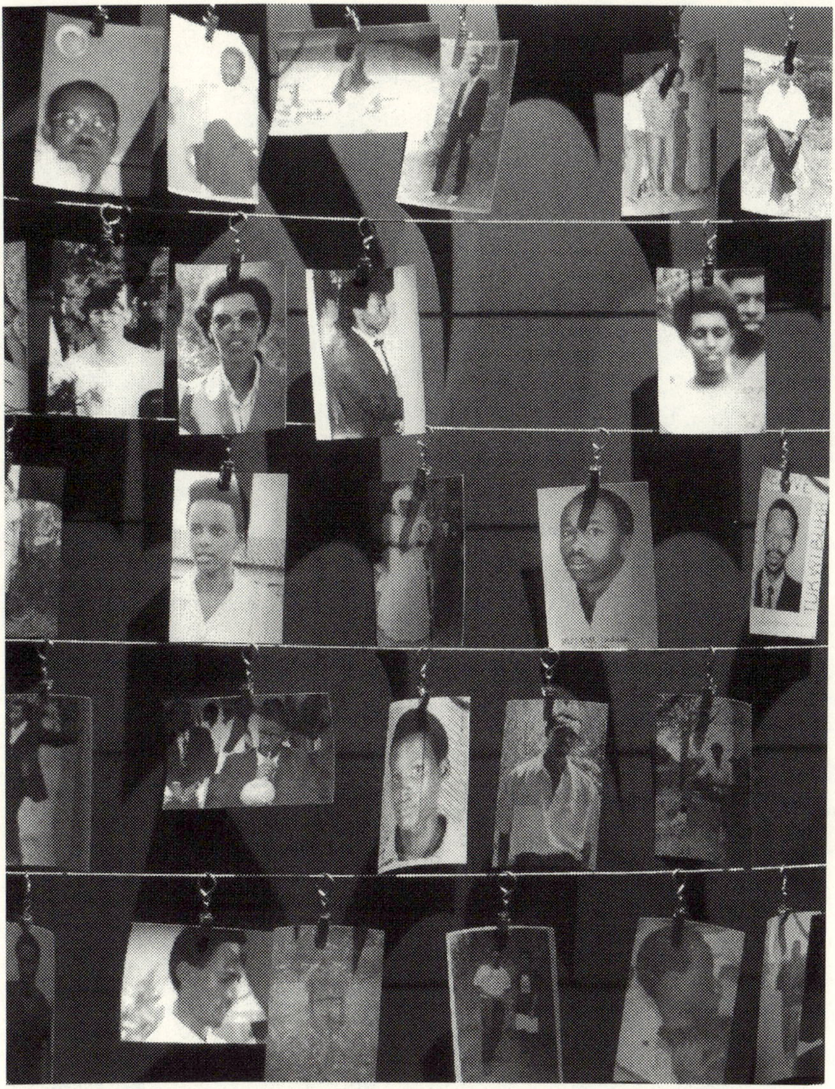

FIGURE 9. Kigali Memorial Centre memorial room of victim photographs. Photo by Adam Jones, PhD / Global Photo Archive / Flickr.

In the next memorial room, the walls are lined with bones laid out in well-lit display cases. Like other genocide memorials throughout Rwanda, this room displays human remains in the effort to depict the extreme violence of the genocide; however, by placing the bones behind glass in a neat and symmetrical display, the effect is much more sanitized and orderly than the gaping wounds of the other memorials. Long bones methodically line the room with skulls in a row in the center; some have visible fractures, perhaps caused by machetes. There is a display case filled with personal artifacts: shoes, a pipe, keys, a rosary. In the background, the names of the victims are read by a disembodied voice; a few moments in this room again gives the visitor a sense of the scale of the genocide. The final memorial room again projects survivor testimony, and here the walls are hung with clothing from the victims, another trope referencing the other memorials throughout Rwanda, but sanitized and hauntingly beautiful in the Kigali Centre. Together with traditional Rwandan clothing are modern, familiar touches for the western visitor: a Superman sheet, a Cornell University sweatshirt. Again, this memorial room seeks to draw the visitor in and demonstrate that this did not happen in some distant place long ago but to people *just like you*.

The final element of the permanent exhibit is the memorial to the children, which consists of large photographs of Rwandan children accompanied by plaques listing the child's name and age and a few facts about the child: favorite food, favorite sport, best friend, last words, and a short description of how the child was killed ("hacked to death by a machete," for example). The simplicity of the memorial and the unthinkable brutality that it conveys is particularly powerful and affective. Again, the visitor exits through a room of photos, which are there for the taking, if a photograph can be any consolation. This is the most emotionally powerful part of the exhibition and elicits a deeply affective response in the visitor not unlike other genocide memorials such as those in Murambi or Ntarama with their staggering displays of bones and corpses; in this way, it complements the historical and intellectual experience of the exhibit and provides the affective commemorative counterpart to the pedagogical strategies used in the rest of the museum. And this kind of affective remembrance in Rwanda's national memorials is not accidental and can be interpreted as deeply political. As Jens Meirhenrich, who has surveyed hundreds of memorials in Rwanda, writes, "It is . . . difficult to formulate critical questions about the legitimacy of the post-genocidal regime when one is face to face—both literally and figuratively—with the legacies of the genocidal regime that preceded it. By remembering the past in a very particular, macabre manner, these memorials facilitate a forgetting of the present" (2011, 289).

THE MEMORIAL COMPLEX

Outside of the main building that houses the exhibition, there is a brilliantly blue pool with a memorial sculpture cradling an eternal flame. Surrounding the building, the grounds of the Kigali Centre hold fourteen mass graves,[15] with the remains of almost 259,000 individuals that were killed and hastily buried in shallow graves in and around Kigali. Every year, during the hundred-day mourning period, additional remains are buried, and the center in Gisozi has become Kigali's graveyard. Next to the mass graves is the wall of names, which reflects the ambitious attempt of the Kigali Centre to collect the names of all who were killed in and around Kigali, which they hope to someday expand to all of Rwanda. The process of collection is arduous, involving door-to-door interviews of people living in and around Kigali, and has severe limitations, as often entire families or even blocks were wiped out, leaving very little memory of who once lived there. Speaking to the difficulty of the task, the wall of names is far from complete; thirty-thousand names had been collected at the time of my visit and only a few thousand engraved on the wall. Next to the mass graves are the "Gardens of Reflection," a beautiful and peaceful space for quiet contemplation and remembrance and "reflect[ion] on how we all have the personal responsibility to prevent discrimination and mass atrocity" (Kigali Genocide Memorial "Burial Place").

Reflecting the sustained importance of confronting Rwanda's violent past, a masterplan for an ambitious expansion, headed by the Aegis Trust, has been drawn up by the British architectural firm John McAslan Architects and Studio Landmarks in Kigali to extensively expand and redevelop the grounds. A Genocide Memorial Amphitheater adjacent to the mass graves was dedicated in 2014, and there are plans to develop the memorial gardens and grounds to include a "Forest of Memory, Stream of Tears and Lake of Reflection" on the south side of the site (Lawson 2014). The mass graves and amphitheater will divide the site into this southern section, focused on remembrance and loss, and a northern section, focused on information about the genocide (Lawson 2014). In the northern section, the masterplan envisions new buildings for the museum and the educational facilities and archive that currently share a small adjacent building. The complex will include a new Genocide Archive of Rwanda,[16] created by MASS Design Group, the firm focused on "design that heals" that is also designing the new Montgomery, Alabama, lynching memorial. It will also include the Kigali School of Genocide Studies and the recently opened Global Center for Humanity, which is intended to serve as a hub for research and education about genocide and conflict prevention for Africa and the world. In the words of the architect, the masterplan is intended to create "a place of shared memory that counters genocidal ideology," reflecting even in the architectural plan the political stakes of memory of the genocide (McAslan).

This development of the site points toward the sweeping missions of many memorial museums to be more than just memorial or museum and points to the Kigali Centre's commitment to peace education, which uses history and memory of the genocide to promote peace and the prevention of future violence. The Rwanda Peace Education Program was launched in December 2013 and is funded by the Swedish International Development Agency and the United Kingdom Department for International Development and seeks to expand on the work the Kigali Centre had been doing to educate school children about the genocide. With this international funding, the Kigali Centre has been able to expand its classroom space and outreach program, which sends teachers and a traveling exhibition around the country. The Kigali Centre has also worked with the Rwandan Ministry of Education to incorporate peace education into the national curriculum. And the ambitions of the Kigali Centre's peace education program extend beyond Rwanda: Aegis Trust and the Kigali Centre are currently working on peace education initiatives in Central African Republic and South Sudan.

It is evident—from the international roots of the Kigali Centre and its inspiration in Holocaust memorialization, the international partnerships it engages in, the international visits and exchange by the museum staff to Germany, the United States, Israel and Poland, and its international ambitions—that the Kigali Centre is decisively part of what we might call the global "memory regime." It emerged from and follows transnational trends in commemoration, and it continues to develop within and with these trends; even memory of the Rwandan genocide is framed within the context of other twentieth-century genocide. Elements of the design are recognizable in memorial museums around the world: the wall of names, the eternal flame, the use of photographs, and the dedicated memorial sculptures and spaces; and the chronological narrative history of the genocide that uses text, images, artifacts, and video footage to support the "full story" echo both the USHMM and the House of Terror and prefigure the Museum of Memory and Human Rights and the 9/11 Museum. As others have noted, the Kigali Centre is a familiar, western-style memorial that many of us have come to expect from memorialization of atrocity (Brandstetter 2010; Caplan 2007). It very much reflects Erll's notion of "traveling" memory, demonstrating how "modes of conveying knowledge about the past have become globalized" (2011, 13).

THE POLITICS OF RWANDAN GENOCIDE MEMORY

The Kigali Centre's elaborate plans reflect the current global need to create memorial museums that do more than solemnly remember the past, instead using genocide memory for education and prevention on a national and international scale. However, despite the center's ambitions, only an estimated 20 percent of the Rwandan population had visited the center in its first five years because it is simply too expensive to get to Kigali. In 2013, the Kigali Genocide Memorial had 65,670 visitors, of whom only 21,834 were Rwandan and 43,836 were international; among those international visitors were UN Secretary General Ban Ki Moon; Samantha Power, US ambassador to the UN; Jared Cohen, the CEO of Google; and Angelina Jolie, UNHCR Goodwill Ambassador (Aegis 2013). This begs the question of for whom, precisely, the museum is intended. And although the center has a relatively sophisticated website and the archive is a large and growing online database of information on the genocide, most of the Rwandan population still relies on radio as their main source of information and has no reliable Internet access. There is clearly a disconnect between the local, national, and international ambitions of the Kigali Centre and the reality in Rwanda, though the goals are admirable and the center is doing what it can to advance them.

The tension between this modern Western museum and the desperately poor, rural, and agrarian population for which it is purportedly intended indicates the broader tension in Rwanda between modernization and memory, reconciliation and redress (Meierhenrich 2011). The Kigali Centre, with its "aesthetic minimalism of a global memorial culture" (Brandstetter 2010), may present its extraordinarily tragic story "in a familiar way" to the western visitor (Caplan 2007) but is at odds with forms and practices of memorialization in the rest of the country, and it belies the ways in which much of the Rwandan population, including many survivors of the genocide, have been abandoned in the name of political and economic modernization. In the effort to propel Rwanda into the twenty-first century, survivors, *lieux de mémoire,* and true confrontation with the causes and results of the genocide have been some of the first victims of Rwanda's development (Meierhenrich 2009; 2011). The shiny, modern Kigali Centre is familiar to the western and international visitors and seems to be appreciated by the Rwandans who do manage to visit it, but has very little or nothing to do with the day-to-day reality for most Rwandans. However, despite the tension and obstacles posed by the uneasy relationship between modernization and memorialization, it is Rwanda's political situation that presents the greatest challenge to center's efforts to translate memory of the genocide into education, peace, and democratic culture.

In any memorial museum, there is both a danger and an inevitability that the museum will serve as an alternative to material reparation, implementation of legal justice, and actual confrontation of the past, becoming instead a symbol onto which a society can project its memory and divest itself of the burden of the past. As James Young writes about the perpetual problem with Holocaust memorialization: "In this age of mass memory production and consumption . . . there seems to be an inverse proportion between the memorialization of the past and its contemplation and study. For once we assign monumental form to memory, we have to some degree divested ourselves of the obligation to remember. In shouldering the memory-work, monuments may relieve viewers of their memory burden" (1993, 5).

Though Rwanda presents a very different context than the late-twentieth-century Holocaust memorialization that Young refers to—in fully reconstructed societies in which there might be a threat that the Holocaust will be forgotten—in Rwanda the danger of allowing the Kigali Centre to replace genuine efforts to deal the past is real. It is a distinct possibility that the center is indeed intended as an alternative to actual confrontation of the present-day reverberations of the past and meaningful acknowledgment and concern for the victims. The government, in its effort to move forward, stifles or simplifies any nuanced discussion of what caused the genocide. It has failed to adequately address even some of the most basic needs of the victims of the genocide, such as housing, land, and livelihood, not to mention its failure to attend to the deep psychological wounds that will haunt generations. And it has neglected all but the six national memorial sites throughout the country. In some ways, the Kigali Centre appears to be a Band-Aid applied by the government to soothe the international community and its own people, legitimate its standing as a "democratic" nation that has come to terms with its past, and avoid addressing the complexity of pre- and postgenocide Rwanda as well as ethnic conflict in the region.

It is essential to remember that in the case of the Kigali Centre, to prevent violence means something different from what it means at other Holocaust and memorial museums around the world: it means to prevent *the very same* (or directly inversed) violence from occurring again. This is a burden that other memorial museums do not have; for them, to prevent violence is an abstract mandate with room for flexibility. For the Kigali Centre, to prevent genocide means to prevent or hinder the violent genocidal ideology that led to the massacre of almost one million friends, neighbors, and fellow citizens in one hundred days. The fight against genocide ideology has been one of the driving forces behind much of the violent conflict in neighboring Democratic Republic of Congo, where lives continue to be shattered and violence and atrocity seem intractable. And neighboring Burundi has seen an ugly resurgence of violence as the government increasingly cracks down on the "opposition" in ways that eerily echo the beginning of the Rwandan genocide (Human Rights Watch 2016).

This is perhaps why comparisons to the Holocaust and other genocides are prevalent in Rwanda, such as in the Kigali Centre's "Wasted Lives" exhibit, which is very different from the USHMM and the House of Terror, which resist broad comparison, leaving the institutions a very abstract mandate to prevent.[17] In the Kigali Centre's comparison of the Rwandan genocide with the Holocaust, there appears to be an effort to demonstrate that the Rwandan genocide was not sui generis and that—like the many genocides that preceded it and the many that will likely follow—it was systematically planned and organized, the result of choices made and steps taken that in retrospect are identifiable and could be interrupted. This troubles some critics, though, as it threatens to create "a simplified and moralized view of the genocide as a replay of the Holocaust" that ignores the actual causes of the genocide and current threats to Rwanda's tenuous peace (Brandstetter 2010). The parallel drawn between the Holocaust and the Rwandan genocide also maintains Rwanda's position in the international community as a victim; this "strategy of suffering" is potent cover for the government's authoritarian tendencies and militaristic actions (Meierhenrich 2011). And while the contextualization of the Rwandan genocide among others is purportedly intended to be about the prevention of future genocide, it is difficult to translate such comparison and knowledge into actual prevention.

The challenge of prevention in the Kigali Centre is enormous, and the attempt in the Kigali Centre is potentially dangerous. As we have seen, the government has imposed a version of the past and the present that often diverges from the known and lived reality of much of the Rwandan population. The genocide, according to both the government and the narrative of the museum, was caused by divisions in Rwandan society forced by colonial rulers, who planted seeds of hatred. This narrative creates a sense of collective victimization that places the blame for the genocide largely on a few "bad apples" and a deadly and pervasive ideology emerging from colonization. Meanwhile the government claims that there is no ethnicity in Rwanda—just one people, reunited after a century of division wrought by the white colonizers. Both of these narratives avoid discussion of ethnic divisions that have plagued the country since well before 1959 and that have not disappeared in the present, but have been forced out of sight. The narratives also obscure the fact that multitudes of Rwandans murdered their neighbors at the command of an overpowering, monoethnic, all-controlling government, which sounds hauntingly similar to the present Kagame regime in Rwanda, especially in light of its actions in the DRC. Rwanda's genocide memorials are complicit in this instrumentalization of genocide memory: in the words of Sara Guyer, "They justify a repressive government by presenting a spectre of past violence as a permanent future possibility, but they also serve as an instrument of repression. Whatever contestation about their legitimacy they generate, the skulls and bones leave visitors speechless" (2009, 161).

By packaging genocide remembrance in a well-curated, compelling, and sophisticated museum, the genocide itself becomes a moment in time; it is contained and discrete. Not only does the museum potentially bear the burden of memory of—and confrontation with—the genocide, it sets it aside as a distinct event with a beginning, middle, and end and firmly sets its precedents in the Holocaust and other twentieth-century genocide. This narrative erases any urgency or historical connection with what is happening in the region and country today. Kagame won a third term in office in 2017, confirming fears that he would become yet another African strongman and ensuring that his silencing of all opposition will continue for at least the next seven and probably seventeen years.[18]

The danger in Rwanda, with a government that has such total control of society and state, is that genocide remembrance in official spaces like the Kigali Centre can be used in a way that advances the government's political and military goals rather than seeking redress for the victims and attempting to learn from the genocide. Claudine Vidal has written about the politicization of genocide commemorations by the regime in Rwanda, commenting that "the ceremonies organized by the regime reveal an inevitable relation of power, first because they capture the silent words of the victims giving them a meaning determined by contemporary goals, and second because they take over the private mourning of the survivors and transform it into a collective mourning in the name of considerations that are not theirs . . . at every commemoration, those in power have instrumentalized the representation of the genocide in the context of the political conflicts at the time" (qtd. in Reyntjens 2008, 201). While the Kigali Centre is not fully under the auspices of the government, it is a public-private partnership, and the government has a strong say in how—and whether—it operates. It is likely that in the acknowledgment and remembrance that it promotes and provides, it has done more good for the Rwandan people than harm. But the past is always remembered according to the dictates of the present, and there is real danger in Rwanda that remembrance of the genocide in the national memorial museum is not about the victims and survivors but about the present political agenda of an increasingly dictatorial regime.

CONCLUSION

At first glance, the Kigali Centre is troubling because it was designed and conceived by a British organization, implying something of a "colonial" memory project foisted on Rwandans—the rampant internationalization of memory. And indeed, it is not at all evident that a museum is how many Rwandans would choose to remember the genocide or that the museum is, in fact, a museum for Rwandans. The museum highlights an uneasy tension in Rwanda between modernization and memorialization and appears to be largely intended for an international audience as a form of legitimating the present regime. But it is the national political forces at play in the museum that are more problematic. The Kigali Centre, rather than self-reflexively facing the past and trying to learn from it, in many ways simply reinforces the government's hegemonic narrative of the genocide.

Rather than a fragmentation of memory and narratives—including those that look critically at the causes and effects of the genocide, as proposed in theories like Olick's politics of regret, Levy and Sznaider's cosmopolitan memory, and Rothberg's multidirectional memory—in the Kigali Centre, genocide memory appears consolidated into the single, dominant version that supports the goals and dogma of the government. This consolidation threatens to usurp for political purposes the memory of those who most need remembrance and acknowledgment and potentially undermines the Kigali Centre's goals of learning from the past, preventing genocide and human rights abuses in the future, and healing this country that is still deeply wounded. However, remembrance alone in Rwanda is not enough to guarantee a peaceful future. At the moment, the antidemocratic inclinations of the current regime are deeply troubling and indicate that perhaps the genocide is not so far behind Rwanda and that "never again" might be more urgent than ever before.

Like the USHMM and the House of Terror, the Kigali Centre grapples with its own particular politics and local context using this increasingly familiar form of commemoration; and like the other two, it has done more than any other similar memorial or institution to crystallize a particular memory and history of the past. Its politics, however, while not as blatant as the House of Terror, nor as abstract and idealized as the USHMM, are perhaps more troubling because of the very tenuous position of Rwanda in a region that is volatile and a nation that is still struggling with tremendous poverty. The Kigali Centre highlights the difficulties of remembering a past that is still an open wound. Today's politics of regret grants political legitimation to regimes willing to confront their past through the use of mechanisms like memorial museums; yet in the Kigali Centre, we see how these mechanisms of political regret and confrontation with the past can easily be put to use in the pursuit of present political and militaristic agendas at the expense of the very memory they are meant to confront. And further, despite the politicization of the past in the Kigali Centre and by the Rwandan government, the "regretful" posture toward the past that the Kagame regime has assumed does indeed appear to legitimate his rule that would otherwise not conform to liberal democratic standards. The past that is presented in the Kigali Centre—despite the efforts of the center and the government to say otherwise—is not yet past, and so the goals and efforts of preventing future violence, dictatorship, or genocide that all memorial museums embrace remain to be truly tested in the case of Rwanda.

5 • THE MUSEUM OF MEMORY AND HUMAN RIGHTS

"A Living Museum for Chile's Memory"

On January 11, 2010, six years after the Kigali Centre opened, the Museo de la Memoria y los Derechos Humanos (Museum of Memory and Human Rights [MMHR]), opened in Santiago, Chile. Like the Kigali Centre, the MMHR was greatly influenced by Holocaust memorialization and is very much a part of the global proliferation of memorial museums as transcultural forms used to come to terms with violent pasts. A stunning glass-and-copper building suspended over a sprawling concrete Plaza de la Memoria, the museum was built on a neutral site to distinguish it and make it more universal than the many Chilean memorials constructed on the sites of torture and detention. The museum is intended to remember and educate about the human rights abuses of the brutal military dictatorship of Augusto Pinochet from 1973 to 1990. Its mission is to reveal the truth about what happened and to "allow dignity for victims and their families, stimulate reflection and debate and to promote respect and tolerance in order that these events never happen again." It is thus both a form of reparation to the victims and a site of education (Museo de la Memoria). And it is also a site that promotes an ethic of "never again": in the words of Ricardo Brodsky, the museum's director, "The political will of Chilean society to see that these events are never repeated is made concrete in the Museum" (2011, 10).

The museum had been almost twenty years in the making. The Chilean Truth and Reconciliation Commission's Rettig Report of 1991 had recommended projects and policies that support memory, such as museums and memorials (Sepulveda 2011, 15). But politics and practical concerns intervened, and it was not until Michele Bachelet was elected president in 2006 that the creation of a museum became a reality. Though a group of human rights NGOs had been negotiating the construction of a Casa de la Memoria to house their vast archive of information about Chile's past human rights abuses, Bachelet, who had herself been tortured by the junta and whose father was killed, swept into office and immediately put into action plans for a government-sponsored memorial museum (Hite and Collins 2009, 19). In the rush to complete the museum before the end of her term in 2010, her administration wrested the project from the human rights NGOs and accelerated a process that many believed should be more inclusive, deliberate, and protracted. The result is today's Museum of Memory and Human Rights, which is meant as a universal, national space of remembrance and education that bridges divergent memories and ideologies of Chile's left and right. But of course, political reality is never as neatly contained as the past is in a museum, especially Chile's complex twentieth-century history. And so while the museum stands as a perfectly realized example of a twenty-first-century memorial museum, one that beautifully and carefully adheres to all the memorial museum tropes that today define the form, the political context of its creation and content compromise its efforts to promote ideals of human rights, democracy, and peace.

STATE TERRORISM IN CHILE

Politically, Chile's history in many ways parallels that of its neighbors in Latin America, just as Chilean efforts to remember and come to terms with that past have followed a similar path. However, Chile's twentieth century started out with greater political stability than its neighbors and saw a period of parliamentary rule give way to presidential rule, with a succession of liberal presidents elected democratically by the populace. In fact, from the 1930s until the 1973 coup, Chile was the only Latin American country to experience no coup d'etats or illegal government turnovers (Loveman and Lira 2007, 45). Despite this relative political calm, the twentieth century in Chile was marked by a series of social movements and demands made by various sectors of society that were often met by political repression (Lira 2011). Though there was a strongly established leftist movement in Chile, the nation was already fractured in 1970, when Salvador Allende—the world's first and only democratically elected socialist—won the presidency with 36.3 percent of the vote, to the right candidate's 34.9 percent and the center-left Christian Democrat's 27.8 percent. Allende's platform promoting swift change and an overthrow of the capitalist system made some Chileans uncomfortable, and almost immediately his presidency was under attack. Opponents of Allende waged a strong media campaign, heightening fears that Allende's presidency was bringing the nation to a civil war, and Chile became an important pawn in Cold War politics. As was a pattern throughout Latin American after the Cuban Revolution of 1959, the United States was deeply involved in attempting to staunch the rise of socialism across the continent. As early as 1963, the United States began using funds to influence politics in Chile, laying the groundwork for a military coup (Lira 2011, 112). By the summer of 1973, divisions within Chile had deepened; the opposition majority in Congress had called for Allende's removal by the military, and many in what was increasingly perceived as a "nation of enemies" expected military intervention (Wright 2007, 50).

On September 11, 1973, the military ousted the embattled Allende government. With the support of the United States, Augusto Pinochet, as commander-in-chief of the army seized power in what was described as a necessary act to "save the nation" (Lira 2011, 111). The attack began at 6 a.m., with the navy taking the seaside city of Valparaiso and then moving into Santiago. When Allende refused to surrender, the military made good on its promise to attack the presidential palace and began the dramatic bombing of La Moneda. From the burning palace, Allende made his last radio address to the nation and took his own life. By 6 p.m., the military had control of the country and announced the coup over the radio, swearing themselves in as the ruling junta and declaring a state of war that suspended civil liberties (Wright 2007, 52). Though the world saw the presidential palace in flames and heard Allende's moving farewell address, the coup went unchallenged, and the junta ushered in a period of terror as the military dictatorship rounded up, detained, tortured, and killed many Chilean leftists and supporters of Allende. Tens of thousands were detained in makeshift centers, like the National Stadium, which became notorious as a symbol of repression. Others were forced into exile. All of it was deemed necessary by Pinochet's regime as an act of saving the nation in the ongoing "war" against Marxism, though the junta had effectively overcome the opposition within weeks of seizing power. While the initial terror subsided, for the next fifteen years Chile was held in the grip of dictatorship and repression as the military secretly and quietly, in an increasingly institutionalized manner, did away with those who opposed its policies.

In 1978, Pinochet declared amnesty for all crimes committed by the military in the years since the 1973 coup. Following this, the Chilean economy began to boom—sometimes termed the "Chilean miracle"—and Pinochet introduced a new constitution in 1980. The constitution was passed in a plebiscite by a supposed 67 percent of the vote, thus establishing Pinochet as leader of Chile for eight more years and ensuring numerous protections for himself and the military (Wright 2007, 81). However, over the course of the 1980s, a lagging economy; the democratization of Chile's neighbors, especially Argentina; a growing domestic and international human rights movement; and several high-profile human rights abuses by the regime renewed the opposition both within and outside Chile. By the time of the constitutionally decreed 1988 plebiscite to determine whether Pinochet's rule would be extended, a strong enough opposition existed to win the "No" vote (Wright 2007, 84). This removed Pinochet from power, allowing for democratic elections in December 1989. Following their successful mobilization of the "No" vote, the center-left coalition called the *Concertación de Partidos por la Democracia* (Coalition of Parties for Democracy, referred to as *Concertación*) won the presidency and swept into power, where they would remain until 2010.

Though Pinochet was democratically removed from the presidency, in the period of transition, he passed a set of "tie-up laws" to ensure his power and impunity would remain intact under the constitution's "protected democracy" (Wright 2007, 184). He extended his leadership of the army for eight more years; passed the Organic Constitutional Law of the Armed Forces, making the military essentially autonomous and outside of presidential, civilian control; and filled the Supreme Court, Senate, and military with loyalists, ensuring that the amnesty law would be upheld. The first democratically elected president, Patricio Aylwin, his hands tied by the fundamentally undemocratic system that he had inherited and counted on for a peaceful transition to civilian rule, resigned himself to mostly symbolic efforts to address the past. As the military and many others in Chilean society maintained that they had been the good guys in the "war" against Marxism, Aylwin set about trying to uncover the truth. He created Chile's first truth commission and carried out a number of symbolic gestures, like reburying Allende and creating memorials.

Despite the power the military and Pinochet maintained, Aylwin and his *Concertación* successors, supported and driven by the strong human rights movement that had arisen in opposition to the junta, continued to seek truth and justice, finding small, incremental ways to ensure the "erosion of impunity on a case-by-case basis" (Wright 2007, 207). Though in most investigations, the government had to guarantee the perpetrators not just amnesty but also anonymity, slowly trials began to take place, the undemocratic pieces of the constitution were revised, and the truth began to be uncovered.

The slow progress began to speed up in 1998. In this year, Pinochet resigned from his position of commander of the army and took the position of senator for life, an honor extended to presidents who had been in office for more than six years, which would grant him continued immunity (Wilde 1999, 474). However, that same fateful year, Pinochet traveled to London for back surgery and was arrested on an outstanding warrant from the Spanish National Court, which had granted itself universal jurisdiction over human rights crimes and had an extradition treaty with England (Wright 2007). Though Pinochet was not extradited to Spain and instead returned to Chile, deemed unfit for trial because of his age and declining health, the case revitalized the Chilean and international human rights movements. Pinochet was stripped of his immunity and charged two more times but was again found unfit to stand trial. Though Pinochet was never punished for his crimes, the power that he had sought to hold onto eroded as Chile looked for ways to confront the past. Pinochet died in 2006, shortly after Michelle Bachelet was elected president and began to make plans for a new memorial museum as yet another form of coming to terms with the past.

HUMAN RIGHTS AND MEMORY IN CHILE AND BEYOND

As the global "Pinochet effect"[1] following his arrest in London demonstrates, Chile's struggle to confront its violent past is intertwined with the broader rise of international human rights in the second half of the twentieth century, which itself is tied to the emergence of memory and coming to terms with the past as a preoccupation for nations and collectives around the world today. Though the Universal Declaration of Human Rights had been adopted in 1948, in response to the atrocities of World War II and the Holocaust, the international human rights regime was not very well established as military dictatorships swept Latin America and enacted their policies of terror and violence. Add to the weak human rights regime the deep involvement of the United States in supporting the military dictatorships in the context of the Cold War, and we see a world that watched passively as human rights were blatantly violated.

However, this passivity did not apply to Chilean society and did not last forever. From the very beginning, there was strong resistance to the military dictatorship by Chilean human rights organizations, many led by the Catholic Church. These groups actively sought to help victims and their families. They also collected documentation, testimony, and other forms of evidence; produced reports and publications; and pressured both the junta and the international community to end the human rights abuses. And the impact of these groups reverberated, "activat[ing] the dormant system of [human rights] protections with implications that extend beyond Chile's tragic human rights calamity" (Ensalaco 1999, 68). Chile's opposition movement was similar to movements in Argentina, such as the well-known Madres de la Plaza de Mayo, and in other Latin American societies in the grip of dictatorship, and the work that these groups were doing was observed and supported by international groups and organizations. Thus the rise of a human rights regime in Latin America contributed to not only bringing down the Latin American dictatorial regimes but also strengthening the international human rights regime, playing a "major role in the development of tougher human rights standards and the tools necessary to enforce those standards" (Wright 2007, 32).

As has been argued, the rise of an international human rights regime is closely connected to the rise of memory, especially memory of violence, atrocity, and human rights abuses, which dominates today (Huyssen 2011; Levy and Sznaider 2010). As is evident in all the museums analyzed in this book, this connection between memory and human rights rests on the notion that memory of past violence and human rights abuses is necessary for coming to terms with and righting the wrongs of the past and thus preventing future violence; there is an ethical duty to remember, especially past violence. This is in part because memory, as a link between past, present, and future, is a "vehicle for assuming (or attributing) responsibility" for rights and wrongs committed in the past at the level of the individual and the collective (Leccardi 2016, 109). A human rights discourse and regime thus depends on memory and the concomitant responsibility of individuals and groups for past actions. And so with human rights comes a set of normative demands regarding memory of abuses of those rights that shape politics today. As Daniel Levy and Natan Sznaider argue, "Memory politics of human rights has become a new form of political rationality and a prerequisite for state legitimacy" (2010, 3). Thus the rise of a human rights movement in Latin America, which helped consolidate and strengthen a global human rights regime, has also helped consolidate and strengthen the centrality and normative expectations of memory in politics around the world today. It is not only the movement for human rights that has moved between Chile and Latin America and the rest of the world but also mechanisms and modes of memory aimed at addressing past human rights abuses.

In Chile, with the restoration of democracy, as fragile as it was, the energy of the human rights organizations that had been aimed toward opposing the dictatorship began to find a new outlet: coming to terms with and commemorating the violence. Following a pattern similar to its neighbors, in Chile memorial sites proliferated across the country, and not just one but two truth commissions were created. Argentina had formed a truth commission to examine the crimes of its dirty war in 1983, and the commission and its report, *Nunca Más*, became a model for Latin American and other countries emerging from dictatorial rule (Wright 2007). Hence in 1991, the National Commission for Truth and Reconciliation was created by Patricio Aylwin, a politically bold move with the military still holding tremendous power. The commission was composed of members from both the left and right under the leadership of a former senator and jurist, Raúl Rettig. It produced what is known as the Rettig Report, which found that more than two thousand people had been killed under the dictatorship. While the Rettig Report was significant in revealing the truth about Chile's recent past, many were not satisfied that this put the past to rest, primarily because it did not name the perpetrators or sufficiently address their use of torture (Lazzara 2011, 87). A second commission, the National Commission on Political Imprisonment and Torture was formed by President Ricardo Lagos, the first socialist president, elected in 2000, to investigate not just murders but also torture and imprisonment. The second commission's report, known as the Valech Report, heard testimony from more than thirty-five thousand people, most of whom were deemed to have been "direct victims" of the regime. The commission was opened for a second time under Michele Bachelet's first term and found an additional nearly ten thousand cases of torture.[2] Both reports recommended as central to the project of reckoning with this violence the creation of memorials and/or a museum as one of the ways to come to terms with the past.

Chile has embraced this recommendation and obligation to remember the victims of the violent regime and to attempt to learn the lessons of the past. The country has more than two hundred memorials to the victims of the military dictatorship, some very well-known like the Villa Grimaldi detention and torture site in Santiago, and many other small, local memorials. Like countries around the world emerging from violence, Chile has enacted the mechanisms that increasingly follow an international set of norms for coming to terms with the past: truth commissions, trials, reparations, and memorials. What was missing, however, was a site where the consolidated collections of the human rights and victims' organizations could be housed—a national memorial and documentation center that could tell the story of the military dictatorship in a way that no one single site could do.

CREATING CHILE'S MEMORIAL MUSEUM

An effort to create just such a site was under way, beginning in 2003 under President Lagos (Hite and Collins 2009). A coalition of human rights NGOs and organizations of families and survivors had collected vast archives of documentation of the military dictatorship and its crimes, which was declared part of UNESCO's Memory of the World Program in 2003, demonstrating its value. The coalition was seeking a permanent home for this collection, a Casa de la Memoria, where the collection could be preserved and displayed to educate about the past. The NGOs believed they had reached an agreement with the Lagos administration that such a site would be created and that the civil society actors themselves would design and run the museum. But then Bachelet came to power and announced that her administration would be creating a museum of memory and that the human rights NGOs would be turning over their archive to be displayed alongside the information gathered in the two truth commissions (Hite and Collins 2009, 21).

This was one of the first tensions in the development of the museum. In the debates and discussions of memory today, in not only academia but also civil society and politics, there is an ongoing question of the process through which memorials are created. As Katherine Hite and Cath

Collins write about memorials in Chile, "Memorials in post-conflict societies are all about process—what should the memorial be about, what groups are involved in the memorial's impetus and design, who builds it, who funds it, who controls the outcome, what dialogues does a memorial trigger, who responds to the memorial once established, and to what degree, and how lasting or fleeting in time does the memorial prove to be?" (2009, 3). This notion does not hold just for Chile, but many scholars of memory and memorialization like James Young (1993; 2016) argue that memory is much less about the finished memorial than it is about the process of its creation. It is through the debates, discussions, and deliberations that true "memory work" happens and the past is truly addressed. Accordingly, memorials today follow an internationally suggested set of best practices that argue for an inclusive process, where various stakeholders, especially the families of victims and survivors, are given a seat at the proverbial table lest their voices are not heard in the development of a museum or memorial. It is also widely agreed that creating a memorial museum takes time and is not something that should be rushed. However, despite these trends that currently drive memorialization around the world, Bachelet's regime worried that if the process was not rushed to completion by the end of her four-year term, it may not ever happen (Andermann 2012, 75), reflecting the deep divisions that remain in Chilean society over Pinochet's rule and legacy.

Thus the museum's creation had to negotiate several key tensions. On the one hand were the civil society groups who had helped to fight and ultimately oust the dictatorship and who wanted greater say in the shape the museum would take. And on the other were Chile's *pinochetistas*, many of whom retained positions of influence and saw memory and memorialization as a political tool of the left that ignored their necessary war against communism. And of course, the museum was created not in a Chilean vacuum but in a region similarly grappling with coming to terms with past political violence and within an international community that not only places normative value on coming to terms with the past but also offers a set of guidelines on how to do so.

And so in September 2007, journalist Marcia Scantlebury was put in charge of the project to create a museum, becoming part of the Presidential Commission for Human Rights Policy. Though a 2007 report conducted by FLACSO (*Facultad Latinoamericana de Ciencias Sociales*/Latin American Social Sciences Institute) to assess the state of memorialization and commemoration of the military dictatorship found that there was not a particular need or desire for national memorial museum (C. Aguilera, personal communication), Bachelet's administration went ahead with plans. Scantlebury and a team of civil society leaders and experts visited memorial museums around the world, including the US Holocaust Memorial Museum (USHMM) in Washington, former concentration camps like Bergen-Belsen and Sachsenhausen in Germany and Auschwitz in Poland, and the apartheid Museum in South Africa to see just what was expected in and of a memorial museum.

Because it was such a rushed process, an architectural competition was held for the design of the building at the same time that one was held for the museum's exhibition design. Estudio America, a Brazilian architectural firm, was selected for the building and Arbol de Color, a design firm based in Santiago, for the exhibitions. Meanwhile, the collection was being gathered from the Memory of the World documentation but also through appeals to families and survivors to donate documents and artifacts. And in a separate process, the script for the exhibition was being composed. This rushed timeframe and its disjointed process meant that the building and exhibition were designed separately, and the script was made to fit the collection that was being gathered, which has had a clear impact on the exhibition, as we shall see.

To enable all this to happen in the narrow timeframe, the Bachelet regime established a private foundation that is funded publically. The foundation not only funded the creation and the operating costs of the museum but, because of its unique public-private status, will continue to operate no matter who is in charge of the government. While those who argue that the creation of a memorial museum should be a long and deliberative process generally cite philosophical reasons, in the case of the Museum of Memory and Human Rights, the practical reasons for taking more time with the creation of such a museum also become evident in the awkward layout of the building and exhibitions and the tensions with the human rights NGOs. But most troubling is the limited context of the museum's narrative; because division remains in Chilean society over Pinochet's rule, the story that the Museum tells is strictly limited to the military dictatorship from 1973 to 1990, meaning much necessary historical context and background is excluded from the story the museum tells. Despite all these tensions, however, the museum opened on January 11, 2010, dedicated by Michelle Bachelet whose presidential term was over. Thus the museum's opening marked the end of two decades of rule by the *Concertación*, which had lost to Sebastián Piñera, the first rightist president to be elected since Pinochet left power.

THE MUSEUM OF MEMORY AND HUMAN RIGHTS

The MMHR is located on the edge of downtown Santiago in a neighborhood undergoing revitalization, which the museum is intended to help spur. It is on a plot of land granted by the Ministry of National Goods and is purposefully in a neutral location on which no particular violence or atrocity occurred to underscore the universality of its message (Sepulveda 2011, 17). The architects, Estudio America, created a building intended to be both bright and solemn; one that symbolizes transparency and conveys a feeling of space and lightness. The dramatic building floats over the vast concrete Plaza de la Memoria, meant to be an "ark where all the reminiscences of Chilean history can be deposited" (Architonic 2009). The museum hangs, suspended like a bridge over a body of water, but in this case the sparkling, greenish museum resembles the water and one imagines—on a hot day, in the blazing sun—the huge, empty concrete plaza feels not unlike Chile's Atacama Desert.

At the base of the sprawling plaza is the discretely marked museum entrance where, behind a small entrance desk, the exhibition begins. Audio guides in many languages are available to augment a visit to the permanent exhibition and accommodate international, non-Spanish-speaking visitors, as much of the exhibition is not translated. In an interesting framing of the museum's permanent exhibition, it begins with a display on truth commissions. A large panel describes truth commissions and how they have been used around the world and in Chile. On the wall hangs a collage of images, forming a "map" of the world; drawing closer, one sees that the images are of human rights abuses around the globe. Below the map are one page summaries of the work of thirty truth commissions, such as those in South Africa, Panama, Argentina, Ethiopia, Bosnia, and Kenya. In glass display cases, the two Chilean truth commission reports reference the centrality to these commissions and their findings to the story the museum will tell. Indeed, the reports provided much of the script of the exhibition, and it is in large part on the basis of their recommendations that the museum was created. This opening exhibit also provides a momentary comparative

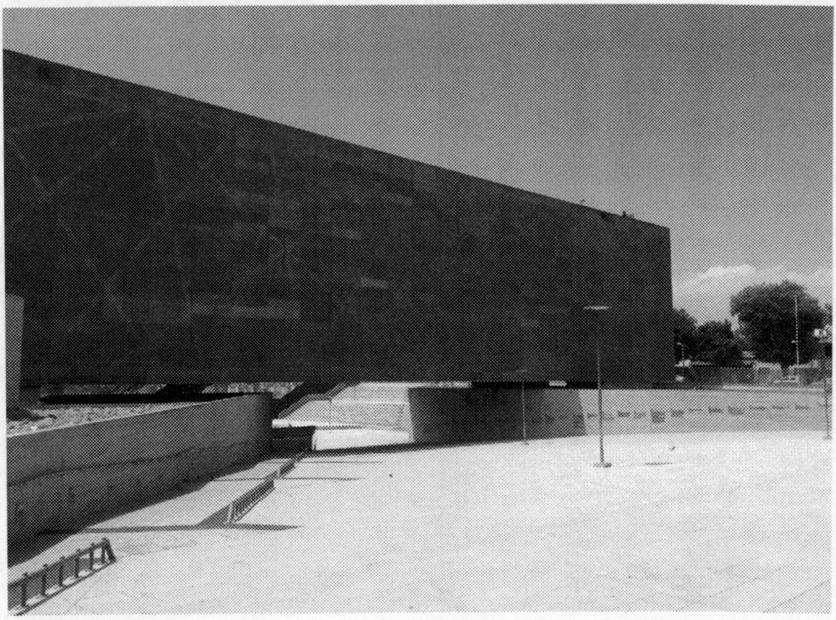

FIGURE 10. Museum of Memory and Human Rights exterior and Plaza de la Memoria.
Photo by Amy Sodaro.

framework, contextualizing Chile within a world of varied forms of political violence demanding truth, accountability, and commemoration. However, the thread of comparison ends here, as does any deeper discussion of the work of Chile's truth commissions.

The other part of the ground floor exhibition complements the truth commissions in its display of a different, but often parallel, form of coming to terms with violence: symbolic reparations in the form of memorials. The focus here is on the more than two hundred memorials to the victims of the dictatorship across Chile. A long, thin map of the country made of stone is the base for photos and brief descriptions of more than seventy memorials that dot the Chilean landscape from the northern tip to the southern. Above these hang a dozen enlarged photos of select memorials. The overall effect is of the tremendous breadth of Chilean memorialization—literally every corner of the country has created memorials, meaning every corner of the country was touched by violence. But with this dual framing of the museum in terms of truth commissions and memorials, the question begins to form of what the museum is. Is it meant to further the work of the truth commissions by presenting documentation and evidence of the truth of what had happened? Or is it a memorial that is a symbolic reparation to the many victims across the country? Is it both? And because the work of both the Chilean truth commissions and memorial projects are so centrally on display, is the museum somehow redundant or unnecessary? At the very least, the museum appears to be wrestling with these kinds of self-reflexive questions about its memory work, and as the visitor puzzles over this with the museum, they are directed to the next floor where the main exhibition begins.

While there was reluctance on the part of the museum's creators to see the exhibition and the museum itself as historical because the past it recounts is so recent, the centerpiece of the museum is in fact a historical exhibit telling the story of the military dictatorship (C. Aguilera, personal communication). Reflecting the controversial—on both right and left—decision taken to depoliticize the violence by focusing exclusively on human rights abuses, the exhibit begins with the morning of September 11, 1973, and ends with the plebiscite of 1988 and, other than the truth commissions and memorials displayed on the ground floor, gives no other context to Chile's recent past. As mentioned, the MMHR's exhibition script is based on reports of the two truth commissions, and much of the documentation and exhibition comes from the human rights organizations' archives[3]—the very materials these groups hoped to house in a Casa de la Memoria that they would oversee. Like the other memorial museums described here, the exhibition uses film, photographs, newspaper articles, official and other documents, testimony, and various other media to tell the story of the dictatorship.

The exhibit begins with the "Area of September 11, 1973." Entering the room, one immediately succumbs to the chaos of (the first) September 11. The exhibit is multimedia—huge images of fearful Chileans in the streets line the wall on one side of the room. Display cases hold a few artifacts like a typewriter and a sign from la Moneda, the destroyed presidential palace. Columns project rotating newspaper headlines from Chile and around the world, announcing the coup. And on the back wall is an eerie image of la Moneda, which does not quite reveal itself to be video or photograph. All around are sounds of bombardment, screams, and expressions of disbelief. It takes a few moments to find the centerpiece of this room, which is a triptych of televisions on the wall to the left, playing footage of the military attack that ousted Allende. The footage is absolutely arresting—the same footage seen in Guzman's well-known film *The Battle of Chile*. One can hardly take one's eyes off of it; and from all appearances on my many visits, most visitors feel the same way and spend a good deal of time watching. Above the televisions is a timeline of the events of the day, beginning at 6 a.m. when the military began to gather at Valparaiso and going until 6 p.m., when the military announced the coup and a curfew went into effect. As we shall see with the "other" 9/11, time has become an important trope in remembering. While Holocaust and other memorial museums also focus on a chronological telling of their histories, in the case of the two 9/11s analyzed here, it is the telling of the events of a single day that forms the most coherent narrative in the museum, pointing toward an intense focus on the minutiae of time but at the expense of deeper understanding and contextualization.

Dotted throughout the room are lighted boxes that provide a more individual experience. Donning headphones, individuals can watch or listen to other documentary footage, such as the swift round-ups of people for detention, the military's announcement of the coup, and Allende's final radio address, when he knows that he will soon take his life. All this audio and image saturation eerily foreshadows the depiction of September 11, 2001, in the memorial museum that is the subject of the next chapter, and reminds us of the now-international exhibitionary language we have for depicting acts of extreme violence. And all the while, the restored la Moneda is in the background; by the end of this part of the exhibit, one realizes that the image is live webcam footage. Why is not as clear, though it suggests a nod to former (socialist) president Ricardo Lagos's efforts to restore Allende's reputation and put la Moneda at the center of Chilean memory of the recent past (Hite and Collins 2009, 15).

It is here that one gets lost and realizes that the clear, controlled path one has come to expect in memorial museums is not present in this one—evidence that the exhibition had to be fit into the existing space (C. Aguilera, personal communication). Not knowing this, a visitor may feel a bit frustrated but can wander, checking room numbers to find the small hallway on the side of the 9/11 exhibit, where the chronology picks up. This part of the exhibition, "The End of the Rule of Law," focuses on the junta's takeover and restructuring of the institutions of Chile, giving the political context of the dictatorship. The left side of the hallway is lined with large photographs of the military junta, each with a scant paragraph of text describing different aspects of the junta's rule, such as its shaping of law enforcement and the political system. The other side of the hallway is lined with display cases of documents, books, and other small artifacts, as well as photographs, newspapers, and newspaper headlines and more detailed information panels.

In addition to the decrees and propaganda of the regime that are on display, there is an emphasis in this section on the junta's use of the media as a tool for its political repression, hence the many newspapers on display. However, as Carolina Aguilera pointed out to me, the museum never clarifies whether the various news accounts on display—articles, newspaper headlines, or televised news stories—are displayed as objective evidence of what had happened or as a demonstration of the junta's ability to manipulate the press and the "reality" of life under dictatorship. Photographs of exiled Chileans, lists of prisoners, and a description of how the regime turned public spaces, like the National Stadium, into places of torture and detention give way to the "Area of International Condemnation." International solidarity with the repressed Chilean population is a theme that will resonate throughout the museum, as though underscoring the "universal" condemnation of the human rights abuses of Pinochet's regime but also contextualizing Chile's experience. And in a striking omission of how this condemnation was in fact not universal, a section on Operation Condor demonstrates the ways in which the Chilean regime was coordinating its repressive policies and practices with the other states of South America but ignores the role of the United States in supporting and promoting the operation.[4] When asked about this omission, Museum Director Brodsky admitted that this should be included, but that the museum's primary goal is to emphasize that what happened is the responsibility of Chile and Chileans and the blame cannot be placed elsewhere.

With slight confusion about the exhibition path again, the visitor rounds the corner to the most dramatic, emotionally charged, and experiential part of the museum: the "Area of Repression and Torture." A dark hallway is lined with black fabric; if one gets close enough, one sees that it is printed with the names of those who were disappeared and tortured by the regime, adhering to the trope of naming victims, though a more subtle yet dramatic take on the wall of names than most memorial museums employ. There is also a small warning about the disturbing content of this part of the exhibit.

In a small, dark room the tactics of the military junta are described in detail. On one wall are descriptions of popular torture methods and a handbook used by Chile's secret police, the *Dirección de Inteligencia Nacional* (DINA; National Intelligence Directorate). Along another, a dark map of Chile is lit up by an astonishing number of red lights marking the locations of detention and torture centers, stretching up and down its long, thin span. More than 1100 clandestine centers have been found, and more continue to be discovered, evidencing the far reach of the DINA (Achtenberg 2013). The room is dominated by a video screen hung over a metal bed. The screen shows nine images of survivors, who recount their torture on grim and heart-wrenching loop. Though the testimony is in Spanish, the English subtitles ensure that many audiences will understand the terrible torture the individuals describe. One after another, they describe the fear, humiliation, and pain that they endured; while the methods of torture vary, almost all of them recall their conviction that they were going to die. It is a stark reminder of the horrors of torture and the impulse to create the Valech Commission to uncover the truth about the tens of thousands of individuals who were tortured. To illustrate the horror further, below the testimony is a metal bed frame, a replica (though only the audio guide will tell you this) of one of the most popular torture techniques, the *parrilla*, or "grill." The *parrilla* was hooked up to electric wires and its victims "grilled" on the

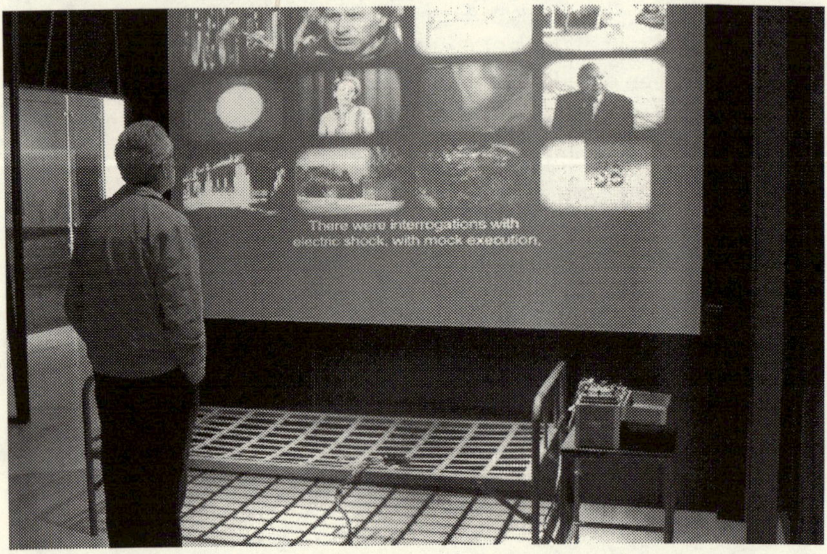

FIGURE 11. Represión y tortura (ALTA) / Area of Repression and Torture. Archivo MMDH.

exposed metal bed slats. Other displays focus on executions and death sentences; letters and other official documents are displayed, although most victims were simply disappeared.

Like the other memorial museums described in this book, this part of the exhibit is highly affective and experiential, encouraging the visitor to feel, for just a few moments, what the victims felt. Through the simultaneous depiction of scale—in the multitude of red lights spanning the nation—and individuality of the victims—in the agonizing testimony—the museum shows the visitor that she too would have likely been caught up in the violence just like the innocent individuals recounting their harrowing tales. In the raw descriptions of humiliation and terror, the visitor cannot help but empathize with the victims, experiencing "a vicarious, spontaneous sharing of affect" (Keen 2006, 208). This experience of empathy is the key to the visitor's internalization of the museum's moral message and is what makes the experience of a memorial museum more powerful than that of mere memorial or museum.

This hauntingly affective room gives way to a room of evidence collected on disappearances and another room on "Findings" that describes some of the most infamous cases of people who were disappeared, whose bodies were later found. One such story is of Marta Ugarte, a communist activist who was disappeared but whose body washed up in a bay. This spurred a search of the bottom of the bay, where railroad ties were found with traces of the clothing that they had been tied to in order to weigh down the bodies so that they may never wash up. Some of those railroad ties are now on display at Villa Grimaldi.

In the hallways awkwardly flanking these rooms is the "Passage of Jail Handicrafts" where items created by prisoners are displayed. There are symbolic and beautiful works, such as dolls referred to as *soporopos*, letters written by prisoners, and various small carvings of seahorses, doves, and other symbolic figures. Perhaps most notable are the copper carvings created by Chilean Air Force general Alberto Bachelet, Michelle Bachelet's father, while he was imprisoned. And countering these small and precious artifacts are two that are large and imposing: a door from the former public jail of Santiago and a watchtower from the Calle Republica 580 torture center. The final section on this floor of the museum is the "Area of the Pain of the Children." The collection of children's drawings of life under the dictatorship, demonstrating the fear and violence that became a part of everyday life, and video testimony of children is drawn from the collection of the *Fundación de Protección a la Infancia Dañada por los Estados de Emergencia* (PIDEE/Foundation for the Protection of Children Damaged by the State of Emergency) and reminds the visitor that the junta's reach extended beyond adults: 150 children were killed and more than one thousand tortured and imprisoned.

From here, the visitor ascends to the third floor and "The Demand for Truth and Justice." While the title of this part of the exhibit may lead one to believe that it will address the period after the military dictatorship when accountability and justice were sought, the narrow context of the museum means that this part focuses on opposition to the regime up to its fall in 1988. The awkward layout of the second floor is replicated on this one, and the long hallway is lined with displays on different groups that fought against the oppression and violence of the junta. Through photos, videos, documents, newspapers, and other artifacts, the work of social institutions like the church and various civil society and human rights organizations to fight the regime is displayed. Thus the internal resistance is granted significant space in the museum, and a section on international condemnation of the dictatorship reminds visitors that Chile was not alone in its resistance and suffering.

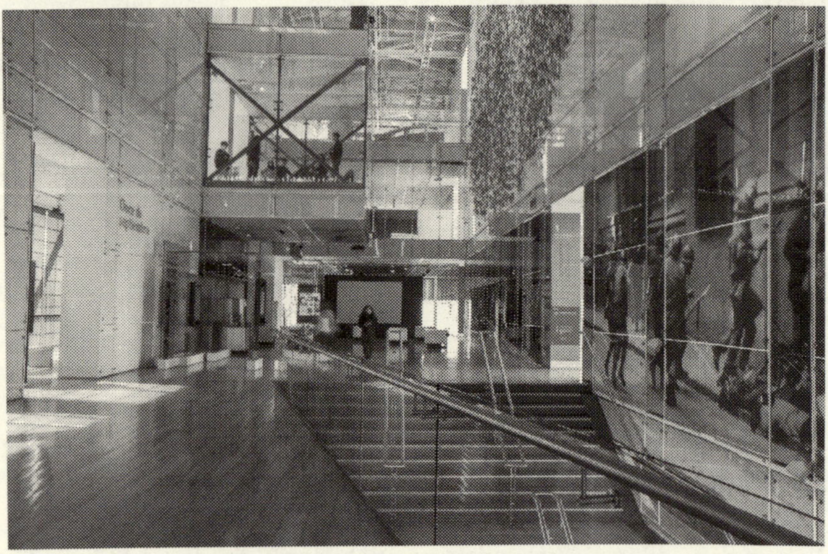

FIGURE 12. Sala 11 de septiembre—Matías Poblete Aravena / Area of September 11, 1973.
Photo by Matías Poblete Aravena, Archivo MMDH.

Inserted in these displays on resistance is the "heart of the exhibit" (*Museo* 2011, 70): a glass box suspended over the exhibit below, facing a massive wall of photographs of the victims that fills the south wall of the museum. The box is lined with Plexiglas "candles" meant to evoke the candles left at the *velatones,* the vigils held by families of the victims and disappeared (*Museo* 2011, 70). The strikingly beautiful "Area of Absence and Remembrance" is the memorial to the victims. Benches overlooking the exhibit below and the photos provide a space of quiet memory and contemplation. But it is also a place for information, as one can look up individuals in a touchscreen database of victims drawn from the Rettig Report. The memorial museum tropes of naming and displaying photographs of the victims, which echoes the Tower of Faces in the USHMM, the House of Terror's courtyard wall of victims, and the Kigali Centre's wall of names and photo memorial, have become fully formed here and foreshadow the similar memorial found in New York's 9/11 Museum. Exhibiting photographs of the victims is central to the work of memorial museums, as it furthers their goals of healing and restoration in the way photographs help return the humanity of the victims that the perpetrators sought to destroy. But displaying photographs of the victims goes beyond restoration; it is also intended to place a burden of empathy and responsibility on the visitor. The photographs of the victims invite the visitor to bear witness in a way that "moves individuals from the personal act of 'seeing' to the adoption of a public stance by which they become part of a collective working through the trauma together" (Zelizer 2002a, 699). Visitors are thus asked, through the act of looking at the photographs, to take responsibility for the past and play an active role in overcoming the trauma of the past and ultimately preventing violence in the future.

The permanent exhibit moves on through the "Area of the Struggle for Liberty," which traces the final decade of the military regime. Growing anger and opposition led to protest and strikes demanding a return to democracy. Opposition media helped spur the resistance of the population, and in 1986, Pinochet's motorcade was attacked. A state of emergency was declared, but the junta was already in its dying days. The exhibit ends with a depiction of the cultural resistance that helped deliver the final blow. Displays on the music and art of opposition bring the visitor to the "Area of the End of the Dictatorship." In this section, the 1988 plebiscite is recounted, in which a resounding "NO" vote at last overthrew the military dictatorship that had terrorized the country for fifteen years. With "NO" ringing in the ears of the visitor, she exits the exhibit, abruptly thrown back out into the narrow stairs descending down from the permanent exhibit. The early display on truth commissions had suggested some kind of exploration of Chile's efforts to uncover the truth and seek justice in the aftermath of such oppression and violence. But that is it. The exhibit and the story of the museum ends, anticlimactically, with the plebiscite.

On the quiet third floor is a display of beautiful *arpilleras*—colorful patchwork tapestries that emerged as an art form during the dictatorship, often created often by families of the disappeared. When I visited, a temporary exhibit was also being installed. There is a small video and audio archive, and in the basement are administrative offices and the documentation center, which is open to the public. Outside, awkwardly hidden in a shaded hallway, are a café and a well-curated gift shop, with local and indigenous arts and crafts and other souvenirs with a human rights emphasis. Apparently there were no plans to include a café and gift shop in the initial design; it was controversial and thought to be in bad taste for people to be eating, drinking, and shopping in a place meant for remembering and contemplating (C. Aguilera, personal communication). But, like other memorial museums around the world, ultimately it was deemed important to give people a place to think and decompress with some nourishment as well as the option to buy something to take away with their memories.[5]

A "PLURAL SPACE"

The MMHR, like the other memorial museums described here, aims to go beyond the traditional functions of a museum collecting and displaying objects. Rather, it has a documentation center that is open to the public for researchers, scholars, and students as well as an oral history archive, where individuals who experienced life under the dictatorship can record their memories and researchers can access the testimonies. The museum offers educational programming, inviting school groups to visit the exhibits and learn about Chile's recent past. It creates temporary exhibits to delve deeper into topics that are not fully covered in the permanent exhibition. For example, when I visited, there was a temporary exhibit on exile and a set of human rights posters on display. And its work extends beyond memory of the recent past and to the larger community through concerts, film screenings, art exhibits, and other forms of public programming. The large memorial plaza is also conceived to be a public space for a variety of uses. Thus while it tells a narrow story of the military dictatorship, it aims to be an institution that is actively engaged in public life and learning.

A large quote on a wall at the entrance to the museum reads "The museum is a school; the artist learns to communicate; the public learns to make connections," demonstrating the MMHR's desire to be a space of education, where there is an interaction between the creators of the museum and the public who visit it. It very much sees itself as part of the public, intellectual, and cultural life of Chile but also a part of international memory discourses. It has hosted seminars, workshops, and lectures for Chilean researchers and students, as well as international conferences and symposia, inviting international memorialization and memory experts like Andreas Huyssen and Tzvetan Todorov. And it is part of a network of similar institutions throughout the region that organizes conferences and workshops on issues related to memory and memorialization. Current and recent memorial museum projects in Colombia, Peru, and Brazil have looked to the MMHR for guidance and assistance (R. Brodsky, personal communication).

Through its public and other programming, the MMHR also seeks to address human rights issues beyond Chile. It has hosted international human rights film festivals and exhibitions, such as the Colombian painter Fernando Botero's series on the abuse of prisoners at Abu Ghraib. Like the other museums in this book, the MMHR sees itself as much more than a museum; it is a vibrant and vital part of the national and international community, contributing to ongoing efforts to come to terms with the past and to build a more peaceful and democratic present and future.

A MODEL MEMORIAL MUSEUM

Ricardo Brodsky, the museum director, writes about the MMHR, "The monumentality of the architecture and the power of the permanent exhibition are the expression of the museum's lasting purpose: to remember the truth and to speak in a voice that crosses generations, using the language and the technical and artistic media necessary to create an experience that is not locked away in the victims themselves, but which rather makes sense to visitors who did not live through this period" (2011, 10). In order to bring visitors into the experience of the pain and suffering of the victims of political violence, the MMHR uses the increasingly familiar global commemorative memorial museum form, which emerged to do just this. As this brief tour of the museum demonstrates—from its architecture, which calls to mind museums like the 9/11 Museum and Libeskind's Jewish Museum Berlin, to its memorial, complete with photographs of the disappeared, eternal flames, and a searchable database, to its exhibits that combine historical information with affective, experiential techniques, and to its goal of morally educating visitors—the MMHR solidly fits the definition of memorial museum. Its inspiration in memorial sites around the globe is evident, as is its international standing within this community of like-minded institutions. The MMHR has membership in international organizations like the International Coalition of Sites of Conscience and the International Council on Museums' Committee of Memorial Museums in Remembrance of the Victims of Public Crimes. Like all memorial museums described here, the MMHR seeks to take Chile's past and translate it into a universal lesson of human rights and democracy for the present and future. And very much like the House of Terror, its goal is to demonstrate to Chileans—especially younger populations—just how bad dictatorship is in order to remind them to work hard at embracing and maintaining democracy.

The MMHR's strict adherence to the many tropes of memorial museums suggests that the form has successfully made its way around the globe and crystallized into its particular shape. In this way, the museum very much suggests that memory—and especially the forms that it takes—has become transcultural in the way that Levy and Sznaider, Erll, and Rothberg suggest. Though Chile's past is quite different from the Holocaust, communism, or genocide in Rwanda, the form in which it is remembered is strikingly similar. In the MMHR, common memorial tropes are borrowed from Holocaust and other remembrance, connecting memory of dictatorship in Chile to other instances of political violence.

As we have seen, memory studies is increasingly focused on memory as a transcultural phenomenon that is not necessarily tied to one particular culture or nation but instead moves through time and space, recycling both form and content. Indeed, the museums in this book appear to embody Astrid Erll's notion of travelling memory, seemingly illustrating "the incessant wandering of carriers, media, contents, forms, and practices of memory, their continual 'travels' and ongoing transformations through time and space, across social, linguistic and political borders" (2011, 11). We have followed the travels of the form and practice of memory in memorial museums from the United States to Hungary, Rwanda, and Chile. This is just a small global sampling, suggesting that as Lucy Bond and Jessica Rapson write, we can view "remembrance as a fluid process in which commemorative tropes work to inform the representation of diverse events and traumas beyond national or cultural boundaries, bridging—but not negating—spatial, temporal and ideational differences" (2014, 18). While the story of the MMHR is particular to Chile, the way in which it is told is not. And of course, the form in which a memory is embodied is important in shaping the meaning of the past (Wagner-Pacifici 1996). Chilean memory of the past is thus shaped by this international form in which it is contained.

But there is reason to be wary of this notion of transcultural memory that travels the world, unaware of borders, especially when we look at the politics of commemoration in a particular context. Susannah Radstone's worries about the globalization of memory studies can easily be applied to the global reproduction of commemorative forms. She writes, "There remains something more than a little paradoxical as well as instrumental . . . about the attempt to produce a fully 'globalizable' version of memory studies [or forms], for memory research, like memory itself (notwithstanding possibilities for transmission and translation) is always located—it is specific to its site of production and practice" (2011, 114). While the forms used to remember past violence may be global, the violence that they remember is located and particular in a way that can be lost in what can seem a generic, one-size-fits-all memory container.

Thus in the context of the MMHR, we see the state terror of Chile's past contextualized globally in the very first display on truth commissions around the world. Chile's past is placed not only in the continuum of the global violence of the twentieth century but also within a global set of "best practices" for addressing past violence as varied as genocide, apartheid, military dictatorship, and ethnic cleansing. The world map and descriptions of truth commissions from around the world demonstrate that Chile was not alone in being victim to political violence nor in the mechanisms used to come to terms with that violence, suggesting the travelling, transcultural nature of memory and its mechanisms. However, when it comes to contextualizing Chile's violent past within the context of Chile's history, the museum is silent. And this lack of context and narrow focus is the most enduring criticism of the museum.

Because of the particulars of the Chilean transition, the museum tells a very narrow and limited story of the past. As was outlined earlier, though

Chile held democratic elections in 1990 and transitioned to democracy peacefully, Pinochet and his supporters ensured a "protected democracy" in which they would enjoy continued power and impunity. Thus the influence of the right and the military did not significantly diminish throughout the transition, and many of Pinochet's supporters and colleagues remained and remain in positions of power in the government and military. As Hite and Collins argue (2009), because of the continued strength of the right and their version of history that sees the dictatorship as a necessary struggle against Marxism, official memorials, like a government-sponsored memorial museum, are more difficult to build than "bottom-up," grassroots memorials because they challenge the memory and story of a still-influential part of the government. Thus though Bachelet had the force of her *Concertación* government behind the creation of the museum, the decision was taken early on to make the story and memory in the museum as politically neutral and palatable as possible. The best way to do this, the museum creators believed, was to focus strictly on the human rights violations that occurred between the 1973 coup and the 1988 plebiscite because there is agreement across political lines that the violation of human rights is wrong.

What this means is that the museum's narrative begins with the coup of September 11, 1973, with absolutely no historical context to situate and explain the coup. This incensed the right in Chile, who believed that the museum's narrative of human rights violations should start earlier and address pre-1973 violations by the left. But the left was also unhappy to have no historical and political context for the violent coup and even more violent repressions that followed; their struggle was in some ways erased in the effort to depoliticize political memory. And the exhibition ends abruptly with the plebiscite and the first democratic election following it. Though the ground floor displays about truth commissions and memorials imply that the museum will address Chile's transition to democracy and the long struggle for transitional justice and truth that it has entailed, again this context is completely lacking. In its effort to construct an apolitical, universal message of human rights, the museum undermines its efforts to reveal and impart the truth about the political past in Chile. Rather, it creates a narrative of "victimization as virtue" (Barkan and Bećirbašić 2015) and presents a decontextualized and depoliticized set of martyrs to some unknown and unnamed higher cause.

This lack of context characterizes the museum as a museum, as well. It was constructed, as noted, on a neutral site with no historical meaning in its effort to promote a universal message of human rights. Because, as we have seen, the human rights movement in Chile is linked to a specific political (leftist) ideology, it was believed that a neutral site would help untangle the politics from the notion of human rights (R. Brodsky, personal communication). However, with the neutral site and the deliberate decision to limit the scope of the museum so dramatically, in many ways what you find in the MMHR is a neutral message without the same kind of impact as an authentic historical site, like Villa Grimaldi, which is deeply moving and widely considered to be a "successful" memorial (Hite and Collins 2009). Villa Grimaldi was a lovely estate just outside of Santiago that was taken over by DINA and became one of the most notorious sites of torture and detention. In 1994, the site was opened to the public and in 1997 was transformed into a "peace park." Today it is dominated by beautiful artworks and mostly resists the urge to reconstruct the instruments of its repression and torture, but a powerful audio guide walks the visitor through the horrors that once occurred on such a peaceful and beautiful site. The experience of Villa Grimaldi is deeply moving, and the power of the place itself reveals a truth and authenticity—a Benjaminian "aura"—that the MMHR cannot.

Thus while the memorial museum form is beautifully realized in the striking glass and copper building, reflecting international expectations and ideals for coming to terms with past violence, in many ways the museum feels rather empty—as if this one-size-fits-all memory container does not quite "fit" Chile's past and its memory. Superficially, the "ill-fit" of the form is evident in the layout of the exhibition: because the architects did not yet have the museum script when they designed the building, they created an awkward container for a memory that had not yet been determined. Thus the path through the exhibit is confusing and not at all intuitive for a frequent museum-goer. But the ill-fitting form goes deeper. While the MMHR checks all the memorial museum boxes in the tropes and trends that it employs, in the truncated story it tells, it is a "partial memory" of the past that leaves the visitor wanting and needing more context to make sense of the violence of Chile's past (Estrada, qtd. in Opotow 2015, 230). And if memory is indeed linked to responsibility, as memorial museums suggest, there is the worry that in the kind of "museification of memory" and "banalizing the past and its potentially destabilizing aspects" in a museum such as the MMHR, the "responsibility of remembering seems to be placed entirely on archives" (or museum, in this case; Leccardi 2016, 116). Of course, the root of this depoliticization and "banalization" is the particular political situation in Chile, which is not at all explicated in the museum, meaning that it cannot address the complexities of memory of political violence in Chile. The museum raises the important question that Bond and Rapson ask, "whether we are right to increasingly think about the past as 'memory without borders' without rigorously questioning whether the most idealistic aspects of memory theory actually reflect the complexity of how commemoration works in practice" (2014, 18). In some sense, all memorial museums have a tension between their desire to create universal messages while attending to the particularities of their pasts. In Chile this tension is even more apparent and complicates and compromises the work of the museum.

CONCLUSION

Brodsky writes, "The task of building a memory must therefore be guided by a moral compass. . . . The goal in the museum's construction of memory is to become a space that assists the culture of human rights and democratic values in becoming the shared ethical basis of our present and future coexistence. Only in this way can we empower our claim of NEVER AGAIN" (2011, 11–12). Just as the other memorial museums described here have a goal to serve as a "moral compass" that helps maintain society's commitment to human rights, democracy, and nonviolence, so the MMHR embraces this ethic of "never again." By exhibiting the antidemocratic human rights abuses of the past, its goal is to deepen a culture of human rights in the present and future. Although Chile has employed truth commissions, trials, memorials, reparations, and other transitional justice mechanisms to this end, it was also deemed necessary to create a memorial museum as a public place in which "never again" can be institutionalized.

However, in negotiating Chile's still precarious political situation, the decision to focus the museum solely on the human rights abuses of 1973–88 sacrifices necessary historical context for a more universally agreeable message. This indicates what Greg Grandin has described as a "shift away from trying to understand the historical causes and social consequences of violence to an almost exclusive focus on how violence is experienced" (qtd. in

Estefane 2013, 164). The danger, of course, is that violence—such as that perpetrated on the bodies of the survivors whose testimony plays in the museum—becomes something inexplicable. But in order to make sense of the past and prevent such violence in the future, the causes and consequences must be explained and understood.

As I have argued in this chapter, the existence of this museum points to the transcultural nature of memory and its forms today. The MMHR is very much a part of what can be seen as a global memory culture. However, in the particular context of Chile's recent past, the form that this memory takes may undermine what the museum seeks to do. Because it is an official institution that needed to be politically acceptable, the MMHR is limited in the ways in which it can confront the past. In seeking to create a robust public institution with a universal message of peace, human rights, and democracy, the creators turned to a neutral site and followed the global memorial museum tropes of remembrance and education. And while the experience of visiting the museum is emotionally powerful and intellectually informative, the past that it contains feels partial and sanitized. Rather than allowing for a travelling, vibrant memory, the museum seems a container that seeks to hold its memory and past still. Michelle Bachelet, trained as a doctor, has said of the past that "only cleaned wounds can heal." However, in the MMHR, the wounds of the past, while well-cleaned and bandaged in the striking building, have been wrenched from the context that would help understand what caused them and how to truly heal them. But the nagging question remains of whether in fact memory and memorial museums can heal; as the museums in this book suggest, whatever healing potential of memory may exist is often eclipsed by political agendas and expediencies.

6 • THE NATIONAL SEPTEMBER 11 MEMORIAL MUSEUM

"To Bear Solemn Witness"

In May 2014, the National September 11 Memorial Museum opened to the public. On the site where the World Trade Center once stood, the museum joins the 9/11 Memorial in remembering and honoring the victims of what was the "largest loss of life resulting from a foreign attack on American soil" (9/11 Museum "About Memorial"). The existence of the 9/11 Memorial Museum suggests that the memorial, two massive reflecting pools in the footprints of the twin towers called Reflecting Absence, is inadequate for this task of remembering, and the museum seeks to be not only a place of memory but also a place "for examining the implications of the events of 9/11, documenting the impact of those events and exploring the continuing significance of September 11, 2001" (9/11 Memorial "Museum"). To fulfill this mission of memory and history, contextualization and documentation, a memorial museum was deemed the necessary commemorative form to contain the history and memory of 9/11.

After the buildings came down and seemingly before the dust had settled on September 11, 2001, conversations began about how to both commemorate the tragic event and redevelop the gaping hole in Lower Manhattan. Discussions abounded: some wanted to turn the site into a park; others wanted to rebuild the buildings, but taller; others proposed a variety of memorials;

and still others advocated leaving the site in ruins (Doss 2011, 28). While it seemed clear from the start that there would be some kind of memorial on the site, it was not clear or inevitable that there would also be a memorial museum, as inevitable as it now may seem (Sturken 2015). What was inevitable is that the redevelopment of the site and the effort to commemorate 9/11 in a way that was meaningful and acceptable to the families of those who were killed and the first responders, as well as to New Yorkers, Americans, and the millions of tourists who flock to the city each year, was contentious from the very beginning. Thus the museum is the result of a protracted process that resembles the discussions and debates surrounding the US Holocaust Memorial Museum (USHMM). However, in this case, rather than a new cultural form of education and commemoration emerging—the memorial museum—we see the difficult process of commemoration of 9/11 resulting in the creation of the by now widely recognized memorial museum form, which in many ways is strained and changed by the complexity of remembering 9/11. In this chapter, I analyze the debates about commemoration of 9/11, with a focus on the decision to create a memorial museum—a cultural form that in this twenty-first-century iteration engages new technologies and modes of remembrance, while reflecting the form's political roots.

REMEMBERING 9/11

September 11, 2001, is a day that changed the world. The clear, blue-skied September morning was shattered by a kind of terrorism that most Americans had never seen and could hardly imagine. Many Americans and people around the world spent the day and night glued to television sets watching the grim events unfold and a search for meaning emerge, as it became clear that this had been a spectacular terrorist attack. An estimated two billion people around the globe witnessed the event,[1] making it truly international, but it was also immediately framed as an attack on America and, in particular, New York City, though of course the Pentagon was also hit and another plane downed in Pennsylvania. And then there were the families. As the initial chaos, fear, and confusion of the morning gave way to the sickening realization of the scale of the loss and destruction, it became clear to many that a new world order was about to emerge.

The discussions about commemoration that began as Ground Zero smoldered and rescue workers searched for survivors indicate just how firmly memory has inserted itself into our contemporary world. The events of 9/11 were captured in countless video recordings and photographs, in voice mail messages and black box recordings from the downed flights; the images seem seared into our collective consciousness. As many tried to erase these images, talk turned to the creation of what Nora refers to as *lieux de mémoire*, or mediated, deliberate, and constructed spaces intended to contain the collective memory of the past. It was not clear from the start just what shape this *lieu de mémoire* would take, but it was evident that the significance of the event and site of commemoration would necessitate a deeply reflective process.

As New York City began to resume its daily routines and the rest of the country mourned and got back to work, at the site that had quickly become known as Ground Zero, a huge rescue effort was under way that turned into recovery as it became clear that no more survivors would be found. Clearing the site of the almost two million tons of rubble became a priority and, with it, recovering artifacts and identifying remains. As this lengthy process plodded on, earnest discussions began about what to do with the site; in the attempt to adhere to the democracy that had been attacked on 9/11, the discussions were intended to be public and inclusive. To guide the process, then Governor Pataki and Mayor Giuliani created the Lower Manhattan Development Corporation (LMDC), which, in 2003, selected a design for the site created by Daniel Libeskind, who has by now become something of a "memorial starchitect." Under his "grand design," which over the years was wrested from his control, a high-profile design competition was called in 2003 for memorial designs. Evidencing the significance of both the attacks and the site, the competition jury was composed of well-known artists and architects, important civic actors and activists, and experts in the fields of memorialization including Maya Lin and James Young.[2]

The jury unanimously selected Michael Arad's Reflecting Absence for the memorial component: two deep memorial pools inverting the towers with water cascading down their sides, which are lined with the names of those who died in a style highly reminiscent of the Vietnam Veterans Memorial. The memorial was initially going to share the space with a cultural center, housing the Drawing Center and the International Freedom Center (IFC), which was intended to be a "living memorial" to 9/11 that told the story through the lens of international struggles for freedom (Dunlap 2005). While controversies immediately surrounded issues like how the names of the victims would be laid out on the fountains,[3] the more vehement outcry was over the cultural center and, in particular, the IFC. Families of the victims were concerned that its exhibits might denigrate America and, more pressingly, that the IFC would detract from the story of 9/11. In response to these fears, they formed a campaign to "take back the memorial" and vigorously argued that the entire site should be dedicated to the memory and story of 9/11. They won and the IFC was evicted from Libeskind's plan in 2005, mollifying some families for the moment.

The underground space of the memorial plaza had been reserved for some kind of museum, and in 2006, serious discussions began about what that museum would look like. At the helm was museum director Alice Greenwald, former director of the USHMM, who was joined by a team of curatorial and other experts, as well as 9/11 family members and community leaders. Set on creating a memorial museum, from the beginning the creators were extremely self-aware of the challenges to the project that lay ahead. They well understood both the normative expectations surrounding the creation of a memorial museum and the particulars of a memorial museum created to such a high-profile and widely witnessed event. To attempt to navigate this difficult terrain, they began the project with a "Conversation Series" intended to bring together memorial, museum, and trauma experts with key stakeholders, including family members, business and religious leaders, politicians, and community members to discuss the potential and pitfalls of the project. They set out with a set of core considerations that demonstrate the self-reflexivity of the project:

- The potential and character of 21st century museums;
- The particular requirements and sensitivities of memorial museums that must balance the concerns of privacy with the imperative to educate;
- The challenge of understanding the Museum's role and responsibility to present visually-difficult imagery without re-traumatizing the public and in an age-appropriate way to younger visitors;
- How the story told in the Museum will contribute to the writing of history, and how the emerging story already echoes key themes of the American historical narrative; and
- The role museums increasingly play as instruments of civic renewal. (9/11 Memorial "Conversation Series Report 2006–2008")

Each year from 2006 to 2013, Conversation Series were held. In the beginning, discussions were more theoretical and broad, such as on the nature and role of museums and the construction of a narrative of 9/11. As the years went by, the discussions became more specific and focused, such as whether and how to tell the story of the many people who jumped to their deaths, whether to display the "composite,"[4] and the depiction of Islam in the museum. One pressing concern was how to display traumatic information without retraumatizing individuals, and for this purpose, trauma experts and counselors were included in the discussions. And throughout the series, a range of museum experts and academics, such as Edward Linenthal and Barbara Kirshenblatt-Gimblett[5] joined the talks, reflecting the desire of this process to adhere to what are increasingly accepted as international "best practices" in the creation of memorial museums.

As the conversation series played out over the years, the creation of the exhibits began under the joint leadership of Thinc Design's Tom Hennes and Local Projects' Jake Barton. As the team began to delve into the event and its meaning in the effort to determine how it should be represented, one striking fact about 9/11 kept returning: how widely mediated, recorded, and witnessed the attacks had been. Realizing that more than half of the world's population likely remembers precisely where they were on 9/11, a driving principle in the museum's design began to emerge, that of letting individuals tell the story of 9/11. This idea of privileging individual memories and stories in the museum was not new for Jake Barton, whose firm had designed the extremely popular StoryCorps oral history project. In a TED Talk on the museum (2013), he describes listening as a form of love and the desire to make "history" out of people's memory. He notes the "symmetry" between the event and how people tell it and how they need to tell it, and from the very beginning, this new mode of what we might think of as "crowdsourcing" history and memory became the key to the construction of narrative in the 9/11 Museum.

As the previous case studies demonstrate, survivor and witness testimony is always a part of memorial museums. In their effort to be both houses of history and spaces of memory, memorial museums use individual testimony to augment the historical artifacts, documents, and narrative displayed in their exhibits. Testimony as memory creates an affective impact that history cannot. It also serves to give the victims voice and points toward the emphasis in memorial museums on the experiences and humanity of the victims and survivors. In the 9/11 Museum, however, the use of "testimony" is quite different from other memorial museums. Rather than memory complementing the historical narrative, the history in the 9/11 Museum is meant to be constructed out of individual memories. Part of this is a function of the new kinds of technology that allowed individuals around the world not only to witness the event but also to record and share their memories and experiences of the event. But it also points to the way that the 9/11 Museum takes memorial museum tropes to a new, twenty-first-century level. The "democratization of memory" that has pushed the memory boom and rise of mechanisms like memorial museums that are meant to bring the experiences and voices of marginalized or silenced individuals into public light is, in the 9/11 Museum, taking on a whole new meaning as individual memories become the foundation of the creation of historical narrative. However, as we shall see, while perhaps the intention was to create a fragmented, "collected" memory of 9/11 sourced from experiences all over the world (Young 1993), the museum instead creates a hegemonic and monolithic memory of the event that is deeply political and problematic.

THE NATIONAL SEPTEMBER 11 MEMORIAL MUSEUM

As the brief background on the museum's creation above demonstrates, the National September 11 Memorial Museum was created in a deliberate, careful process that drew upon the growing collective body of knowledge and expectations about how to remember a traumatic past through the construction of a memorial museum. In many ways, the process of creating the 9/11 Museum is the logical conclusion of decades of "memorial museum mania"[6] across the globe that has contributed to an international set of norms and best practices; hewing to these norms and processes, the process of creating the museum indeed seems to be a model of "memory work." And just as 9/11 marked the geopolitical end of the twentieth century, in many ways commemorating it marks the end of twentieth-century commemorative forms; the process outlined above has created a massive, highly sophisticated, state-of-the-art, twenty-first-century memorial museum.

The finished museum boasts of 110,000 feet of exhibition space "in the archaeological heart of the World Trade Center site," and whether intended to or not, the museum cannot help but to shock and awe visitors—from the twenty-four-dollar entrance fee, to the massive scale of the building and artifacts on display, to the breadth of the collection and minute-by-minute account of the morning of 9/11, to some of its overt omissions. Visitors enter the museum through the memorial plaza, where it is tucked into a corner of the site, which is dominated by Arad's pools. For someone who has visited other memorial museums, the pavilion's steel beams enclosed in a skin of glass, designed by the Norwegian firm Snøhetta, seems typical of the sleek, industrial concrete and steel "architecture of memory." The similarity to Daniel Libeskind's Jewish Museum in Berlin, the USHMM, and the Museum of Memory and Human Rights (MMHR) in Chile is instantly striking. And, as is not uncommon at Holocaust museums, the first encounter one has at the 9/11 Museum, after the often extraordinarily long lines, is airport-style security. Once in the building, visitors must empty their pockets and remove their coats to walk through metal detectors. While perhaps this should make one feel secure, it rather reminds that this is a place that has the potential to be dangerous and that visitors should be alert and fearful.

Inside the pavilion, one can go upstairs to an auditorium and café or descend down into the museum proper, which is located at bedrock, seven stories below the ground and designed by New York firm Davis Brody Bond (DBB). Whichever way the visitor goes, she is met in the pavilion by the skeletal remains of the WTC buildings, two "tridents" that are massive in scale. In creating the museum, DBB set four principles to which they would adhere: scale, memory, authenticity, and emotion (Sturken 2015, 478). We shall soon see how memory, authenticity, and emotion play out, but scale is the first thing that strikes a visitor—initially, the scale of the memorial itself and then the scale of the museum represented first in those tridents, which give a taste of what is to come. As a driving principle of its design and a key aspect of the experience of the museum, the sheer scale of it all is deeply important to the story and memory the museum creates about 9/11. As Marita Sturken argues, the scale of the site, the memorial, and the museum "all converge to convey the sense of 9/11 as an event of massive importance" (Sturken 2015, 478).

Acutely aware of the heavy significance of the event one is about to witness, the visitor begins the descent to the museum. On the first lower level, the daylight that had streamed in through the glass of the Pavilion is gone, and muted lighting and somber dark wood shifts the visitor into quiet, serious museum mode. Past the information booth, the exhibit begins with a huge photograph of the Twin Towers on the morning of September 11, the sun streaming behind them, a spot where many visitors pause for photographs. Breaking the levity, a massive map on the wall shows the trajectory of the planes that morning as they set off on course and then gruesomely changed direction with deadly intent. Here the first bottleneck of visitors occurs as this story we feel we know so well begins to be explicated. Viewing the photo and map, one becomes aware of a cacophony of voices, and as the overview of the events begins to sink in, visitors can begin to make out what the voices are saying. The voices overlap—men and women, many with accents from across the globe. It is a recording of individuals (417 of them to be precise) recounting their memories of 9/11, some of whom were nearby and others thousands of miles away.

As the words of the voices begin to come into focus, so too does a series of columns that lead the visitor forward and onto which are projected words that together create the shapes of continents. If one stands at the right angle, the columns converge to create a map of the globe. Beyond this map, images of people witnessing the event are projected onto further columns. This at

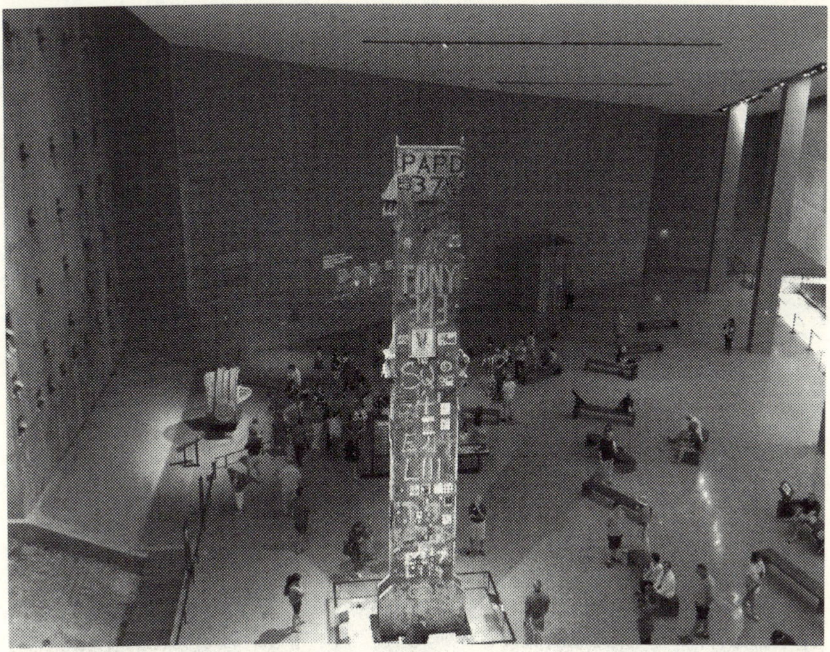

FIGURE 13. View from the platform of the Foundation Hall, with the Last Column in the center and the slurry wall on the left.
Photo by Amy Sodaro.

once reminds the visitor that 9/11 was an event witnessed and felt around the world and also invites the visitor to become a witness to the event as well. And as we shall see, witnessing in the museum becomes an important ethical act and a democratic duty. As one listens, the visitor realizes that like the map, the voices also converge. The individuals from France, England, Morocco, California, and New York finish each other's sentences. What at first seems to depict the multiplicity and fragmentation of individual memories of the day begins to literally form into one coherent narrative: collected memory becoming collective.[7]

Down the ramp past the voices, the visitor reaches a stunning viewing platform overlooking the slurry wall, which was constructed to hold back the waters of the New York Harbor from the World Trade Center buildings. Surrounding it in the cavernous Foundation Hall are scattered massive artifacts, at the center of which is the Last Column.[8] As one gapes yet again at the scale, the depth of the museum begins to sink in, and the visitor must descend yet again to the exhibitions. Another long hallway leads the visitor down past photos of the site before and after the attacks and past projections of the very first 9/11 memorials, the missing posters that desperate

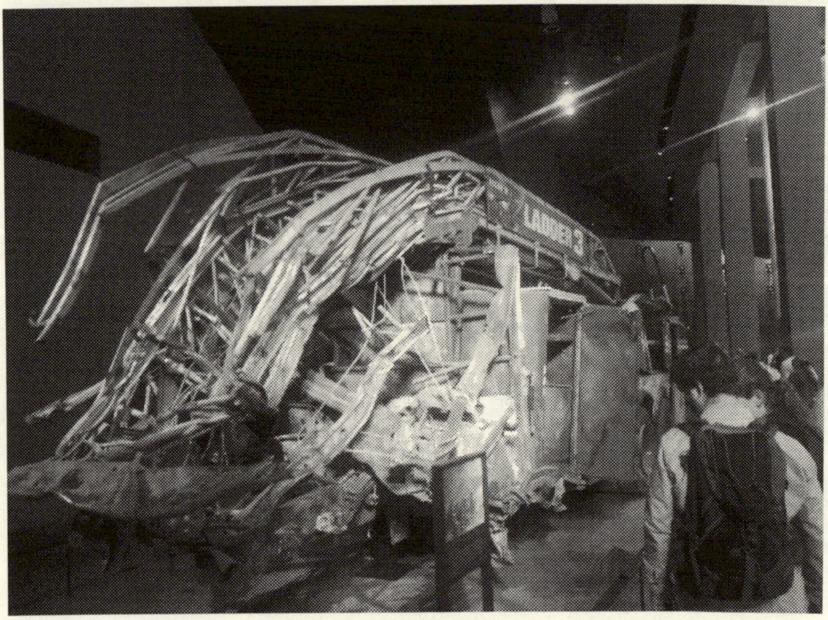

FIGURE 14. Ladder 3 fire truck.
Photo by Amy Sodaro.

loved ones posted around the city. At the bottom of the ramp is yet another viewing platform, this one overlooking the striking and immense memorial artwork by Spencer Finch, "Trying to Remember the Color of the Sky on that September Morning." The almost three thousand pieces of paper—one for each victim—in almost three thousand different shades of blue remind both of the number of the victims and of the beautiful day that changed the world forever. Set into the blue collage is a quote from Virgil's *Aeneid*: "No day shall erase you from the memory of time." Meant to be a testament to the healing and enduring power of memory, the quote has been deeply controversial. In the original context, the "you" were two Trojan perpetrators who were brutally slaughtered after they viciously attacked their enemies. Classicists argue that the original context of the quote makes it more applicable to the perpetrators of 9/11 than its victims (Dunlap 2014). Nevertheless, the quote hangs in massive scale on the wall and also adorns various tchotchkes in the gift shop.

Down one last set of stairs and past the remnant of the "Vesey staircase," which many people used to escape the burning buildings, the visitor is at last in the cavernous Foundation Hall and unsure about where to go. Straight ahead is a cube wrapped in aluminum—the base of one of the memorial reflecting pools, which contains the memorial—and around the corner are more massive artifacts and the other building footprint. It's not clear which way the visitor is intended to proceed, but perhaps in the logic of a museum that constructs its narrative around individual experiences the individual should decide for herself. Here, we will begin with the "Historical Exhibit." Unlike the creators of the MMHR in Chile, who were reluctant to use the term or field of history to describe their recent past, in the 9/11 Museum this exhibit suggests that a mere decade after 9/11, it is an event that necessitates historical framing. In describing the need to create the museum, filmmaker Steven Rosenbaum, who documented the events of 9/11 and the creation of the museum, explains that we oddly know little about 9/11 and argues that "complex nuance and historic detail are at risk of being lost to history" without a museum to tell that history (2012). Thus one anchor of the museum is the historical exhibit, called simply "September 11, 2001."

THE HISTORICAL EXHIBIT

Entering the historical exhibit, the museum experience dramatically changes. Photography is allowed in Foundation Hall, where selfie-sticks, iPads held high, and people posing in front of mangled firetrucks and pieces of the buildings feel almost a part of the exhibit. As the crush of visitors squeeze their way through a revolving door, they are reminded that no photography is allowed inside the historical exhibit. Instead, apparently, all senses are to be focused on learning the history of 9/11. And while the pavilion, the descent, and Foundation Hall are all characterized by their sweeping scale and massive proportions, suddenly the museum feels cramped, claustrophobic, chaotic, and uncomfortable. Thus begins the 9/11 experience.

Once inside one is thrust, in multimedia, into the events of the day. Through images, documents, videos, artifacts, and a constant din of overlapping audio background, the museum endeavors to show the visitor how the gorgeous, blue-skied September day was shattered. It immediately becomes apparent that the exhibit follows a timeline. In the way that all memorial museums tell a chronological story following a controlled path, so too does the 9/11 Museum. But instead of spanning months or years, this timeline spans minutes—102 of them, from the time the first plane hit the north tower at 8:46 a.m. until the north tower collapsed at 10:28 a.m. The timeline snakes along the wall with details about what was happening in the sky and on the ground flanking the passing of the minutes, taking us from Lower Manhattan, to the Pentagon, to Shanksville, Pennsylvania, and back to Lower Manhattan. Surrounding the timeline, the senses are assaulted by the images of destruction—the airplane slamming again and again into the south tower; flames leaping from the gaping holes in the buildings; people screaming and running for their lives. Huge artifacts, like twisted ambulances, remind the visitor of the scale of destruction, while small personal belongings like wallets, eyeglasses, shoes, and backpacks, remind of the human scale.

But most powerful and affective is the audio. The soundtrack to the exhibit is a clamor of voices of victims, family members, survivors, talking heads, and witnesses to the event. There are screams and shouts of disbelief, sirens wailing all around, incredulous newscasters trying to make sense of what was happening even while trying to explain it to their viewers, and the voices of the victims themselves in the voice mail messages they left

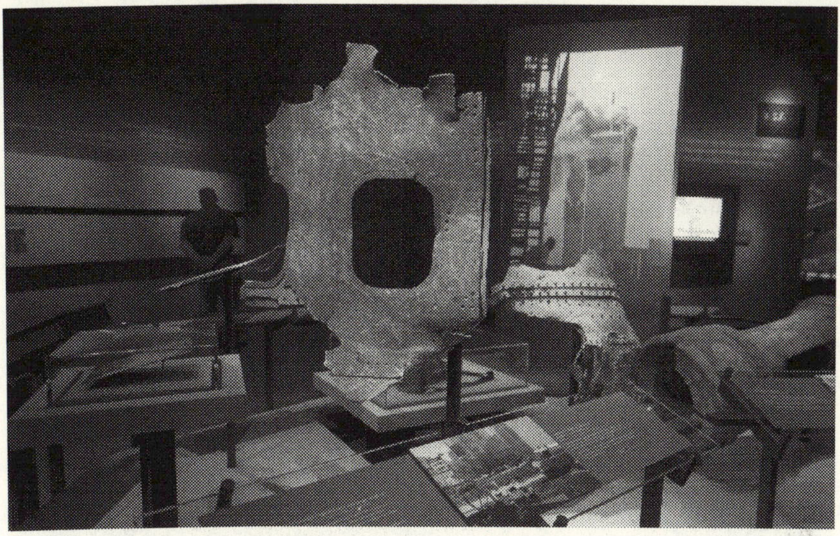

FIGURE 15. Detail of the historical exhibit.
Damon Winter / *The New York Times* / Redux.

for their loved ones. As noted, testimony is an intrinsic and essential part of all memorial museums, but no others offer the voices of the victims who no longer have a voice, and the effect is deeply affective.

If one wants to delve emotionally deeper, there are other moving and affective recordings and testimonies in the alcoves set off from the main exhibit, with signs warning of the "disturbing material" inside and podiums holding tissues discretely tucked into the corners. One of the lead designers, Tom Hennes of Thinc Design, described their efforts to make the space what they referred to as "safe enough—providing enough safety to allow the experience to enter us in the museum, but not so safe that we don't stretch our own horizons and come to new insights about ourselves and others" (2014). Visitors who wish to "stretch their horizons" can enter these alcoves and there, in the dark, listen to stories of those who escaped the building. Visitors can hear the recordings from the hijacked flights' black boxes and the calls made by the flight crews and passengers to their loved ones and to air traffic controllers. One can follow Flight 93 to its heroic end in a Pennsylvania field. Visitors can witness the people who were forced to jump to their deaths in an almost beautiful still photograph of people falling through the sky and in the heart-wrenching quotes on the wall of those who witnessed it. One in particular stands out: "She had a business suit on, her hair was all askew . . . This woman stood there for what seemed like minutes, then she held down her skirt and then stepped off of the ledge . . . I thought, how human, how modest, to hold down her skirt before she jumped . . . I couldn't look any more." Together with this witness, the visitor is also witness to the impossible choices that people were forced to make that horrific morning.

The intensity of the day begins to ebb after the buildings fall. The chaotic audio collage of sirens and screams gives way to a mournful, monotonous beeping of the Personal Alert Safety System (PASS) device that firefighters wear to notify others if they are in distress. Time slows as the visitor walks in disbelief—like those who were there that day—through the wreckage. Twisted metal reminds of the destruction, and the images are so large and powerful that one almost feels herself coated in the white dust that settled over the city. And with the settling dust, a deep sadness overtakes the fear and trauma of the preceding rooms. As one moves through the immediate aftermath of search, rescue, and recovery, which has a dual emphasis on the destruction of the attacks and the courage of the first responders, the magnitude of the task of recovery becomes almost overwhelming, serving to remind the visitor of the triumph of the very existence of the museum.

After the solemnity of rescue and recovery, the chronology that so rigidly guided the events of 9/11 suddenly ruptures as the historical exhibit turns to a set of disjointed rooms focused on before and after 9/11. From the horrors of the day, visitors step into a strange room of kitschy portrayals of the Twin Towers—a model of the towers stands in the center, and the walls are lined with movie posters and other pop culture references, saving the towers from their architectural banality. This jarringly nostalgic room is followed by a room focused on the 1993 WTC bombing. Those iconic towers were the victim of not one but two terror attacks—a stark reminder of their symbolic power and the persistence of the terrorists who want to harm America. With an ideological connection between the WTC attacks established, the visitor moves on to two rooms focused on the rise of Al Qaeda and the perpetrators of the attacks. The centerpiece of this historical contextualization of 9/11 is an almost seven minute video, narrated by Brian Williams, that traces the emergence and establishment of Al Qaeda. In his newscaster voice, speaking at a breakneck pace, Williams delivers a staccato overview of Al Qaeda and their murky grievances against the United States. A wall of panels opposite the film repeats much of the same information, with some supplemental detail, and together these are supposed to give visitors the context they need to understand the 9/11 attacks and their ongoing significance. Largely because of the film, the museum garnered criticism in its early days for not doing enough to distinguish Al Qaeda from the peaceful practice of Islam; indeed, some of the terminology used in the museum—"fringe elements of Islam," "Islamist" and "jihad"—could potentially conflate Islam and terrorism in the minds of some. There is a small panel that gives a visual depiction of the miniscule position of Al Qaeda within Sunni Islam, but in the museum's one hundred thousand square feet of exhibition space, this tiny graphic is easy to miss. From my experience, most visitors watch some or all of the video and perhaps glance passingly at the information panels; after all, one has just emerged from an emotionally draining experience, and "we all know" who committed the attacks.

The final section of "Before 9/11" has two small rooms devoted to the hijackers who carried out the attacks. In these two small rooms, the difficulty of representing perpetrators in a memorial museum becomes highly apparent. All memorial museums focus on victims, pointing to an underlying fear that representing the perpetrators or explaining their actions might lead to understanding or condoning them; this is no different in the 9/11 Museum. The plan to include the perpetrators in the exhibit was controversial from the start. Some viewed the decision as "appalling," a form of tribute and "honor" to the terrorists. Others argued that a historical exhibition must tell the history of what had happened, which has to include the perpetrators (Cohen 2012). Particularly polemical was the decision to exhibit photographs of the perpetrators, so a compromise was struck: as one moves from the first to the second room focused on them, small photographs of the hijackers and their names are displayed, arranged according to the flights they hijacked, and hung at knee level. It was clearly a conscious, if awkward, decision to not only morally and politically but also physically ensure that their status in the narrative and displays in the museum is lower than that of victims, survivors, and rescuers. In this part of the exhibit, there are other uncomfortable omissions as well. Under a reproduction of a letter from September 10, 2001, called "The Last Night," only one line of translation is offered, though the full letter written in Arabic intrigues those who wish to really attempt to understand the motivation behind 9/11. The historical exhibition was developed under extreme pressure from family members and others who believed that including the stories of the perpetrators would allow them a say in the creation of historical narrative. So while the perpetrators are named and photographed and their motivations touched on, the space given to them is limited and kept very much on the periphery of the story the museum is telling. This keeps the focus on the victims and reminds us with whom we are to identify when we remember and process the events of 9/11.

There is more space devoted to "After 9/11," most of which is focused on how America united in the aftermath of violence. A huge wall is devoted to the proliferation of the American flag in the days and weeks following 9/11. Posters of the missing give faces and names to those whose destruction one has just witnessed, and other makeshift memorials, like messages of sadness and hope scrawled onto walls and doors, take one back to those early hours and days as witnesses struggled to make sense of what had happened. Newspaper headlines and magazine covers give evidence of how a whole nation and world grappled with the attacks and around the room videos depict the responses of talking heads, politicians, late night talk show hosts, and others. Though the difficulty of making sense of the attacks is acutely felt in this section, even more evident is the way that America—and the world—was united in grief, mourning, and resolve.

The final room, "Beyond Recovery," opens with a set of questions about the ongoing effects of 9/11, like who should be held accountable? How do we know what happened? Sprinkled around these head-scratching questions are words that they might call to mind: memory, proof, extremists, remains, terrorism, enhanced interrogation. Answers to the questions are attempted around the room, with small panels of text and images giving cursory information. Tucked into this part of the exhibit, under the heading "How Can America Protect Its Citizens from Terrorism?"—and afforded the same space the museum gives to addressing conspiracy theories—is the only acknowledgment of the wars in Iraq and Afghanistan; the United States' use of torture, unlawful detention, and the PATRIOT Act; and the continued threat of terrorism. The museum's scant mention of the wars in Afghanistan and Iraq contextualizes them within the "Global War on Terror" and is primarily aimed at celebrating the heroism of the troops and suggesting that war was a necessary response to 9/11: a photograph of a bomb in Afghanistan dedicated to memory of the victims, a sign designating a navy camp in Iraq "Let's Roll,"[9] a note left at the site of the crash of Flight 93 by someone who joined the military because of 9/11. And while there are two dull reproductions of anti-(Iraq) war flyers, they are dwarfed by a color photograph of a sign toted at a prowar rally reading "We gave peace a chance, we got 9/11." There is a photograph of detainees at Guantanamo, but other than the inclusion of "enhanced interrogation" in the spread of words related to the big questions, this is as close as the museum comes to addressing the US use of torture and unlawful detention in the aftermath of 9/11. Rather, this section is dominated by four large, gruesome photographs of the attacks "linked to" or "influenced by" Al Qaeda in Bali, Madrid, London, and Mumbai. These terrible images, followed by the carnage one has just witnessed, remind us that terror remains a very real threat. The visitor is thus comforted by the nearby photograph of President Bush signing the PATRIOT Act, a reminder that the American government is doing everything it can and must do to protect its citizens from another 9/11. Indeed, after the experience of the historical exhibition, it seems that any and all tactics for protecting Americans are critically needed and fully justified.

IN MEMORIAM

The other anchor of the museum is the memorial, In Memoriam, which occupies the other building footprint. The walls of the room are lined with photos of the almost three thousand victims of 9/11 and the 1993 WTC attack. The color photos are all the same size and fill the walls of the large room, reminding the visitor of the staggering scale of loss. If one gets close, the individual photos attest to the individuality of the victims who were lost. But stepping back and viewing the room as a whole, the photos lose their individuality and become one massive victim of hateful ideology. Inside the room is a smaller, darkened cube with a glass floor through which the bedrock can be seen. It is lined with benches, and projected on the walls, one at a time, are more details about individual victims, such as their age and interests, additional photographs, and reminiscences by family and friends. This same information can be looked up in the touch table databases around the room, very much like the searchable database at the MMHR in Chile. And scattered throughout the room are display cases with personal belongings of the victims—phones, rings and wallets, ear muffs and stuffed animals, combs and glasses. The memorial, which so strikingly reminds one of the tower of photos in the USHMM, the courtyard lined with victims' faces in the House of Terror, the memorial room of photographs in the Kigali Centre, and the Area of Remembrance in the MMHR, attests to the innocence of the victims, who were simply going about their daily routines when suddenly they were taken by an act of extreme violence. Having just been "through" the attacks, the visitor/victim can't help but identify and empathize with these thousands of victims who are depicted as being just like her.

BEYOND THE MUSEUM

True to the memorial museum form, the 9/11 Museum experience does not have to be limited to a visit to the exhibitions. Rather, the museum has a robust set of educational and public programs and a sophisticated website intended to reach far beyond the already massive audience of the museum itself. Like the other museums in this book, the 9/11 Museum is actively collecting testimony from individuals and visitors—not just those who were there during the attacks, but any individual with a memory of the day. It is thus creating a vast oral history archive, which it has used and continues to use to construct its narrative. In this way, it takes the notion of the museum as an interactive and democratic space to an extreme that is practically unprecedented. While the other museums here seek to involve visitors, those who did not directly witness the events are not a part of the writing of history. This effort to involve visitors (and the estimated 2 billion people who witnessed the event) in the museum's telling of history demonstrates a new, more interactive and wide-reaching role that museums imagine for themselves today. And it is largely twenty-first-century media and technology that makes it possible, which the museum has greatly relied on in its design and development.

Utilizing technology, the museum thus attempts to make sure that even those who cannot physically visit the museum can have a virtual 9/11 experience. The museum's website has an interactive timeline, not unlike the one that structures the historical exhibit. In this way, anyone can trace the minutes and seconds of that day. It also offers an interactive, virtual tour of the museum and memorial in which visitors can select their own paths, customizing their experiences. It has timelines of the recovery of the site and resources on everything from the health of recovery workers to recent terror attacks.

For those wishing to go deeper, the museum and website offer robust educational resources. In addition to school visits, the museum hosts professional development for teachers and summer programs and workshops for students and offers online lesson plans and teaching guides for those who are not local. There is a museum ambassador program for high school students who spend a year working at the museum, researching, writing, and giving artifact talks. There are also family programs that use stories and art to teach younger children about 9/11. And for those on the other end of the educational spectrum, scholars and graduate students, the museum's website has an archive of primary sources related to 9/11 (9/11 Memorial "Primary Sources"), including such documents as Osama Bin Laden's "Declaration of Jihad against Americans" from 1996, a full translation of the terrorists' "Last Night" letter of September 10, 2001, the congressional authorization for the use of military force in response to the attacks, the text of the PATRIOT Act, and numerous speeches and remarks by politicians. There are also many webcasts available that feature experts speaking on topics ranging from memorialization and memory to Middle East history and security.

The museum also has an active schedule of public programs meant to further examine issues around terrorism and 9/11, to fulfill its "mission to explore the global impact of 9/11 and its continuing significance" (9/11 Memorial "Public Programs"). A recent sampling of public programs include a talk by photographer Andrea Booher on "Hope at Ground Zero," a discussion with Henry Kissinger on security and the Middle East, a presentation by scholar Katherine E. Brown on the women of ISIS, and a talk by Manhattan district attorney Cyrus Vance on the competing demands of immediate responses to crises versus longer term security. Thus, like the other museums in this book, the 9/11 Museum seeks to go well beyond the exhibiting of artifacts and documents, striving to be a public space for the asking and answering of difficult contemporary questions. Though also like the other museums, of course, most people's experience of the museum is in fact limited to a visit to its exhibitions.

BEARING WITNESS IN THE MUSEUM

Visiting the museum is a moving, powerful, and sometimes overwhelming experience. And for visitors to Holocaust and other memorial museums, it is also largely familiar. There are common exhibitionary tropes like the narrative structure, emphasis on victims, audio and video testimony, multimedia and interactive displays, a memorial space with photographs and details about the victims' lives; even the architecture is similar, though on a very large scale. However, there are also some ways in which the 9/11 Museum is dramatically different from other memorial museums, suggesting a new twenty-first-century iteration of the form that politicizes the past in new—and deeply troubling—ways.

Memorial museums have as a key function documentation of past violence so that it cannot be denied or forgotten. As the museums analyzed in this book demonstrate, their artifacts, testimony, and other forms of documentation serve as evidence of the violence that occurred; the museums are intended to literally bear witness to past violence. From the moment one enters the 9/11 Museum, it is clear that this is a different kind of event being remembered—one that was witnessed globally. Rather than bringing to light that which had been hidden, like the genocidal murder, torture, or disappearances that other memorial museums display, the 9/11 Museum is not so much museum as witness but a museum *about* witnessing. The museum crowdsources memories of 9/11 to create a history of that day. The attacks of 9/11 were so heavily mediated—by the media itself, but also by individual witnesses—that there is little that needs to be witnessed in and by the museum.

If we think of the 9/11 Museum as a museum about witnessing in a very twenty-first-century fashion, perhaps the most noteworthy part of the exhibition is its use of audio recording—from recordings of the hijacked airplanes' cockpits, to voice mail messages from family members who never made it home, to news reports and individual remembrances, the experience of the museum is predominantly audio. Lead designer Jake Barton described the museum as a "listening experience," and indeed this is central to not only the experience of the historical exhibit but the larger goals of the museum's creators. The hope was to avoid a single story line and instead allow visitors to reconstruct narratives on their own, using the artifacts on display. According to director Alice Greenwald, "Witnesses are the way into the museum" (Kuang 2014). Further, the act of witnessing is conceived by the designers as an ethical act. Tom Hennes, the other lead designer writes, about witnessing: "By maintaining the first-person voice throughout, and by continuously re-grounding the exhibits in lived experience, we have sought to create conditions where people feel comfortable moving out of their own experience to witness the events and others' myriad responses to them with greater empathy and an increased sense of how they themselves relate to 9/11. By witnessing others, and being witnessed by others in the museum, we are all brought into closer contact with our own humanity" (Hennes 2014). However, while the museum's creators intended to democratize memory in the hope of avoiding the creation of a single, hegemonic narrative and history of 9/11, they have actually done quite the opposite. Just as in the opening corridor, the overlapping memories of more than four hundred people who witnessed the event from near or far are stitched together into one "memory" of the day, throughout the historical exhibit, the individual testimonies and memories all reinforce the same story of 9/11. The "collected memory" of many individuals is aggregated into one shared and cohesive collective memory of the day (Young 1993; Olick 1999). While individuals were in different places with different vantage points, together their memories form a shared narrative and history of the events of September 11.

This coherence of the memories of diverse and disparate individuals about such a complicated event is possible because of the limited context of the museum. Temporal context is often politically determined, as we have seen in the other case studies in this book. As the 9/11 Museum was being created, a pressing question that the designers had to engage was the question of when 9/11 began and ended. The simplest answer—and what was ultimately decided upon—is that 9/11 began at 8:46 a.m. on Tuesday, September 11, 2001, and, though the museum suggests that its impact is still not over, in the museum's telling, 9/11 essentially ended when Ground Zero had been cleared. This narrow temporal contextual focus, like in the MMHR, accomplishes several things at once.

First of all, it allows for a narrative that is relatively simple to tell in a museum: a compelling plot line that follows a clear chronology and is moved along by innocent victims, brave heroes, and evil perpetrators. In fact, this adherence to the chronology of the day through the timeline is one of the most striking things about the historical exhibit. As has been noted, chronological exhibits in memorial museums are a common trope and conform to expectations of how historical museum narratives should be structured. But most memorial museums tell a story that spans months or years. In the 9/11 Museum, most of the story spans 102 minutes, so it is a very different use of chronology.

Literary scholar Justin Neuman has coined the term "chronomania" to describe the "obsession with time and temporal disruption that characterizes representations of 9/11," which he argues obscures meaning (2011).

While his focus is on the 9/11 Commission Report and various key political speeches after 9/11, his concept works well to describe the obsession with time in the museum. The timeline is nothing if not chronomaniacal, suggesting to visitors that the important question in understanding 9/11 is not why but *when*. Just as the museum's emphasis on witnessing collects the memories of individuals into one shared memory/history of the day, its emphasis on time "by refashioning disaster as chronology . . . aims to replace victims with knowers—first by establishing an authorial subject in command of its perceptual, technological and temporal fields, and second, by attempting to shape personal and collective understandings of 9/11 by securing events unfolding in multiple locations and witnessed in myriad ways on a single, immanent timeline" (Neuman 2011). The timeline becomes all important—the anchor to an understanding of the day that obscures deeper meanings.

This chronomania of the timeline leads us to the second way in which the narrow contextual focus of the museum works: to depict 9/11 as a rupture that occurred "out of the blue," the blue in this idiom of course being the sky. This notion of 9/11 as an event that occurred out of the blue is quite literally suggested in the frequent representational focus on the beautiful September day that was ruptured when planes fell out of the perfect blue sky. The museum's massive wall of sky blues underlines this idealized gorgeous blue from which 9/11 came out, and this is indeed a tempting way to think of that day. It is also a way of remembering 9/11 that is very much encouraged in wide-ranging representations of the day in large part because it allows us to forget about the causes of the event. The framing of 9/11 as a rupture has become very important politically. As Neuman writes, "The disappearance of history at the heart of chronomania denies the narratives that would consider the role played by American policies in creating the material conditions out of which 9/11 arose and substitutes for them dystopian imaginings of greater violence yet to come" (2011).

And this brings us to the third key function of the narrow focus of the museum on the events of the day: this allows the museum—and as Neuman's work shows, other representations of 9/11—to avoid confrontation with the politics behind the cause and consequences of 9/11. This is deeply problematic in a memorial museum. Because they are both museum and memorial, an important feature of memorial museums is their ability to give context to the violence that occurred. Memorials can effectively remember victims and often inspire some kind of moral reflection, but museums are able to tell a more complete story that combines affect with understanding in order to convey a moral message. And so memorial museums to political violence are meant to take painstaking steps to contextualize the violence so that visitors are better able to comprehend what happened and why. However, of the more than one hundred thousand feet of exhibition space in the 9/11 Museum, very little is devoted to context. The two small rooms on the origins of the 9/11 attacks can hardly address the complexity of the motivations behind the attacks and extremist terrorism more generally, and the lack of any meaningful discussion of the two wars, which continue to embroil American resources and military personnel, or the accelerated rise of extremist terrorism belies any claim the museum can make to contextualizing the events within contemporary American and global society.

Rather, the museum's focus on the events and *trauma* of the day—at the expense of historical contextualization—tell a story of 9/11 that is deeply affective and emotional. In its minute detail of the destruction and traumatic rendering of the 102 minutes, the museum's historical exhibition gives visitors such a forceful emotional experience of 9/11 that they cannot help but come away from the historical exhibition deeply horrified and angry. And while the story the museum tells is one of a wounded America, all visitors, because of the ethical implications of their role as witness to the events, are invited to identify with the individuals and values that were attacked. And the museum goes further than simply promoting American values and ideals such as democracy and freedom. It presents a simple, Manichean image of the world, in which the good "us" (Americans, and by extension, visitors to the museum) was attacked by the evil "them." The museum takes pains to ensure that the perpetrators of this violence are depicted as "outsiders"—literal in that they were not US citizens and had spent hardly any time in this country and metaphorical in that they espoused an ideology that is radically foreign to most visitors of the museum. Further, in the effort to not grant the perpetrators too much space or voice, the context given to their ideological position is superficial and sheds little light on the deeper causes of the rise of global terrorism. The museum creates an evil other against which the glorious USA triumphs and will continue to triumph. It is ultimately a highly nationalistic museum that serves a Durkheimian, nineteenth-century museological purpose of "renewing the sentiment that the group has of itself and of its unity" (1965, 420). It serves the purpose of bolstering American national identity, drawing all those who visit into its Manichean world of "us against them." Like the nationalist underpinnings of the House of Terror and the narrative of national revival in the Kigali Centre, the 9/11 Museum's narrative of the past is deeply nationalistic and divisive.

CONCLUSION

All the museums examined here are important as tourist sites, a function that greatly impacts the ways in which they confront the past. However, the 9/11 Museum, because of the global impact of the event, the highly public process of redeveloping the site, and its location in the heart of New York City, is especially shaped and challenged by its role as a destination for the millions of tourists from across the globe who visit New York each year. In many senses, its role as a premier tourist destination has, more than anything else, shaped the institution and how it in turn shapes an understanding of and narrative about the past. Similar to the way the MMHR in Santiago had to negotiate the delicate politics of a country still divided, in the case of the 9/11 Museum, the creators had to try to accommodate not only the divergent responses and desires of a range of deeply involved stakeholders but also many other members of the nation and world with some kind of perceived connection to the site. And similar to the MMHR's solution of limiting the context of the museum's narrative, we see a narrow focus in the 9/11 Museum on the events of that September morning at the expense of any deeper historical contextualization or reckoning.

On the one hand, this allows for people from a wide range of backgrounds and experiences to have a meaningful encounter with the events of the day. Those who were there are taken back to that morning; those who watched the events on television are taken a bit closer to the mediated experience of watching on TV; and those who did not witness it firsthand have the opportunity to "see what it was really like."[10] But much more troubling is the way that this narrow focus on the events of the morning allows the museum to avoid confrontation with the important questions that 9/11 raised and continues to raise. The chronomania of the museum and its role as a tourist site simplify the complexity of 9/11 in a way that reproduces a Manichean narrative of good and evil in the world today. Marita Sturken describes this problem in terms of American tourists: "The mode of the tourist, with its innocent pose and distant position, evokes the American citizen who participates uncritically in a culture in which notions of good and evil are used to define complex conflicts and tensions" (2007, 10). Tourism is an innocent endeavor; it is a fleeting encounter with the past by someone who is free from its weight and burden. The very nature of tourism demands simplification in the effort to make the past something that can be easily consumed and digested (Sturken 2007). And in the 9/11 Museum, the visitors are indeed placed in the innocent, distant position of tourist who is offered up a simplistic version of the past for consumption. After "consuming" 9/11 in a way that is suggested in the museum to elicit thorough understanding, the tourist can then cross the street for high-end shopping, artisanal food, and lovely views of the Hudson River.

If the cultural forms we use truly do shape the ways in which events enter into our collective memory, we have good reason to be wary of what collective memory is being crystallized by the National September 11 Memorial Museum. The museum has exceeded four million visitors since its opening and so promises to impart a particular "prosthetic memory" of 9/11 to many millions of visitors in coming years. But the danger is that this memory will strengthen the kind of outsider/insider division and triumph of the glorious nation that has the potential to contribute to new forms of twenty-first-century violence. In recent months, the United States and Europe have seen a wave of hateful, divisive, and intolerant ideology sweeping political and social life, evidenced in the United States by the election of Donald Trump as president. The values that the museum is meant to promote, such as democracy, freedom, and tolerance, appear to be under very real threat today for many Americans and others around the world. In particular, the Trump administration's focus on the threat of terrorism in the effort to sow fear and bolster support for exclusionary and xenophobic policies like the immigration [Muslim] ban, demonstrate just how ripe the memory of 9/11 continues to be for manipulation and mobilization. And it cannot help to have the 9/11 Museum constructing a national narrative of 9/11 that echoes the divisive and exclusionary political rhetoric from the right. While we can hope that the museum will find a way to stand up for the values it is meant to promote, the traumatic and divisive ahistorical narrative created in and by the museum can potentially help fuel the kinds of dangerous ideology and rhetoric that threatens them.

7 • MEMORIAL MUSEUMS

Promises and Limits

> Perhaps too much value is assigned to memory and not enough to thinking.
>
> —Susan Sontag (2003)

Memorial museums are intended to be about both memory and thinking in the form of historical understanding; they are also aimed at inspiring emotional, affective responses and empathy. This is a broad mandate for any cultural institution; add to this their focus on the most sensitive of subject matter and memorial museums emerge as very complex institutions. In this final chapter, I would like to suggest a few broad conclusions about the form that can be drawn from these five case studies and reflected in dozens of other memorial museums around the world.

Through these case studies, I have endeavored to trace how and why the memorial museum form has emerged and how it is used around the world in the attempt to come to terms with past violence and atrocity. I have concluded that there are three primary functions that memorial museums are created to fulfill. The first is what we can consider their "museum" function—that is, their role as a mechanism of truth-telling about history and preserving the past; in this sense, they aspire to be houses of history where the past is uncovered, documented, and preserved, and the "truth" about what happened is revealed to their visitors. The second is what we can consider their "memorial" function, which is to serve as a space of healing and repair; in this they are a form of symbolic reparation that seeks to give acknowledgment to the victims and serve as a solemn space of mourning and remembrance in the effort to help heal and repair a community. The final function embodies what is most new and unique about these museums and is the very reason that this hybrid form has emerged: they are intended to morally educate visitors to internalize an ethic of "never again." Memorial museums consider themselves to be first and foremost a warning to the present and the future about the dangers of division, ideology, intolerance, and hatred. Their most lofty goal is to prevent future genocide, human rights abuses, and violence, and in their robust efforts to do so, they radically depart from many other forms of commemoration.

PRESERVING THE PAST: MEMORIAL MUSEUMS AS TRUTH-TELLING MECHANISMS

Like other mechanisms for dealing with past conflicts, such as truth commissions or criminal prosecutions, one of the primary functions of memorial museums is to serve as a record of the past and to reveal and preserve the truth about what happened. This was the initial impulse behind the preservation of concentration camps like Majdanek and Auschwitz-Birkenau immediately following World War II, which were early precursors to what has crystallized into the memorial museum form today. Lest it be forgotten what horrors were suffered on the sites, they were preserved. In the immediate sense, this preservation was pragmatic: should justice be sought, the evidence would be on hand to support accusations against perpetrators of the tremendous atrocities committed in the camps. But there was also a more enduring purpose for the preservation of the concentration camps that came out of a sense that the camps and the terrible past that they represented would be something that the future could learn from, reflecting memory's utilitarian or consequentialist function. Similarly, memorial museums have at the center of their mission the function of preserving the past in order to tell the truth about what happened to present and future generations and to preclude those who might deny the history.

Museums have always been concerned with material culture and remains. History museums collect documents and artifacts in the name of preserving and telling history; natural history, science, and anthropology museums similarly collect specimens and artifacts not just for display but for scientific study; art museums' functions are based on their collection of the authentic works of art, which have meaning and value precisely because of their authenticity and which are used for the study and preservation of art history.[1] The museum as a cultural and educational form in society is charged, at least in part, with this function of preserving the past and its physical remains.

These material remains of the past, such as documents, photographs, films, and artifacts, serve as evidence of what happened, especially when dealing with violence, human rights abuses, and genocide. In some cases, such as Tuol Sleng Genocide Museum in Phnom Penh, Cambodia, the detention center was left as it was found by the Vietnamese liberators of the city as "evidence" of the crimes committed and this evidence—including photographs, torture instruments, and documentation by the perpetrators—has recently been used in long-delayed international criminal proceedings against former Khmer Rouge leaders.[2] In other cases, like the District Six Museum, in Cape Town, South Africa, the material remains on display in the museum serve as evidence of what once existed and is now gone.[3] A map on the floor reconstructs a neighborhood that was razed to the ground, and artifacts, photographs, and other documents are the only physical reminders of the past. In the cases studied here, the use of artifacts, documents, and photos as material evidence may not be as obviously functional as in the cases of Tuol Sleng or District Six, but it serves a similar purpose. The material remains of the past are intended to document what happened thoroughly and convincingly so as to suppress any efforts to deny the events and to persist as a record for posterity of man's inhumanity to man.

Further, as centers for scholarship, memorial museums seek to tell the story of the past in a way that is more in-depth and self-reflexive than their history museum precursors were able to. As we have seen, the growing awareness over the twentieth century of the social and political manipulations of the past in the service of the nation-state resulted in a new, apparently more reflective way of relating to the past, with a focus on its negative aspects, the victims or groups that were silenced or left behind, and righting its wrongs. Memorial museums, as products of this shift to the "politics of regret," are not intended, therefore, to underpin the dominant versions of the past that the nation-state would have told—generally focused on the triumph and glories of the nation—but are intended to be more balanced, critical, and reflective in their telling of the past. They are also intended to be open to new scholarship and research on the past, hence their extensive programs of conferences, lectures, book launches, and other fora for sharing research and scholarship. However, each museum also has its own relationship to history, authenticity, and truth, as we've seen, which can complicate their efforts to be houses of history, truth-telling, and preservation that embrace the new historiographical trends of the late twentieth and early twenty-first centuries.

The USHMM has amassed the largest collection of Holocaust-related artifacts and documentation in the world: it has a vast database of photographs and documents that are accessible on its website and in its archive; it has acquired an authentic railway car from Poland, trees from Lithuania, milk tins from the Warsaw ghetto, and piles of personal belongings from Auschwitz; and it has hours of survivor video testimony playing on loop, recounting for visitors what "actually" happened, though individual memory is notoriously faulty. What it could not bring to Washington DC, the USHMM has reproduced: a cast of the ghetto wall of Warsaw reproduces it precisely, and a perfect reproduction of the Auschwitz "Arbeit Macht Frei" sign welcomes the visitor to *l'univers concentrationnaire*. Thousands of miles from the "scene of the crime," the USHMM has placed a significant emphasis on authenticity and re-creation of the sites of suffering to bolster its mission as a site of preservation for future generations of the truth of the Holocaust. One of its primary purposes is to stifle any potential or real instances of Holocaust denial, and with the vast amounts of real and re-created material and documentary, photographic, and filmed evidence that it displays, the museum seems very well positioned to accomplish this goal; only one who is completely blinded by hatred could maintain denial in the face of such compelling evidence.

The USHMM is also a huge center for scholarship on the Holocaust. The museum's Jack, Jason and Morton Mandel Center for Advanced Holocaust Studies is an extremely active center for research on the Holocaust, sponsoring fellowships, faculty and teacher trainings, conferences and lecture series, workshops for scholars, and publications, including the journal *Holocaust and Genocide Studies*. Its purpose is "to shed new light on significant topics, fill gaps in the literature, and facilitate access to study of the Holocaust for scholars and the general public" (USHMM "About the Mandel Center"). It acknowledges that our understanding of the history of the Holocaust is expanding and changing, and it seeks to accommodate this by putting itself at the center of the new scholarship. Unlike history museums of the nineteenth century, the USHMM attempts to both capture and flow with the nuance of history and historiography, including asking difficult questions and raising contentious issues, and remain at the forefront of Holocaust research. Though as we have seen, despite all these efforts, it remains a highly Americanized telling of the Holocaust, infused with American principles and ideals.

The House of Terror has a slightly different truth-telling mission and relationship to scholarship and historiography. While indeed its intent is to document the "truth" about life under communism, it is not necessarily outright denial that it is fighting, but rather, the possibility of the Hungarian people, especially younger generations, forgetting or not understanding just how terrible communism was. For the House of Terror, a large part of enforcing remembrance of the horrors of communism is challenging what it views as the dominant historiography that places the Holocaust and fascism at the center of totalitarian evils of the twentieth century and creates the perceived taboo of comparing fascism and communism. Therefore, central to the House of Terror's mission is questioning the scholarly positions that the museum's creators see as dominant, especially in Western Europe and the United States. In the effort to document and preserve the absolute terror of communist "occupation" in Hungary, though, the House of Terror undermines what could be one of its greatest strengths in fulfilling its mission, which is the power of the historical space in which it is located. The House of Terror is in a building steeped with history, but apparent disregard for authenticity in its displays, exhibitions, and reconstructions takes the power from the building. Ironically, it should be one of the most "authentic" museums examined in this book and so be able to provide compelling material evidence of what happened, but it instead is the most theatrical, resulting in a deeply cynical rendering of the past. Much of the museum's "evidence" of communist crimes and terror is manipulated in a way that undermines the museum's efforts at preserving and disseminating the truth about the past.

The Kigali Centre is also intended to preserve the truth of what happened to prevent and forestall efforts at genocide denial. As an unprecedentedly well-documented genocide, there seems to be little space for denial, and the museum has compelling photographic, documentary, and testimonial evidence of the hundred-day genocide. Though it is not on the site of a particular massacre, the more than 250,000 individuals buried on the site postgenocide give it a heavy air of authenticity and lend further credence to its tale that is, unfortunately, all too believable.

However, as we have also seen, increasingly in Kagame's Rwanda, denying the genocide or questioning the official version is a highly punishable crime and one that tends to be invoked anytime someone of public import voices opposition to Kagame's regime or policies. Therefore, the museum must tread an extremely careful line between telling and preserving the truth about the genocide and serving as a form of government propaganda intended to prop up a dictatorial regime. At the moment, until it takes a harder look at the postgenocide massacres by the RPF, the ongoing consequences of the genocide in the DRC, and the repressive policies of the present regime, it threatens to lean more toward propaganda than documentary and truth-telling. As long as the genocide remains a political tool—for use by all sides—truth-telling will be very difficult, as will being at the center of new scholarship on the genocide if the museum and its associates must follow the official history.

Like the others, the Museum of Memory and Human Rights (MMHR) also seeks to reveal and preserve the truth, in this case about Chile's fifteen-year military dictatorship. Chile's fraught transition to democracy did not allow for immediate confrontation with the past beyond attempting to uncover the truth about what had happened. Following the recommendations and findings of the two truth commissions, then, the museum reflects Chile's efforts to reveal the truth in a way that can help the country move forward. The nature of state terrorism in Latin America and Chile was deeply secretive, especially disappearance as a tactical strategy by the junta. While the bodies of those disappeared may never be recovered, the hope in Chile and throughout the region is that at least the truth about what happened to them can be told. The MMHR is a key mechanism for telling this truth in a way that can reach a broader audience than a truth commission report or the proceedings of a criminal trial. Thus the museum has provided not just a home for the substantial archives collected by the human rights NGOs in Chile but also a permanent space where Chileans can go to learn about their recent past. Because Chilean politics remain divided today, however, the truth that the Chilean museum tells is perhaps only partial, with a very narrow focus on the years of dictatorship that hinder deeper understanding of the causes of the abuses that are so well documented in the museum.

The 9/11 Museum, like the House of Terror, is also on an authentic historic site and seeks to harness the power of the site in its truth-telling and preservation efforts. The colossal slurry wall, tridents, and other pieces of the Twin Towers speak to the enormity of the buildings and their destruction. And like the USHMM, the 9/11 Museum has a massive collection of documents, photograph, artifacts, and audio recordings. However, unlike the other of the museums in this book, 9/11 is an event that was highly mediated and globally witnessed even while it was unfolding, meaning the truth does not necessarily need to be revealed and preserved. Nevertheless, it was deemed important to create a museum full of documentary and material evidence to preserve the truth of the event. In its acknowledgment of the conspiracy theories, the exhibit suggests that part of the museum's purpose is to counter those who believe that the attacks were even more heinous and nefarious than they actually were. But proving these theories wrong is not the purpose of the museum. Rather, it preserves the "truth" about 9/11 as a reminder to the United States and the world of the innocence and good of America in the face of a new, radical evil. The "truth-telling" of the museum is a way to bolster US national identity and invite into the fold all those who are "with us," dividing the world into good versus evil. Further, the terrible tale of September 11 that the museum tells serves to justify US political and military responses to 9/11 that have gone against the very American ideals the museum purports to uphold.

Of course in all these cases, the intention of memorial museums to be truth-telling mechanisms that preserve the past for posterity assumes that there is some "truth" in the past worthy of—and requiring—preservation. Like Hannah Arendt's image of Walter Benjamin as a pearl diver searching for the hidden meanings of the past, memorial museums seek to dredge from the depths of the past pearls of truth that they deem essential to preserve and musealize for the future. However, which pearls they excavate and bring to the surface and how they are displayed and narrated does much to shape our present understanding of the past. A close reading of these museums' exhibitions tells us more about the present's needs and desires vis-à-vis the past than about the past itself. True, the photographs, documents, film footage, and other artifacts from the past are existential realities and serve as evidence that can help us understand what happened and prove that indeed massive crimes were committed. However, which pieces of "evidence" are chosen and how they are arranged and presented can dramatically shape the story of the past into a narrative that fits present needs. The past as told in these museums is indeed composed of pearls of "truth," but how they are put together—artfully as in the USHMM or more crudely as in the House of Terror—can change and shape our reading and understanding of history, from a subtle emphasis on American values to a disturbingly imbalanced, highly political maneuvering for political power in the present.

HEALING THE PRESENT: MEMORIAL MUSEUMS AS SPACES OF REPAIR AND REMEMBRANCE

The second primary function of memorial museums, and one that is as important as preserving a record of the past, is what we might consider their memorial function: memorial museums are a form of reparation, solemn remembrance, and healing. They are intended, to varying degrees depending on how much time has lapsed, as spaces for survivors and families to find peace and healing that comes from public acknowledgment and recognition of the wrongs that they or their loved ones suffered and that is provided by a public space in which their memory is preserved and honored. Throughout human history, individuals and communities have used public ceremonies and spaces to commemorate their loved ones, and memorial museums serve a similar function to cemeteries, memorials, and other forms of public remembrance and acknowledgment of loss. This is based on the assumption that memory is necessary as a part of healing; though of course this assumption overlooks the potential of memory to incite violence, divide people, and open old wounds.

Despite this other very real potential of memory, memorial museums are built upon the assumption that memory heals, and accordingly each of these memorial museums has at least one purely memorial component that is intended to be a space for quiet contemplation and remembrance: the USHMM has the Hall of Remembrance where an eternal flame burns and where hushed visitors sit and contemplate what they have just seen in the exhibit or light candles in memory of the victims. The House of Terror has the memorial Hall of Tears, where eerie lights wave gently on delicate crosses, echoing the memorial trope of the eternal flame and evoking a cemetery. Not only does the Kigali Centre have the Children's Memorial and memorial rotunda, but the entire site is a memorial, with mass graves beautifully landscaped into the rose gardens and around the memorial fountain, where an eternal flame burns. The eternal flame is replicated, and includes photographs, in the MMHR's Area of Remembrance, where quiet contemplation is just one function; visitors can also gather information about victims in the database. This effort to restore individual humanity through photographs and life details is even more robustly realized in the 9/11 Museum where the memorial room not only displays a photo of each victim but also has searchable databases and projects individual profiles.

And of course, upstairs and outside are the gigantic memorial pools if the memory in the museum does not suffice.

Each museum also has, as a central part of its mission, a memorial function aimed at this perceived power of memory to heal individuals and communities: the USHMM is intended "to preserve the memory of those who suffered"; the House of Terror is built to be a "monument to the memory of those held captive, tortured and killed in this building." The Kigali Centre, for which memory and healing is more pressing, has deemed itself a "permanent memorial to those who fell victim to the genocide and serves as a place for people to grieve those they lost." The MMHR is envisioned as the "country's most significant effort to recuperate buried words and return to its own self pieces of its lost heart" (Zurita 2011, 27). And the 9/11 Museum sets as a goal that "the lives of every victim of the 2001 and 1993 attacks will be commemorated as visitors . . . learn about the men, women, and children who died" (9/11 Memorial "Museum").

Public projects of commemoration can do much to provide a sense of restoration to individuals and communities and can help assuage some of the suffering. The mere existence of each of these museums, and their very high profiles in their own countries and around the world, means that the suffering of the victims of the Holocaust; communism (and fascism) in Hungary; the Rwandan genocide; torture, detention, and disappearance under Pinochet's regime; and the terrorist attacks of 9/11 have been duly acknowledged by a government that prioritizes recognition of wrongs committed, redress for suffering, and a new direction for the future. These museums also create communities of and for victims, survivors, and families, providing a space for shared memories, pain, and understanding. Survivors work or volunteer in some of these museums, such as at the USHMM, the Kigali Centre, and the 9/11 Museum, perhaps finding some sense of relief in sharing their stories with each other and visitors.

But the function of repair and restoration goes beyond individual or even community remembrance and these museums are not for the victims or survivors alone; as forms of symbolic reparations, memorial museums have important social, political, and international roles to play. As symbolic reparations, memorial museums attempt to turn the knowledge that their historical, truth-telling side produces—at least in part—into public acknowledgment of the suffering of victims. This recognition and the acknowledgment of victimization are considered to be two of the first steps toward healing and repairing both the individual lives that have been broken and the social fabric that has been shredded. And there is hardly a more effective place for this to happen than an expensive, state-sponsored museum that is prominent not only among the national public but also on the international stage.

To see how memorial museums function as a form of symbolic reparation and seek to repair at the individual, social, and international levels, it is useful to return again to Hannah Arendt's notion of the "promise" (1958). I have argued that memorial museums are built as a promise to the future that such violence, intolerance, hatred, and atrocity will not be allowed to occur. This message is aimed not only toward those who suffered and their families but also toward society more broadly—including perpetrators, bystanders, and those with no experience of the atrocities and crimes being remembered—as well as toward the international community. Not only is the promise of memorial museums evident to their local, national, and international visitors, but the museum itself is an external symbol to the world that the present (and future) regime(s) will not allow such violence to recur. Memorial museums serve as society's "prosthetic conscience"—a social contract with the present and future.

The memorial museum as promise to its own public and to the world is evident in the speeches made at the opening of the museums studied here; the creators of these museums and the politicians who dedicated them were clearly looking to the ruins of the past as the basis on which to promise a better future. President Clinton called the USHMM "an investment in a secure future against whatever insanity lurks ahead," assuring America and the world that America had learned from her lessons of inaction during the Holocaust (1993). At the opening of the House of Terror, Viktor Orbán promised, "We now lock fear and hatred behind bars, because we do not want them to have a place in our future lives" (House of Terror Guide, 67). In Rwanda, Kagame opened the Kigali Centre looking to the future: "We cannot turn the clock back nor can we undo the harm caused, but we have the power to determine the future and to ensure that what happened never happens again" (2004). Michele Bachelet, in opening the MMHR, echoed Kagame, saying, "We cannot change the past. All that remains for us is to learn from what we have lived. This is our responsibility and our challenge" (Kornbluh and Hite 2010). And on opening the 9/11 Museum, Barack Obama declared that the museum would not only capture "the true spirit of 9/11—love, compassion, sacrifice" but "enshrine it forever in the heart of our nation" (2014).

Each of these museums stands as a symbol that the regime responsible for its creation acknowledges and remembers the destruction wrought by other regimes of violence and, through this acknowledgment, promises to be different. While each context is different, the message is the same: this negative and violent past is behind "us" and that healing for survivors, families, the nation and all of human kind can begin, since the evils of the past have been locked up in display cases and musealized for posterity. Implicit in the creation of memorial museums, then, is that the past is truly past. In this sense, memorializing through a (state-sponsored and official) museum is a luxury available to those nations and communities that are no longer in conflict and have the political, social, and economic means to put the past behind them. This underlines the legitimating potential of memorial museums as public way of demonstrating the "door has been slammed" on the violent past (Orbán, qtd. in Rev 2008, 78) and that a new direction has been set for the future. Thus the regime that builds a memorial museum sets itself apart from the previous, destructive regimes and sees a brighter, more peaceful and liberal-democratic future ahead.

However, again we must take into account the particular political and cultural context of each museum. In the United States, it was President Carter who started the USHMM project fifteen years before Clinton dedicated the museum with his sweeping rhetoric, and Carter's motivation was purely political. In Hungary, Orbán and his Fidesz Party built the House of Terror as a central part of their difficult reelection campaign, dedicating it as a promise to their constituents on the eve of an election they would lose. In Rwanda, the Kigali Centre is caught up in the Kagame government's hegemonic discourse on the genocide, dissenters of which are jailed or worse. The MMHR tiptoes so carefully around contemporary politics that it hardly is able to tell its story, and the 9/11 Museum goes so far as to seem to justify blatantly nondemocratic, damaging, and deadly actions by the US government. It is therefore the *rhetoric* around making a promise to the future and drawing the line between past and present, between that regime and this, that unites these museums and the museums' politics dramatically limit the possibility that such a promise will be effective.

SHAPING THE FUTURE: MEMORIAL MUSEUMS AS SITES FOR MORAL EDUCATION

While memorial museums are intended to present an accurate record of the past and serve as a form of reparation, restoration, and healing, their primary goal, as both museum and memorial, is to morally educate their publics to embrace democratic values and internalize the moral imperative of "never again." Museums always serve the purpose of education; however, memorial museums seek to balance their intellectual-historical narratives with affective-emotional experiences that will impact the visitor more fully and, in this way, morally transform her to come away from the museum with a new moral sensibility. While precisely what this sensibility is may differ from case to case—in the USHMM and 9/11 Museum, it's an embrace of American values of democracy, freedom, innocence, and (a particular form of) tolerance; in the House of Terror and the MMHR, it's the value of democracy over dictatorship; and in the Kigali Centre, it's the dangers of divisionism and genocide ideology—in each museum, the goal is to create a newly moral public that will work to prevent future violence. It is not enough to reach the mind of the visitor so that she comes away with a more thorough understanding of the past; the museums also strive to reach the visitor's heart, so she absorbs the lessons of history and actively puts those lessons to work in the present and the future. They attempt to use empathy, affect, and emotion to educate the visitor against what Adorno referred to as the "coldness of reason," which he believed lies at the heart of modern society and its most damning moment—Auschwitz.

Of course, many other memorials today have such preventative aspirations built into them; Santayana's dictum that "those who cannot remember the past are condemned to repeat it" is one of the dominant justifications underpinning the memorial frenzy of the day. We have seen that there appears to be a strong ethical demand to remember, based in part in the belief that memory can help prevent violence in the future. Around the world, human rights memorials are being constructed at a dizzying rate as communities, societies, and nations struggle to learn from past violence and prevent it in the future. However, it appears that experiential memorial museums are perceived to be especially well-equipped to create an emotional *and* intellectual experience that will morally impact the visitor in a way that a memorial cannot do, creating Alison Landsberg's "prosthetic memory" with all of its ethical potential. It is their particular ability to reach visitors' hearts *and* minds and their lofty goals of morally transforming their publics that set memorial museums apart from other forms of commemoration and makes them a unique and entirely new cultural form for remembering the past.

As I have noted, museums play a particular role in society; they are spaces of education that produce and disseminate what Carol Duncan calls "secular knowledge," which "functions in our society as higher, authoritative truth" (1995, 90). Despite our postmodern skepticism of "truth" and "history," even today we tend to visit museums expecting a degree of authenticity, objectivity, and truth that we may not expect from a more artistic and abstract form of commemoration like the Memorial to the Murdered Jews of Europe in Berlin or the Vietnam Veterans Memorial in Washington, DC. Museums are still presumed to be houses of history, with the "facts" and "evidence" laid out in an objective manner that tells us the truth about what happened. The experience of a museum is different from more abstract forms of commemoration, and the "higher, authoritative truth" of a museum is clearly believed to have a powerful impact on visitors, and so museums are considered an important—if not essential—way to deal with a difficult past.

Museums also provide a regulated and mediated experience beyond that of a different kind of memorial; most if not all memorial museums use a controlled path that leads the visitor not only through the narrative but also through the experience of the exhibition, and each step of the way is highly mediated with a particular visitor experience in mind, though of course visitors bring their own experiences and backgrounds to their visits and may have a completely different experience than that which is intended. But unlike memorials that are clearly open to multiple interpretations and experiences, memorial museums do not appear to allow for the same level of interpretative freedom. This makes their messages and experiences especially powerful, as museums are a voice of authoritative truth; this is especially true of the state-sponsored "official" memorial museums like those I have considered here.

Further, museums create a particular audience experience. Tony Bennett describes the "exhibitionary complex" in which the crowd both sees the exhibition and sees itself as part of the exhibition, thus learning self-regulation—"a society watching over itself" (1999, 341). For Bennett, the museum works not unlike a panopticon in that its visitors internalize the discipline they acquire, knowing that they are being watched. He describes the history of the museum as intended to provide spiritual uplift for the working class masses; part of the goal of early museums was to teach the lower classes self-regulation that would persist outside the museum in their social life. Similarly, memorial museums wish to see their visitors take a moral message away with them that will help improve society. Memorial museums, in attempting to reach the "heart" of the visitor, work to create a personalized experience of the exhibit—one that the visitor can connect to her own life and experience. But at the same time, the museum experience is a public one, and the fact that one is "experiencing" the suffering of the past with others is extremely important. If indeed part of the function of the museum is to create a self-regulating public, then a memorial museum takes it a step further and seeks to create a *morally* self-regulating public. Not only are the museums' visitors aware of and so internalize how they behave while experiencing the exhibition, but the memorial museum also seeks for them to internalize, with the discipline of being watched, the moral lesson of the past that they have learned in the museum, leading to a new moral discipline in everyday life. Together with self-regulation in how they experience the past, memorial museums' visitors are intended to also internalize the values that oppose the horrors on display in the museum in a way that they will carry into the future.

But how is it, exactly, that museums attempt to make the leap from a powerful emotional experience in the museum to a moral transformation and shift in moral sensibility that will be sustained beyond the museum visit? The primary way that they attempt to do this is by making their visitors *identify* with the "victims," in this way instilling them with *empathy* and the ability to connect the past and its trauma to their own lives.

The methods through which they do this vary according to the message and goal of each museum, as well as who the museum's primary audience is. The USHMM, for example, is primarily aimed at a US audience, almost all of whom are too young to have any direct experience of the Holocaust; therefore, it aims to bring this distant traumatic experience closer to home in a way that encourages visitors to make connections to their own lives. In addition to the many experiential and affective exhibit components described earlier, the most obvious method is the identity card given to each visitor as they enter the permanent exhibit; divided by gender, the passport-like "identities" are there to accompany the visitor through the permanent exhibit.[4] The cards give some basic biographical information about an individual victim or survivor of the Holocaust, with details such as where and when he or she was born, his or her experience under the Nazi regime, and his or her ultimate fate. In this way, the nameless and faceless millions whose story the museum is telling are condensed into one individual with whom the visitor "experiences" the Holocaust.

The exhibition's experiential tactics make the visitor a part of the Holocaust "experience" with this individual. This begins already in the elevator that ascends to the beginning of the exhibition, in which one cannot escape the terror and disbelief of the American service man describing the camps. Released from the elevator, the visitor becomes a player in the Holocaust script, standing opposite the American service men at Ohrdruf with a similar gaping look of disbelief at the pit of bodies that confronts her. The horrors continue throughout the exhibit, as the visitor is first bombarded by "history" and then swept into the inconceivable evil of the Holocaust itself; the Warsaw ghetto is re-created to make the visitor "walk in the steps" of those who perished there before being "transported" in an actual train car to pass under the ominous Auschwitz sign, following the path of the millions that entered and never returned. The architecture of the building and the design of the exhibition are also intended to create spaces of claustrophobia to help re-create the experience of the Holocaust's victims; there are moments when escape appears to be impossible. In re-creating *l'univers concentrationnaire*, the museum forces the visitor into the role of victim, aiding their sense of identification with those who perished and with the individual whose ID they hold.

Similarly, the House of Terror is aimed at a national audience of individuals who may not have a personal memory of the events; as Schmidt and her cocreators averred, the museum was created to show young Hungarians the terror of living under communist occupation (M. Schmidt, personal communication). Therefore, the exhibit centers on the national trauma of Hungary's occupation(s). Each room is punctuated by a quote that "every Hungarian will know," and throughout, the founding myths of post-1989 Hungary are highlighted: Hungary throwing off the chains of occupation and Hungary for Hungarians (A. Mathe, personal communication). Dark spots on Hungary's past, such as its own Arrow Cross movement and collaboration with both the fascist and communist occupiers, are drastically minimized and internal "enemies," such as the Arrow Cross or Hungarian Communist Party, are portrayed as a small core of bad apples, while the "real" Hungarians were innocent victims. The narrative of the exhibition creates a Hungarian "us" that won the struggle against "them," thus drawing in young Hungarians to identify with their past. As Zsolt Horvath argues (2007), in Hungary's present political rhetoric and in the museum *all* Hungarians are victims and so too then are all who identify and empathize with them, as one cannot help but do in the museum.

Like the USHMM, the House of Terror also uses highly experiential techniques to encourage identification with the victims of the occupiers and encourage empathy with the innocent Hungarians who were terrorized. Throughout, not only do the audio devices allow the visitor to hear individual stories of terror and suffering, but also the act of listening to the old-fashioned phone or communist-era surveillance headphones takes the visitor back in time to experience what it was "really like." Haunting music sets the mood, and the lighting and other effects underscore the visceral experience; the building itself, with its winding rooms, tight spaces, and maze-like interior helps flesh out this experience of the past and the Kafkaesque nightmare of totalitarianism. Finally, the visitor's very long descent to the bowels of the terrible building, in an agonizingly slow elevator filled with terrible description of political execution, begins the claustrophobic climax of the exhibitionary experience, as the visitor is encouraged to enter the torture and detention cells. Squatting in cells that are too low to stand in, or standing in cells that are too narrow to sit in, the visitor's experiential immersion in the innocent and victimized Hungarian past is complete, and the visitor is meant to come out of the exhibit understanding what the thousands of victims of the communist (and fascist) regime(s) underwent. This empathy, then, is intended to underpin an appreciation for the (right-wing) democracy that replaced communism, despite its apparent difficulties.

The Kigali Centre has a slightly different aim, as its terrible past is more recent, and so the question of identification and connection to the present is not as pressing; many visitors to the museum experienced the genocide all too acutely and do not need to be made to feel as if they did. Nevertheless, as I've pointed out, the museum is also very much aimed at international visitors as well as Rwandans (mostly Tutsi) who returned to the country from exile following the genocide. Therefore, the museum uses many similar tactics to make the visitor who may not have direct experience of the genocide identify with what happened. One of the key ways that the Kigali Centre does this is in its efforts to emphasize the individuality of the victims, through their photographs, testimony, and personal belongings, to encourage further identification. This tactic is especially evident in the haunting memorial rooms in which one is surrounded by the material remains of the destruction; while the bones are oddly impersonal reminders of the terror, stripped of anything but wounds that would identify the individual from which they came, the photographs and the personal effects like clothing have an immediacy that visitors can connect to. Rwandan visitors clearly identify intensely with these artifacts, evidenced by the fact that the photos are often taken. But even international visitors cannot help but identify and empathize. The color family photos of birthdays and other celebrations, the Cornell University sweatshirt, the huge, innocent eyes of the extralarge photos in the children's memorial individualize what is a staggering trauma and draw the visitor in to identify with the individual victims who are portrayed *just like them*. And while the genocide happened far away, it is not far from the visitor's mind that the international community failed to prevent or stop it.

The MMHR similarly seeks to restore individual identity to the victims in a way that helps visitors identify with them and their suffering. This is evident in the memorial photos that line the wall of the museum, but even more affective in the section on the torture tactics of the junta. Here, in a dark and foreboding room, and over the most heinous instrument of torture of all, the *parilla*, the visitor watches the agony of individuals describing the ways in which they were tortured. The stories of different individuals, on a split screen, alternate and together form a disjointed but all too frighteningly coherent description of pain, humiliation, and terror and the effort of the torturers to strip all humanity from their victims. While visitors may not be able to feel or imagine such terrible abuses, the individuals who experienced it are immediate in their words and images, and their suffering is contagious. Any abstract historical understanding of the institutional inner-workings of Pinochet's regime, for example, are immediately elapsed as one listens to the anguishing stories. To counter this dehumanization, the exhibits on the artifacts created by prisoners give a sense of the hope that persisted in the face of such torture, which is almost more affecting than the tortured testimonies themselves. The victims, though tortured so heinously, retained their humanity and hope.

The 9/11 Museum similarly uses testimony, photographs, architecture, and artifacts to experientially draw the visitor in to make her identify with the victims. However, as a truly twenty-first-century museum, it has a powerful tool that the others do not: the use of audio recordings of the victims themselves before they died. While all the museums here use audio effectively—historical recordings, testimony, music, and other sound effects—it is the voices of those who were killed on 9/11 that are particularly haunting and that inspire deep empathy and identification. Again and again, a husband leaves voice mail messages for his wife, assuring her that he is OK; with each beep of the answering machine, the visitor imagines her agony listening to those messages knowing that he did not make it out of the burning building. Frantic 911 calls and dispatches capture the immediacy of the event and the terror that it instilled—reminding one of the meaning of terrorism, which has become abstract in today's discourse. Frightened passengers on the doomed planes call their loved ones to say good-bye; their terrible composure forces the individual to wonder what her response would be in the face of impending death. These audio recordings draw the visitor deep into the fear, chaos, and destruction of 9/11, but also the love and compassion expressed that day in an extremely affective and powerful way, and remind the visitor that the victims were just like her, simply going about their innocent daily routines, targeted for nothing they had done, but simply for being free.

This effort to make the visitor "experience" the past in a way that leads to empathy with the victims, however distant and different they might be, is intended to create Landsberg's "prosthetic memory." In experiential spaces of our contemporary mass culture, such as memorial museums, visitors who are brought face to face with the past can actually form a memory of a past trauma. But this "prosthetic memory" is not of the actual event itself but of the "mass-mediated experience of a traumatic event" (2004, 19). This potential for individuals to form a memory of a past that was not actually experienced by way of a mediated cultural form is celebrated by Landsberg as opening the door to ethical and moral transformation. Like the creators of the museums described in this book, she sees in prosthetic memory the potential to effect progressive social and political change. Prosthetic memory, because it does not require that an individual actually experience the event, takes away any "biological or ethnic claims of ownership" of the past; according to Landsberg, "Rather than atomizing people, prosthetic memories open up collective horizons of experience and pave the way for unexpected political alliances" (2004, 143) and "opens up memories and identities to persons from radically different backgrounds" (2004, 11). In this, Landsberg argued, prosthetic memory can bring about real change. Prosthetic memory thus has a synergistic connection to Levy and Sznaider's cosmopolitan memory imperative or Rothberg's multidirectional memory, in which memories of diverse and divergent pasts are not in competition but compatible, and in fact, the traumatic past of one group may help another to articulate and remember their own.

The use of experiential learning to inspire empathy and identification in order to alter the moral sensibility of the visitor is precisely what memorial museums aim and purport to do. However, as the histories and contexts of the museums examined here demonstrate quite clearly, the past is always subject to interpretation, which is usually political, and the hope or belief that a prosthetic memory of a traumatic past can transcend group or national ownership and is devoid of the exclusivity of other, more traditional forms of memory (such as nineteenth-century memorials and monuments) is overly optimistic. These museums are political projects, and as lofty as their intentions to morally educate their publics might be, the messages conveyed by memorial museums tend to fall in line with the dominant political agenda of the creator(s). While the past might appear to be open to claims of ownership by any and all visitors, the prosthetic memory created by the museum is of a very particular version of the past; and as we have seen, despite the transnational forms and movements of memory, it is still a national past that is much more hegemonic than the museums acknowledge. In this sense, rather than liberating and holding the potential for political and social change, prosthetic memories as formed in memorial museums might simply reinforce hegemonic, national views of the past, present, and future. Yet they have an undeniable force derived from the affect, emotion, and empathy that forms them and, in this way, are potentially even more dangerous than previous forms of hegemonic memory. Rwanda is the obvious case to watch for the potential dangers of prosthetic memory, but Hungary's continued swing to the far right and the wave of right-wing populism in the United States also reflect the potential danger of the kind of nationalistic narrative of the past displayed in these museums.

THE UNSTATED GOALS OF MEMORIAL MUSEUMS

While memorial museums have a set of explicitly stated goals that encompass preserving the past and "telling the truth," serving as a space of reparation and healing, and morally educating their publics, they have another set of implicit functions on the national and international level and are—whether stated or not—tools of political legitimation intended to demonstrate that the regimes that build them have come to terms with the past, made amends to the victims, and promised a better future.

Carol Duncan argued that art museums serve a legitimating function in the modern nation-state. We can easily apply her words about art museums in the nineteenth and twentieth centuries to memorial museums in the late twentieth and early twenty-first centuries: "Having a [memorial] museum is a sign of political virtue and national identity—of being recognizably a member of the civilized community of modern, liberal nations" (Duncan 1995, 89). Memorial museums are continuing to be built around the world at such a tremendous rate in large part because they serve this sort of legitimating function. For countries transitioning to democracy (or attempting to), coming to terms with past violence, or working to placate groups that feel that they have been victimized, memorial museums provide a way to publicly recognize suffering and victimization, close the door on the past with the promise of a better future, and produce and disseminate knowledge about the past to morally and civically educate their publics. And as I have noted, during the late twentieth and early twenty-first centuries, facing the past through the lens of political regret has been high on the agenda for many, many nations as central to their ambitions to be recognized as legitimate political players in the international community. It is no wonder, then, that they are looking to do this in part through the use of memorial museums.

Memorial museums also mark (or purport to) the fact that the past is over; they provide a way—as we have seen especially in the case of Rwanda and Chile—to draw a thick black line between past and present, making the past a distinct and terrible entity that is just that: past. This is crucial for new governments and/or nations that are attempting to differentiate themselves from what came before and promising their people a better future. President Clinton did this at the opening of the USHMM, when he promised the American people that such regimes would not be allowed to flourish under his watch; Orbán and Fidesz used the House of Terror as a way to slam the door on the past, forever ending foreign, totalitarian occupation and mapping a new course for Hungary's future. The Kigali Centre and Kagame have set the Rwandan genocide apart as a discrete event with beginning, middle, and end, placing the Rwanda of the past, with its racial and ethnic divisions and pervasive genocide ideology, very much apart from the Rwanda of the present and future. The MMHR turns the page on the past with the 1988 plebiscite, not even acknowledging the divisive politics that continue today. And the 9/11 Museum contains its narrative primarily to a mere 102 minutes with no substantive recognition of the consequences of 9/11 and the United States' response that continue to reverberate today. As I've noted, this sort of memory is a luxury for those who are able to demonstrate that the past is truly past, and claiming such can be a large step toward political legitimacy and international recognition of a new regime or its policies, especially in an age in which the "politics of regret" is a central principle of legitimation. Thus perhaps the most important goal, though unstated, is to claim international political legitimacy for the regime creating the museum and the domestic and international actions and policies it pursues.

However, as this study has shown, in the words of Faulkner, "the past is never dead. It's not even past." As much as these regimes would like to use memorial museums to leave the past behind, the museums themselves reveal the battles of the past, present, and future raging in the communities, publics, and nations that build them. Perhaps the greatest insight that we can gain from them is that there is no one version of the past that existentially determines the present and future, but rather that past is always changing, open to interpretation and representation and ready to be put to use in and by the present for whatever political ends are so desired.

Our present relationship to the past is conflicted. On the one hand, we recognize that it is socially constructed and often mobilized around present needs and desires; on the other, we hope to get from it some essential "truth" that we can learn from in order to create a better future. However, these positions vis-à-vis the past are uncomfortable bedfellows. We are skeptical of the tools that we are using at the very same moment that we are using them to work toward progress and a more perfect world. The postmodern rejection of the promises of modernity belies the modern idea underpinning memorial museums: through knowledge and education, we can learn from the past to create a present and future. Revealing the political nature of memorial museums presents a difficult challenge to some of the fundamental presumptions behind their creation—that education leads to prevention, that there is an inherent value in commemoration of atrocity and trauma, and that memory has a direct connection to democracy. Rather, as these cases suggest, while well-intended, the rhetoric around prevention, democracy, and peace may be just that—rhetoric. Rather, the negative past is simply the new battleground on which to fight present battles, and following Halbwachs, this past is socially constructed by and for the present according to the political realities of the day. Whatever "truths" the past might hold are at the service of the present, and so these museums tell us much more about the present societies that construct them and the expectations of the international community vis-à-vis the past than they do about the terrible and tragic pasts that they are remembering.

CONCLUSION

On the surface, these memorial museum initiatives appear to be a highly innovative, ambitious, and effective way to come to terms with a difficult past. They represent what is most noble in our convictions: we can learn from past mistakes through engaged and open dialogue and education about the past and thus create a better present and future built upon empathy with our fellow human beings. They also represent an ambitious attempt to confront the past and to make amends and right historical injustice. The fact of acknowledgment of victimization and injustice alone is important, and expensive initiatives like these museums can go a long way toward righting wrongs. In their ambitions, they also strive for something totally new in the project of commemoration—a self-reflexivity and reflection that was not present in previous memorials and monuments. These museums seek to present the past in a way that does not forestall dialogue and understanding but contributes to an ongoing discourse between and among a variety of diverse publics, across past, present, and future. In this way, they are intended to be bulwarks of democratic values and to symbolize a commitment to nonviolence, tolerance, and peace.

And yet, it is impossible to divorce the political reality from the rhetoric and good intentions. Memorial museums are at heart political projects. This does not mean that the good intentions are not there or are deliberate facades for more devious political projects. Rather, it appears that memory today, despite all the good intentions, continues to support and sustain the dominant narratives of the past as delineated by the existing powers that be and their priorities. True, today these priorities are focused on the negative past and fall within the "politics of regret," but rather than critical spaces of reflection on the negative past, memorial museums tend more toward a celebration of the present as—and because it is—distinct from the past; by exhibiting what is most terrible in the past, they reinforce the superiority of the present. This is surprisingly not so far from the mobilization of memory in the nineteenth century around the political agendas and goals of the hegemonic nation-state.

However, there is reason to hope that these museums will actually contribute to a more peaceful and democratic present and future. Their visitor books and online review sites like TripAdvisor are filled with passionate pledges to never forget so that "never again" can such violence occur, suggesting that individual attitudes are shaped by the experience of memorial museums. However, it is clear that despite the global proliferation of memorial museums calling for "never again," again and again violence, genocide, and atrocity are committed, often with the international community's full knowledge. So even if indeed individual attitudes are altered in a meaningful way, societal change does not necessarily follow, and memorial museums' (and memory's) imperative to aid in the prevention of future violence seems hollow.

Despite the collapse of modernity's belief in progress, memorial museums continue to cling to the notion that confronting the negative past can lead to a better future, reflecting broader assumptions about the ethical duty to remember. Indeed, the theories engaged in this book positing an increasingly transnational, traveling, cosmopolitan, or multidirectional memory are hopeful that with globalization's shrinking of the world, individuals and collectives will be more interconnected, their negative pasts interwoven and articulated in ways that ameliorate division and, ultimately, reduce violence and suffering. Memorial museums are an important part of this effort to learn from the past and bridge past, present, and future with the goal of creating a better world. And yet, what we have seen in recent months is a rejection of globalization, cosmopolitanism, interconnection, and critical engagement with the past and its lessons. Rather, as right-wing populism ascends and nativist, xenophobic and isolationist ideologies take hold, memory and the past are being mobilized to undo the progress that has been made toward a more interconnected and cosmopolitan world. In the calls to "Make America Great Again" or Brexit's move to "take back control," we see a powerful nostalgia for a time when the world was not so interconnected and when hegemonic power structures were safely intact. It appears that to some degree the progressive potential of memory has been usurped, and we shall have to find new ways to imagine and articulate our relationship to the past in this new political climate. Memorial museums will doubtless play a role as the politics of the past are renegotiated. However, it's not clear if this role will be to reinforce the hegemony of the nation and its power structures or to uphold the values of inclusion, tolerance, and democracy that memorial museums are meant to embody and that seem to be currently under attack.

NOTES

INTRODUCTION

1. Dark tourism, also referred to as thanatourism, refers to tourism at sites of grief, death, and suffering and has been receiving increased scholarly attention in recent years. The seminal book on the topic is *Dark Tourism: The Attraction of Death and Disaster* by J. John Lennon and Malcolm Foley (2000), but there is a growing body of scholarly works on the topic.
2. In this way, they might be considered what Elzbieta Matynia would call "spaces of appearance" for performative democratic practice (2009).

CHAPTER 1: THE EMERGENCE OF A NEW FORM

1. Anecdotally, a quick search on TripAdvisor shows that the museums in this book are all listed in the top ten things to do in their cities, with the exception of the House of Terror in Budapest, which is, however, in the top 10 percent of recommended things to do.
2. Sigmund Freud's psychoanalytic theories perhaps best represent this belief that the past is always present; as he writes, "In mental life nothing which has once been formed can perish" (1961, 16). The past for Freud is a reality that shapes the individual in the present, a notion that was dramatically challenged by Halbwachs's theory of the social construction of memory.
3. Zygmunt Bauman stridently and compellingly makes this argument in *Modernity and the Holocaust* (1989).
4. This is an argument excellently illustrated by Elazar Barkan and Belma Bećirbašić in their work on the former Yugoslavia (2015).
5. The International Center for Transitional Justice, the leading organization in the field and that has defined the field itself and its academic study, lists on its website the six pillars of transitional justice: criminal prosecutions, truth commissions, reparations programs (both material and symbolic), gender justice, security system reform, and memorialization efforts. See http://ictj.org/en/tj/#1 [Accessed February 4, 2011].
6. Several widely cited surveys of US museum visitors found that for the vast majority of those surveyed, museums were considered to be one of the most trustworthy sources of historical information, even more so than books or relatives (AMS 2001; Reach Advisors 2008). More recently, even as trust has diminished among the US public in many spheres of society like politics and media, another Reach Advisors poll of seven thousand participants found that museums ranked 6.4 on a scale of 1–10 for trustworthiness, above NPR and Wikipedia (Reach Advisors 2015).

7. Jeshajahu Weinberg, former director of the USHMM, has written about what differentiates it from other history museums; he highlights that its point of departure is not the collection but rather the story of the Holocaust. It is, according to him, "an attempt at visual historiography . . . a narrative museum" (1994). However, I prefer the term experiential, as it better captures the essence of memorial museums.

8. Parabolic speakers are speakers able to focus their sound very precisely, so a visitor can stand under or in front of one and essentially be the only person able to hear the speaker.

9. Thomas Cushman (2003) makes this excellent point about the emerging field of genocide studies and its basis in the belief that by studying genocide, we can find a way to prevent it, though genocide itself is often rooted in these modern ideas that society can be perfected. However, genocide itself increasingly relies on the tools of modernity for its perpetration, which complicates the idea that through education we can prevent it.

CHAPTER 2: US HOLOCAUST MEMORIAL MUSEUM

1. The full report from the commission can be found at https://www.ushmm.org/information/about-the-museum/presidents-commission [Accessed February 13, 2017].

2. See, for example, Barbie Zelizer (2002b), "Photography, Journalism & Trauma," in *Journalism after September 11*.

3. Most notably, in 2005, Yad Vashem reopened after a ten-year, $100-million renovation, the centerpiece of which is the Holocaust History Museum, a forty-thousand-square-foot museum intended to bring "Holocaust remembrance well into the 21st century" (http://www.yadvashem.org/yv/en/museum/overview.asp#!prettyPhoto [Accessed July 7, 2015]).

4. For an excellent discussion of "the six million" as a Holocaust icon, see Stier 2015.

5. Wiesel's writings on the Holocaust, especially his book *Night* (which is frequently read by high school students), have greatly influenced America's reading of the Holocaust. He sees it as something that can never be understood but must be remembered for the sake of humanity. Almost incapable of being represented, the Holocaust to Wiesel is almost only comprehensible and approachable through survivor testimony and is totally unique in history (Linenthal 1995, 4).

6. Arguments about the uniqueness of the Holocaust are usually framed in terms of the six million (Jewish victims) versus the eleven million (six million plus five million other victims). This figure—eleven million—was the invention of Simon Wiesenthal, another prominent Holocaust survivor in the United States who is a proponent of the inclusion of other victims.

7. The Museum Council was expanded at this time, in late 1979, to include fifty-five presidential appointees, who are chosen by the president from a list of candidates compiled by the current council members. Five members each are selected from Congress and the Senate. The term for an appointee is five years, and they can be reappointed.

8. TripAdvisor recently listed it as the number-four attraction in Washington, DC (2016).

9. Subsequently a Smithsonian National Museum of the American Indian was constructed, and the Smithsonian's National Museum of African American History and Culture has just opened; both of these museums focus not primarily on genocide and slavery but on celebrating culture and heritage.
10. Tim Cole, for example, argues that Yad Vashem's recent renovation was a "response to the challenge to its monopoly over the 'Holocaust' coming from Washington, DC" (2000, 136).
11. For an excellent discussion of the United States' failure to respond to genocide again and again over the course of the twentieth century, see Samantha Power's *A Problem from Hell: America and the Age of Genocide* (2002).

CHAPTER 3: HOUSE OF TERROR

An earlier version of this chapter appeared as "Haunted by the Spectre of Communism: Silence and Spectacle in Hungary's House of Terror," in *Silence, Screen, and Spectacle: Rethinking Social Memory in the Age of Information*, edited by Lindsey Freeman, Benjamin Nienass, and Rachel Daniell (Berghahn, 2014), and is being used with permission from Berghahn.

1. The Fidesz (Young Democrats) Party was formed in the 1980s and was one of the main opposition forces in the movement against communism. Throughout the years, it has had several ideological shifts but has remained right-wing or center-right and swept the 2010 election on a right-wing populist wave.
2. Throughout the region, a number of museums devoted to remembering fascism and communism embody a similar set of tensions in their remembrance of these two totalitarian regimes. Some examples include the Museum of Occupations in Tallinn, Estonia, and the Museum of Occupation in Riga, Latvia, which both tell the story of occupation first by the Soviets, then the Nazis, and again the Soviets; the Museum of Genocide Victims in Vilnius, Lithuania, which also tells the story of fascism and communism, with a focus on the communist genocide; and the Topography of Terror in Berlin, a museum and documentation center on the former SS and Gestapo headquarters in Berlin flanked by the Berlin Wall. A different tension is found in museums devoted solely to communism, such as the DDR Museum in Berlin and Prague's Museum of Communism, between depicting the terror of communist totalitarianism and producing a seeming nostalgia for everyday life under communism. As we shall see, this tension is also present in the House of Terror.
3. For example, until 1989, the exhibitions and displays at Auschwitz did not mention the specificity of the Jewish victims/victimization in the death camp and instead referred only to the Polish victims of fascism (Young 1993).
4. For example, just after the transition, the new democratic government tried to right the problem of inflation by allowing a dramatic rise in fuel prices, which resulted in a days-long blockade of the streets of Budapest in October 1990; fearing further unrest, the government capitulated and continued to subsidize fuel (Bohle and Greskovits 2009, 54).

5. Schmidt (personal communication) anecdotally tells the story of the opening of the museum when a group of survivors of communism visited with a group of youth, aged six to sixteen. The survivors were quite unhappy with the museum, instead expecting something more traditional; however, after visiting the exhibit with the youth, their minds were completely changed and they loved the museum.

6. Altering a World Heritage site building like this was a point of huge contention and controversy, though Schmidt happily asserts that the controversy over the facade gave the museum more publicity than it could have hoped for and ultimately backfired for the museum's detractors.

7. The museum's soundtrack was composed by Ákos Kovács.

8. The phones throughout the museum also play testimony, political speeches, and so on, none of which is translated.

9. The House of Terror website does tell you that no executions were carried out at 60 Andrassy, though it's never explicitly said in the exhibition: http://www.terrorhaza.hu/en/exhibition/basement/reconstructed_prison_cell.html [Accessed April 2, 2011].

10. In an interview, Aron Mathe explained that the concept of the memorial comes from a story told to Kovacs, the exhibition designer, by his grandfather, who fled Hungary under communism by affixing torches to bamboo poles that waved in the wind and distracted the border guards, allowing him to cross the border undetected.

11. The perpetrators are defined as those "who took an active part in establishing and maintaining the two Hungarian totalitarian terror regimes . . . as well as those who held responsible positions in the executive orders of these two regimes" (Exhibition guide).

12. This wall of perpetrators is highly controversial, especially as many are still alive and have indeed gone free. Maria Schmidt told me the story of a man who came to her and begged her to take down his photo because his second wife, whom he had recently married, did not know that he had been a member of the political police and would divorce him if she found out; his children had already found his photo in the museum and were not speaking to him.

13. The journalist and author Anne Applebaum, for example, is listed as an associate on the museum's website; when asked about her relationship to the museum, she said that she doesn't really have one but stayed in an apartment maintained by the XXI Century Institute once while doing research in Budapest.

14. Anecdotally, most Hungarian intellectuals I have met refuse as a matter of principle to visit the museum.

15. Unfortunately I do not have the space or time here to devote to a discussion of the Uprising Museum, which deserves its own chapter or book.

16. This museum, called Emlekpont, which translates to "point of remembrance in time," is intended to encapsulate the memories of the town of Hódmezővásárhely from 1945 to 1990. See http://www.emlekpont.hu/eng/index.html [Accessed April 2, 2011].

17. Aron Mathe showed me the artifact storage room, which was hardly larger than a closet with only a few dusty volumes and several midcentury artifacts on its shelves.

18. The planned memorial depicts an eagle, representing Germany, descending on the angel Gabriel, a symbol of Hungary, with a plaque stating that it remembers all of

the victims of the German occupation. Critics rightly argue that this not only fails to recognize Jews as the primary victims of the Holocaust but, worse, depicts Hungary as an innocent victim, when in fact the Hungarian government and portions of the population were highly complicit.

CHAPTER 4: KIGALI GENOCIDE MEMORIAL CENTRE

An earlier version of this chapter appeared as "Politics of the Past: Remembering the Rwandan Genocide at the Kigali Memorial Centre," in *Curating Difficult Knowledge: Violent Pasts in Public Places*, edited by Erica Lehrer, Cynthia E. Milton, and Monica Eileen Patterson (Palgrave Macmillan, 2011) and is being used with permission from Palgrave Macmillan.

1. Much of the ethnic distinction is based on appearance and greatly exaggerated. Tutsi are supposedly taller, lankier, with a thinner nose, lighter skin, oval face, and straighter hair—in other words, they look more like Europeans; Hutu are supposed to be shorter and stockier with a wider nose, darker skin, and curlier hair. All of this is rooted in European "race science" of the late nineteenth and early twentieth century and Jonathan Hanning Speke's "Hamitic hypothesis" of a "superior race of negroes" (Des Forges 1999).
2. To this day, it is still unknown who shot down President Habyarimana's plane. At the time, Hutu leaders claimed it was the RPF and used this as an excuse to start killing Tutsis, though today it is more widely believed that it was Hutu extremists dismayed at the moderation of Habyarimana, who had recently signed a cease-fire agreement with the RPF, toward the Tutsi population. Today there are others who believe that Kagame gave the orders to shoot down the plane in order to sabotage the cease-fire and ensure full military victory of the RPF over the Hutu leaders; clearly this is a highly controversial claim in Rwanda today.
3. In 1999, the government created the National Unity and Reconciliation Commission (NURC) as a semi-autonomous body intended to educate about and promote unity and reconciliation. See http://www.nurc.gov.rw/index.php?id=83 [Accessed November 2, 2015].
4. In Kinyarwanda, *interahamwe* means "those who stand together" and refers to the armed Hutu militias that were largely responsible for perpetrating the genocide.
5. Most recently, Patrick Karegeya, Rwanda's former external intelligence chief, was found murdered in a hotel in Johannesburg, South Africa, in 2014; many believe Kagame ordered the killing.
6. In October 2010, the UN released a report, "DRC: Mapping Human Rights Violations 1993–2003," that implicates the RAF and Rwandan government in genocide in the DRC. The release of the report was a serious international test of the Kagame regime, which has enjoyed impunity for crimes committed in postgenocide Rwanda and Congo. However, Kagame has powerful friends, and the UN accusations fell on largely deaf ears in the international community.

See http://www.ohchr.org/EN/Countries/AfricaRegion/Pages/RDCProjetMapping.aspx [Accessed November 2, 2015].

7. These ambitious plans include Rwanda's Vision 2020 (http://edprs.rw/content/vision-2020 [Accessed November 2, 2015]), which was implemented in 2000 and seeks to develop Rwanda from an agricultural to a knowledge-based, middle-income economy by 2020.

8. The term *gacaca* comes from "lawn," referring to how members of the *gacaca* sit on the lawn to listen to cases and consider appropriate punishments (Rettig 2008).

9. The image of piles of bones stacked in churches is one that often comes to mind when thinking about genocide commemoration in Rwanda; and the most prominent genocide memorials outside of the Kigali Centre, such as the churches in Nyamata and Ntarama and the technical school in Murambi, still display the bones, bodies, and clothing of the thousands of people killed on the sites.

10. There are now also Holocaust Museums in Durban and Johannesburg.

11. In addition to funding from the Clinton Global Initiative, funding was secured from the Waterman foundation in the United Kingdom, the Swedish and Belgian governments, the British department of education, among others.

12. Aegis created a documentary, *Our Memory, Our Future*, that describes the creation of the center: Aegis Trust. (n.d.). *Our Memory, Our Future: Creating the Kigali Memorial Centre* [DVD]: Aegis Trust.

13. For example, the USHMM and other Holocaust and memorial museums have had small exhibits on other genocides or comparing genocide, though these kinds of exhibits have generally been supplementary to the permanent exhibit, not an integral part of it.

14. All of these senior leaders of the genocide have been indicted, tried, and convicted by the ICTR: http://www.unictr.org/Cases/tabid/204/Default.aspx [Accessed February 16, 2017].

15. Each grave is four meters wide by eight meters deep; the coffins in each grave are all different sizes and can hold the remains of many individuals, as it is primarily bones that have been recovered; often it is difficult or impossible to identify the remains or find complete remains.

16. The growing archive has evolved out of the many materials collected to create the museum exhibition that did not end up on display. In 2010, the Aegis Trust, in partnership with CNLG and with support from University of Southern California Shoah Foundation, University of Texas Libraries, Austin, and the NIOD Institute for War, Holocaust and Genocide Studies in the Netherlands, officially launched the archive, which continues to collect survivor testimony, perpetrator confessions, film footage, artifacts, photographs, documents, and scholarly work related to the genocide. All of this will be available online through the archive's digital database: http://genocidearchiverwanda.org.rw/index.php/Welcome_to_Genocide_Archive_Rwanda. The archive is intended to be the largest repository of information about the 1994 genocide in the world and is expanding rapidly, with a number of specialized programs in addition to collecting, preserving, and digitizing its collection. For example, in collaboration with IBUKA, the central Rwandan survivors' organization, the archive manages a victim's database that

compiles biographical information on victims; not unlike the databases at the Museum of Memory and Human Rights in Santiago and the 9/11 Museum, the purpose is to restore the humanity and memory of those killed. The archive is also engaged in mapping sites of genocide and reconstruction. Interactive maps with virtual tours of genocide memorials and key sites connected to the genocide are available on the website.

17. Though it could (cynically, but perhaps correctly) be argued that in the House of Terror, prevention means preventing the Socialists from gaining political power, as they are the successor party to the communists.

18. The changes to the constitution allowing him to run for a third seven-year term also allow for him to run for two additional five-year terms, meaning that he could be in office until 2034.

CHAPTER 5: MUSEUM OF MEMORY AND HUMAN RIGHTS

1. The term comes from the title of a 2006 book by Naomi Roht-Arriaza, *The Pinochet Effect: Transnational Justice in the Age of Human Rights* (University of Pennsylvania Press), and reflects the global implications of Pinochet's arrest on international transitional justice and human rights.

2. A summary of the Valech Report is available on the website of the US Institute for Peace: http://www.usip.org/publications/commission-of-inquiry-chile-03 [Accessed February 12, 2017].

3. Most of the documentation comes from the collections of these human rights organizations: Fundación de Ayuda Social de las Iglesias Cristianas (FASIC), Corporación de Promoción y Defensa de los Derechos del Pueblo (CODEPU), Fundación de Protección a la Infancia Dañada por los Estados de Emergencia (PIDEE), and TeleAnalisis (Sepulveda 2011, 19).

4. This is dramatically different from a tour that I took of the former detention and torture center in Buenos Aires, ESMA (Escuela Superior de Mecánica de la Armada/Navy Mechanical School), which emphasized at every possible turn the role of the United States in installing and supporting Argentina's military junta.

5. There was a huge uproar over the 9/11 Museum's gift shop and café when the museum opened. Families were outraged at the "crass commercialism" of a gift shop on a site deemed sacred by many (Phillip 2014; also see Sturken 2015). The symbol of such crass kitsch became a cheese plate, in the shape of the United States with hearts marking the three sites of the planes crashing (Chung 2014). The museum was also forced to scale back plans for a café serving comfort food and artisanal booze by celebrity chef Danny Meyers. While the outrage over the 9/11 Museum café and gift shop was particularly visible, most memorial museums have to negotiate this tension and ultimately seem to decide to include shops and cafés.

CHAPTER 6: NATIONAL SEPTEMBER 11 MEMORIAL MUSEUM

1. By some estimates, a third of the population watched the events unfold live and another third knew about the events within twenty-four hours, making it truly a twenty-first-century "media event" (Dayan and Katz 1994).

2. The full list of jurors is available here: http://www.911memorial.org/design-competition [Accessed July 13, 2016].

3. The layout that was agreed upon is one described by principle designer Jake Barton of Local Projects as "meaningful adjacency." His firm designed an algorithm that determined what he refers to as the "geography of event," arranging the names of individuals according to where they were (Barton 2013).

4. The composite is a controversial chunk of material that experts estimate is approximately five floors of one of the towers melded together by the heat; the controversy lies in the belief by many that it contains human remains, though experts have concluded that it does not because of the high heat that created it. Discussions on the composite and other controversial artifacts and concepts can be found here: http://www.911memorial.org/museum-planning-conversation-series.

5. Edward Linenthal is a well-known American historian who wrote books on the USHMM and the Oklahoma City Memorial. Barbara Kirshenblatt-Gimblett is a professor of Performance Studies at New York University and is the project director of the new POLIN Museum of the History of Polish Jews in Warsaw.

6. This is a take on the title of Erika Doss's book *Memorial Mania: Public Feeling in America* (2010).

7. This is a distinction made by Jeffrey Olick (1999) between collected memory—the collected memories of individuals (a concept also used by James Young [1993])—and collective memory that occurs sui generis within a group.

8. The Last Column is the final steel beam that was removed from the site. Rescue workers covered the column with messages and tributes, and it has taken on a heavy symbolic meaning as a sign of resilience and heroism.

9. These were the last words famously spoken by Todd Beamer, a passenger on Flight 93, who made a call to an airphone supervisor, Lisa Jefferson, when it became clear that the flight had been hijacked and described to her the passenger's plan to attempt to thwart the hijackers by flying the plane into the ground.

10. I visited the museum with a group of students who were very young when 9/11 occurred, and this was an anecdotal response of a student when asked what she thought about the museum.

CHAPTER 7: PROMISES AND LIMITS

1. This reflects Walter Benjamin's concept of the aura of an object, described in "The Work of Art in the Age of Mechanical Reproduction" (1936).

2. The Extraordinary Chambers in the Courts of Cambodia was established in 2006 as a national Cambodian tribunal with assistance from the United Nations in order to bring to trial the most senior leaders of the Khmer regime. Five individuals have been brought before the court, two of whom died before their trials were completed and three of whom are serving life sentences for their crimes.

3. District Six was a neighborhood in downtown Cape Town that was cleared of its black and colored population to become white only. The occupants were sent to live in desolate townships outside of Cape Town, and the District Six neighborhood was left an empty plot of land and largely remains so today.

4. The ID cards were originally age- and gender-specific to encourage even greater identification, and the story of the individual's fate was meant to unfold with each stage of the exhibition. Though the concept has been simplified, clearly the effort to make individuals identify with the victims remains strong.

REFERENCES

9/11 Memorial. "About Memorial." Accessed July 8, 2016. http://www.911memorial.org/about-memorial.

———. "Museum." Accessed February 13, 2017. https://www.911memorial.org/museum.

———. "Museum Planning Series Conversation Series Report, 2006–2008." Accessed August 2, 2016. https://www.911memorial.org/sites/all/files/Conversation%20Series%202006%20-%202008_0.pdf.

———. "Primary Sources." Accessed July 10, 2016. https://www.911memorial.org/911-primary-sources.

———. "Public Programs." Accessed July 10, 2016. https://www.911memorial.org/public-programs.

Achtenberg, Emily. 2013. "In Chile, Remembering 9/11: Reflections." NACLA/*Rebel Currents,* September 30. Accessed August 2, 2016. http://nacla.org/blog/2013/9/30/chile-remembering-911-reflections.

Aegis. 2013. "Annual Report." Accessed January 22, 2017. http://genocidearchiverwanda.org.rw/images/d/db/Aegis_Annual_Report_2013.pdf.

Andermann, Jens. 2012. "Showcasing Dictatorship: Memory and the Museum in Argentina and Chile." *Journal of Educational Media, Memory, and Society* 4 (2): 69–93.

Anderson, Benedict. 1991. *Imagined Communities: Reflections on the Origin and Spread of Nationalism.* New York: Verso.

Architonic. 2009. "Museum of Memory and Human Rights." Accessed February 16, 2017. https://www.architonic.com/en/project/estudio-america-museum-of-memory-and-human-rights/5100625.

Arendt, Hannah. 1973 [1951]. *The Origins of Totalitarianism.* New York: Harcourt Brace & Company.

———. 1955. *Men in Dark Times.* New York: Harcourt Brace.

———. 1958. *The Human Condition.* Chicago: University of Chicago Press.

Assman, Jan. 1995. "Collective Memory and Cultural Identity." *New German Critique* 65: 125–33.

Barkan, Elazar. 2003. "Restitution and Amending Historical Injustices in International Morality." In *Politics and the Past: On Repairing Historical Injustices.* Edited by John C. Torpey. Lanham, MD: Rowman and Littlefield, 91–102.

Barkan, Elazar, and Belma Bećirbašić. 2015. "The Politics of Memory, Victimization, and Activism in Post-conflict Bosnia and Herzegovina." In *Historical Justice and Memory.* Edited by Klaus Neumann and Janna Thompson. Madison: University of Wisconsin Press, 95–113.

Barton, Jake. 2013. "The Museum of You." TED Talk, May. Accessed July 13, 2016. https://www.ted.com/talks/jake_barton_the_museum_of_you?language=en.

Bauman, Zygmunt. 1989. *Modernity and the Holocaust*. Ithaca, NY: Cornell University Press.

Benjamin, Walter. 1969 [1936]. "The Work of Art in the Age of Mechanical Reproduction." In *Illuminations*. Edited by Hannah Arendt. New York: Schocken, 217–51.

Bennett, Tony. 1999. "The Exhibitionary Complex." In *Representing the Nation: A Reader*. Edited by David Boswell and Jessica Evans. New York: Routledge.

Berenbaum, Michael. 1993. *The World Must Know: The History of the Holocaust as Told in the United States Holocaust Memorial Museum*. New York: Little, Brown.

Bickford, Louis, and Amy Sodaro. 2010. "Remembering Yesterday to Protect Tomorrow: The Internationalization of a New Commemorative Paradigm." In *Memory and the Future: Transnational Politics, Ethics, and Society*. Edited by Yifat Gutman, Adam Brown, and Amy Sodaro. New York: Palgrave Macmillan.

Blustein, Jeffrey. 2008. *The Moral Demands of Memory*. New York: Cambridge University Press.

———. 2015. "How the Past Matters: On the Foundations of an Ethics of Remembrance." In *Historical Justice and Memory*. Edited by Klaus Neumann and Janna Thompson. Madison: University of Wisconsin Press, 74–92.

Bohle, Dorothee, and Bela Greskovits. 2009. "East-Central Europe's Quandary." *Journal of Democracy* 20 (4): 50–63.

Bond, Lucy, and Jessica Rapson. 2014. *The Transcultural Turn: Interrogating Memory between and beyond Borders*. Berlin: De Gruyter.

Brandstetter, Anna-Maria. 2010. "Contested Pasts: The Politics of Remembrance in Post-Genocide Rwanda." Ortelius Lecture, Netherlands Institute for Advanced Study in the Humanities and Social Sciences. Accessed August 2, 2016. http://www.nias.knaw.nl/Publications/Ortelius_Lecture/Ortelius_06_Brandstetter.

Brodsky, Ricardo B. 2011. "A Living Museum for Chile's Memory." In *Museo de la Memoria y los Derechos Humanos* museum guide. Santiago, Chile: Ograma, 9–12.

Brog, Mooli. 2002. "In Blessed Memory of a Dream: Mordechai Shenhavi and Initial Holocaust Commemoration Ideas in Palestine, 1942–1945." *Yad Vashem Studies* 30: 297–336.

Buckley-Zistel, Suzanne. 2006. "Remembering to Forget: Chosen Amnesia as a Strategy for Local Coexistence in Post-Genocide Rwanda." *Africa* 76 (2): 131–50.

Buruma, Ian. 1994. *The Wages of Guilt: Memories of War in Germany and Japan*. New York: Farrar, Straus, and Giroux.

Cairns, Alan. 2003. "Coming to Terms with the Past." In *Politics and the Past: On Repairing Historical Injustices*. Edited by John Torpey. Lanham, MD: Rowman and Littlefield, 63–90.

Caplan, Pat. 2007. "Never Again: Genocide Memorials in Rwanda." *Anthropology Today* 23 (1): 20–22.

Centro de Memoria Histórica. 2015. "Sobre el Museo." Accessed January 23, 2017. http://www.centrodememoriahistorica.gov.co/museo/museo/sobre-el-museo.

Chung, Jen. 2014. "This 9/11 Cheese Plate May Be The 9/11 Museum's Most Tasteless Souvenir." *Gothamist*, May 22. Accessed February 12, 2017. http://gothamist.com/2014/05/22/photo_finally_you_can_buy_a_911_che.php#photo-1.

Clinton, William. 1993. "Remarks of President William J. Clinton at the Dedication Ceremonies for the United States Holocaust Memorial Museum." United States Holocaust Memorial Museum, April 22. Accessed February 13, 2017. https://www.ushmm.org/research/ask-a-research-question/frequently-asked-questions/clinton.

Cohen, Patricia. 2012. "At Museum on 9/11, Talking Through an Identity Crisis." *New York Times*, June 2. Accessed August 2, 2016. http://www.nytimes.com/2012/06/03/arts/design/sept-11-memorial-museums-fraught-task-to-tell-the-truth.html.

Cole, Tim. 2000. *Selling the Holocaust: From Auschwitz to Schindler; How History Is Bought, Packaged and Sold*. New York: Routledge.

Cotter, Holland. 2016. "Review: The Smithsonian African American Museum Is Here at Last. And It Uplifts and Upsets." *New York Times*, September 15. Accessed January 25, 2017. https://www.nytimes.com/2016/09/22/arts/design/smithsonian-african-american-museum-review.html.

Coughlin, Brenda, and Jeffrey K. Olick. 2003. "The Politics of Regret: Analytical Frames." In *Politics and the Past: On Repairing Historical Injustices*. Edited by John Torpey. Lanham, MD: Rowman and Littlefield, 37–62.

Crownshaw, Richard. 2011. "Introduction." *Parallax* 17 (4): 1–3.

Cushman, Thomas. 2003. "Is Genocide Preventable? Some Theoretical Considerations." *Journal of Genocide Research* 5 (4): 523–42.

Dayan, Daniel, and Elihu Katz. 1994. *Media Events: The Live Broadcasting of History*. Cambridge, MA: Harvard University Press.

De Cesari, Chiara, and Ann Rigney. 2014. *Transnational Memory: Circulation, Articulation, Scales*. Berlin: De Gruyter.

Dekel, Irit. 2013. *Mediation at the Holocaust Memorial in Berlin*. New York: Palgrave Macmillan.

Des Forges, Alison. 1999. *Leave None to Tell the Story: Genocide in Rwanda*. New York: Human Rights Watch.

Diner, Hasia. 2009. *We Remember with Reverence and Love: American Jews and the Myth of Silence after the Holocaust, 1945–1962*. New York: New York University Press.

Doss, Erika. 2011. "Remembering 9/11: Memorials and Cultural Memory." *OAH Magazine of History* 25 (3): 27–30.

Duncan, Carol. 1995. "The Art Museum as a Ritual of Citizenship." In *Exhibiting Cultures: The Poetics and Politics of Museum Display*. Edited by Ivan Karp and Steven D. Lavine. Washington, DC: Smithsonian Institution Press, 88–103.

Dunlap, David W. 2005. "Governor Bars Freedom Center at Ground Zero." *New York Times*, September 29. Accessed August 2, 2016. http://www.nytimes.com/2005/09/29/nyregion/governor-bars-freedom-center-at-ground-zero.html.

———. 2014. "A Memorial Inscription's Grim Origins." *New York Times*, April 3. Accessed June 16, 2016. http://www.nytimes.com/2014/04/03/nyregion/an-inscription-taken-out-of-poetic-context-and-placed-on-a-9-11-memorial.html.

Durkheim, Émile. 1965. *The Elementary Forms of Religious Life*. New York: Free Press.

Ensalaco, Mark. 1999. *Chile under Pinochet: Recovering the Truth*. Philadelphia: University of Pennsylvania Press.

Equal Justice Initiative. 2016. "EJI Announces Plans to Build Museum and National Lynching Memorial." EJI, August 16. Accessed January 23, 2017. http://eji.org/news/eji-announces-plans-to-build-museum-and-national-lynching-memorial.

Erll, Astrid. 2011. "Travelling Memory." *Parallax* 17 (4): 4–18.

Estefane, Andrés. 2013. "Materiality and Politics in Chile's Museum of Memory and Human Rights." *Thresholds* 41: 158–71.

Faulkner, William. 1975 [1951]. *Requiem for a Nun*. New York: Vintage.

Freedom House. 2016. "Nations in Transit 2016: Hungary." Accessed January 17, 2017. https://freedomhouse.org/report/nations-transit/2016/hungary.

Freud, Sigmund. 1961. *Civilization and Its Discontents*. New York: W. W. Norton.

Gopnik, Adam. 2014. "Stones and Bones: Visiting the 9/11 Memorial and Museum." *New Yorker*, July 17. Accessed August 2, 2016. http://www.newyorker.com/magazine/2014/07/07/stones-and-bones.

Gourevitch, Philip. 1998. *We Wish to Inform You That Tomorrow We Will Be Killed with Our Families: Stories from Rwanda*. New York: Picador.

Guyer, Sara. 2009. "Rwanda's Bones." *Boundary 2* 36 (2): 155–75.

Halbwachs, Maurice. 1980. *The Collective Memory*. Translated by Francis Ditter Jr. and Vida Yazdi Ditter. New York: Harper and Row.

———. 1992. *On Collective Memory*. Edited by Lewis A. Coser. Chicago: University of Chicago Press.

Hansen-Glucklich, Jennifer. 2014. *Holocaust Memory Reframed: Museums and the Challenges of Representation*. New Brunswick, NJ: Rutgers University Press.

Hartman, Geoffrey. 1996. *The Longest Shadow: In the Aftermath of the Holocaust*. Bloomington: Indiana University Press.

Hennes, Tom. 2014. "Reflections on the Opening of the 9/11 Memorial Museum." *TED Blog*, May 22. Accessed August 2, 2016. http://blog.ted.com/reflections-on-the-opening-of-the-911-memorial-museum-from-the-lead-exhibition-designer/.

Hite, Katherine, and Cath Collins. 2009. "Memorial Fragments, Monumental Silences and Re-Awakenings in 21st-Century Chile." *Millennium: Journal of International Studies* 38 (2): 379–400.

Hobsbawm, Eric. 1994. *The Age of Extremes: A History of the World, 1914–1991*. New York: Vintage.

Hodgkin, Katharine, and Susannah Radstone. 2003. Introduction to *Contested Pasts: The Politics of Memory*. New York: Routledge, 1–22.

Horvath, Zsolt. 2007. "The Redistribution of the Memory of Socialism: Identity Formations of the 'Survivors' in Hungary after 1989." In *Past for the Eye: East European Representations of Communism in Cinema and Museums after 1989*. Edited by Oksana Sarkisova and Péter Apor. Budapest: Central European University Press, 247–73.

Human Rights Watch. 2016. "Burundi: Abductions, Killings, Spread Fear." Accessed February 25, 2016. https://www.hrw.org/news/2016/02/25/burundi-abductions-killings-spread-fear.

Hungarian Spectator. "House of Fates." Accessed February 25, 2016. http://hungarianspectrum.org/tag/house-of-fates/.

Hunt, Lynn. 2007. *Inventing Human Rights: A History*. New York: W. W. Norton.

Hutton, Patrick. 2000. "Recent Scholarship on Memory and History." *The History Teacher* 33 (4): 533–48.

Huyssen, Andreas. 1995. *Twilight Memories: Marking Time in a Culture of Amnesia*. New York: Routledge.

———. 2003. *Present Pasts: Urban Palimpsests and the Politics of Memory*. Stanford, CA: Stanford University Press.

———. 2011. "International Human Rights and the Politics of Memory: Limits and Challenges." *Criticism* 53 (4): 607–24.

Inglis, David. 2016. "Globalization and/of Memory: On the Complexification and Contestation of Memory Cultures and Practices." In *Routledge International Handbook of Memory Studies*. Edited by Anna Lisa Tota and Trever Hagen. New York: Routledge, 143–57.

Irwin-Zarecka, Iwona. 1994. *Frames of Remembrance: The Dynamics of Collective Memory*. New Brunswick, NJ: Transaction Publishers.

Jelin, Elizabeth. 2007. "Public Memorialization in Perspective: Truth, Justice and Memory of Past Repression in the Southern Cone of South America." *International Journal of Transitional Justice* 1 (1): 138–56.

Jick, Leon A. 1981. "The Holocaust—Its Use and Abuse within the American Public." *Yad Vashem Studies* 14: 303–18.

Jones, Sara. 2011. "Staging Battlefields: Media, Authenticity and Politics in the Museum of Communism (Prague), the House of Terror (Budapest) and Gedenkstätte Hohenschönhausen (Berlin)." *Journal of War and Culture Studies* 4 (1): 97–111.

Jordan, Michael J. 2010. "Rise of the Hungarian Right." *Foreign Policy*, July 13. Accessed July 17, 2017. http://foreignpolicy.com/2010/07/13/rise-of-the-hungarian-right/

Judt, Tony. 1992. "The Past Is Another Country: Myth and Memory in Postwar Europe." *Daedalus* 121 (4): 83–118.

———. 2005. *Postwar: A History of Europe since 1945*. New York: Penguin.

Kagame, Paul. 2004. "Excerpts: Kagame Marks Genocide." *BBC*, April 7. Accessed February 16, 2017. http://news.bbc.co.uk/2/hi/africa/3609001.stm.

———. 2012. "Speech by President Paul Kagame at the Closing of the Gacaca." Gacaca, n.d. Accessed November 2, 2015. http://gacaca.rw/opinion/speech-by-president-paul-kagame-at-the-closing-of-the-gacaca/.

Karp, Ivan. 1992. Introduction to *Museums and Communities: The Politics of Public Culture*. Edited by Ivan Karp, Christine Mullen Kreamer, and Steven D. Lavine. Washington, DC: Smithsonian Institution Press.

Keen, Suzanne. 2006. "A Theory of Narrative Empathy." *Narrative* 14 (3): 207–36.

Kigali Genocide Memorial. "Burial Place." Accessed February 16, 2017. http://www.kgm.rw/memorial/burial-place-gardens/.

———. "Our Mission." Accessed February 16, 2017. http://www.kgm.rw/about/our-mission/.

Kis, János. 1991. "Postcommunist Politics in Hungary." *Journal of Democracy* 1 (3): 3–15.

Kiss, Csilla. 2006. "The Misuses of Manipulation: The Failure of Transitional Justice in Post-Communist Hungary." *Europe-Asia Studies* 58 (6): 926–40.

Klein, Kerwin Lee. 2000. "On the Emergence of Memory in Historical Discourse." *Representations* 69: 127–50.

Kornbluh, Peter, and Katherine Hite. 2010. "Chile's Turning Point." *The Nation*, January 17. Accessed August 3, 2016. https://www.thenation.com/article/chiles-turning-point/.

Kuang, Cliff. 2014. "The Near-Impossible Challenge of Designing the 9/11 Museum." *Wired*, May 14. Accessed August 2, 2016. http://www.wired.com/2014/05/911-museum-3/.

Kundera, Milan. 1980. *The Book of Laughter and Forgetting*. New York: Alfred A. Knopf.

Landsberg, Alison. 2004. *Prosthetic Memory: The Transformation of American Memory in the Age of Mass Culture*. New York: Columbia University Press.

Lawson, Hannah. 2014. "After the Genocide." *Ribaj*, July 2. Accessed February 10, 2017. https://www.ribaj.com/culture/after-the-genocide.

Lazzara, Michael J. 2011. *Chile in Transition: The Poetics and Politics of Memory*. Gainesville: University Press of Florida.

Leccardi, Carmen. 2016. "Memory, Time and Responsibility." In *Routledge International Handbook of Memory Studies*. Edited by Anna Lisa Tota and Trever Hagen. New York: Routledge, 109–20.

Lennon, John, and Malcolm Foley. 2000. *Dark Tourism: The Attraction of Death and Disaster*. London: Thompson Learning.

Lessa, Francesca, and Vincent Druliolle, eds. 2011. *The Memory of State Terrorism in the Southern Cone*. New York: Palgrave Macmillan.

Levy, Daniel, and Natan Sznaider. 2005. "The Politics of Commemoration: The Holocaust, Memory and Trauma." In *Handbook of Contemporary European Social Theory*. Edited by Gerard Delanty. New York: Routledge, 289–97.

———. 2006. *The Holocaust and Memory in the Global Age*. Philadelphia: Temple University Press.

———. 2010. *Human Rights and Memory*. University Park: Pennsylvania State University Press.

Linenthal, Edward T. 1995. *Preserving Memory: The Struggle to Create America's Holocaust Museum*. New York: Viking.

Lira, Elizabeth. 2011. "Chile: Dilemmas of Memory." In *The Memory of State Terrorism in the Southern Cone*. Edited by Francisca Lessa and Vincent Druliolle. New York: Palgrave Macmillan.

Local Projects. Accessed January 25 2017. https://localprojects.net/work.

Loveman, Brian, and Elizabeth Lira. 2007. "Truth, Justice, Reconciliation, and Impunity as Historical Themes: Chile, 1814–2006." *Radical History Review* 2007 (97): 43–76.

Majdanek. "The Mission." Accessed February 13, 2017. http://www.majdanek.eu/en/mission.

MASS Design. Accessed January 25, 2017. https://massdesigngroup.org/.

Matynia, Elzbieta. 2009. *Performative Democracy*. New York: Routledge.

McAslan. "Kigali Memorial Centre." Accessed January 19, 2017. http://www.mcaslan.co.uk/the-initiatives-issue/kigali-memorial-centre/102.

Meierhenrich, Jens. 2009. "The Transformation of Lieux de Mémoire: The Nyabarongo River in Rwanda, 1992–2009." *Anthropology Today* 25 (5): 13–19.

———. 2011. "Topographies of Remembering and Forgetting: The Transformation of Lieux de Mémoire in Rwanda." In *Remaking Rwanda: State Building and Human*

Rights after Mass Violence. Edited by Scott Straus and Lars Waldorf. Madison: University of Wisconsin Press, 283–96.

Meyerhoff, Harvey. 1993. "Remarks of Harvey Meyerhoff, Chairman of the Council, at the Dedication Ceremonies for the United States Holocaust Memorial Museum." *United States Holocaust Memorial Museum*, April 22. Accessed February 13, 2017. https://www.ushmm.org/research/ask-a-research-question/frequently-asked-questions/meyerhoff.

Muramira, Gashegu. 2016. "Construction of Genocide Museum Begins in Uganda." *New Times*, April 10. Accessed January 27, 2017. http://www.newtimes.co.rw/section/article/2016-04-10/198833/.

Museo de la Memoria. Accessed January 13, 2016. http://www.museodelamemoria.cl/.

Museo de la Memoria y los Derechos Humanos. 2011. Museum guide. Santiago, Chile: Ograma.

Neuman, Justin. 2011. "9/11 Chronomania." *The Immanent Frame* (Social Science Research Council blog). Accessed June 20, 2016. http://blogs.ssrc.org/tif/2011/09/09/911-chronomania/.

New York Times. 2008. "In Transit: A Wonderful Museum of Terror in Budapest." Accessed February 10, 2017. https://intransit.blogs.nytimes.com/2008/08/20/a-wonderful-museum-of-terror-in-budapest/.

Nietzsche, Friedrich. 1967. *On the Genealogy of Morals*. Translated by Walter Kaufmann. New York: Random House.

Nora, Pierre. 1989. "Between Memory and History: *Les Lieux de Mémoire*." *Representations* 26: 7–24.

———. 2002. "The Reason for the Current Upsurge in Memory." *Transit Online*, November 22, 2002. Accessed July 4, 2017. http://www.iwm.at/transit/transit-online/the-reasons-for-the-current-upsurge-in-memory/.

Novick, Peter. 1999. *The Holocaust in American Life*. New York: Houghton Mifflin.

Obama, Barack. 2014. "Remarks by the President at 9/11 Museum Dedication." White House Press Release, May 15. Accessed July 10, 2016. https://www.whitehouse.gov/the-press-office/2014/05/15/remarks-president-911-museum-dedication.

Olick, Jeffrey K. 1999. "Collective Memory: The Two Cultures." *Sociological Theory* 17 (3): 333–48.

———. 2007. *The Politics of Regret: On Collective Memory and Historical Responsibility*. New York: Routledge.

Opotow, Susan. 2015. "Historicizing Injustice: The Museum of Memory and Human Rights, Santiago, Chile." *Journal of Social Issues* 71 (2): 229–43.

Orwell, George. 1949. *1984*. New York: Harcourt Brace.

Phillip, Abby. 2014. "Families Infuriated by 'Crass Commercialism' of 9/11 Museum Gift Shop." *Washington Post*, May 19. Accessed February 12, 2017. https://www.washingtonpost.com/news/post-nation/wp/2014/05/19/families-infuriated-by-crass-commercialism-of-911-museum-gift-shop/?utm_term=.0741f1b5cb6c.

Power, Samantha. 2002. *A Problem from Hell: America and the Age of Genocide*. New York: Harper Perennial.

Radstone, Susannah. 2011. "What Place Is This? Transcultural Memory and the Locations of Memory Studies." *Parallax* 17 (4): 109–23.

Renan, Ernst. 1882. "What Is a Nation?" Lecture delivered at the Sorbonne.

Rettig, Max. 2008. "Gacaca: Truth, Justice, and Reconciliation in Postconflict Rwanda?" *African Studies Review* 51 (3): 25–50.

Rev, Istvan. 2008. "The Terror of the House." In *(Re)visualizing National History: Museums and National Identities in Europe in the New Millennium*. Edited by Robin Ostow. Toronto: University of Toronto Press, 47–89.

Reyntjens, F. 2004. "Rwanda, Ten Years on: From Genocide to Dictatorship." *African Affairs* 103 (411): 177–210.

———. 2011. "Constructing the Truth, Dealing with Dissent, Domesticating the World: Governance in Post-Genocide Rwanda." *African Affairs* 110 (438): 1–34.

Rieff, David. 2016. *In Praise of Forgetting: Historical Memory and Its Ironies*. New Haven, CT: Yale University Press.

Rosenbaum, Steve. 2012. "Building a Museum at Ground Zero." *TED Blog*, May 1. Accessed August 2, 2016. http://blog.ted.com/building-a-museum-at-ground-zero-steve-rosenbaum-on-the-ted-blog/.

Rosenberg, Tina. 1995. *The Haunted Land: Facing Europe's Ghosts after Communism*. New York: Random House.

Rothberg, Michael. 2009. *Multidirectional Memory: Remembering the Holocaust in the Age of Decolonization*. Stanford, CA: Stanford University Press.

Saunders, Doug. 2011. "Hungary's Strongman Spooks Europe." *Globe and Mail* (Toronto), January 29, F5.

Savage, Kirk. 1999. "The Past in the Present." *Harvard Design Magazine* 9 (Fall). Accessed April 8, 2011. http://www.gsd.harvard.edu/research/publications/hdm/back/9savage.html.

Schudson, Michael. 1992. *Watergate in American Memory: How We Remember, Forget, and Reconstruct the Past*. New York: Harper Collins.

Schwartz, Barry. 1982. "The Social Context of Commemoration: A Study in Collective Memory." *Social Forces* 61 (2): 374–402.

———. 1996. "The Expanding Past." *Qualitative Sociology* 19 (3): 275–82.

Sepulveda, Maria Luisa. 2011. "Museo de la Memoria y los Derechos Humanos." In *Museo de la Memoria y los Derechos Humanos* museum guide. Santiago, Chile: Ograma, 15–21.

Sontag, Susan. 2003. *Regarding the Pain of Others*. New York: Picador.

Sorin, Gerald. 1997. *Tradition Transformed: The Jewish Experience in America*. Baltimore, MD: Johns Hopkins University Press.

Stier, Oren Baruch. 2015. *Holocaust Icons: Symbolizing the Shoah in History and Memory*. New Brunswick, NJ: Rutgers University Press.

Sturken, Marita. 1997. *Tangled Memories: The Vietnam War, the AIDS Epidemic, and the Politics of Remembering*. Los Angeles: University of California Press.

———. 2007. *Tourists of History: Memory, Kitsch, and Consumerism from Oklahoma City to Ground Zero*. Durham, NC: Duke University Press.

———. 2015. "The 9/11 Memorial Museum and the Remaking of Ground Zero." *American Quarterly* 67 (2): 471–90.

———. 2016. "The Objects That Lived: The 9/11 Museum and Material Transformation." *Memory Studies* 9 (1): 13–26.

Terrorhaza. "Museum." Accessed February 13, 2017. http://www.terrorhaza.hu/en/museum.

———. "Permanent Exhibition." Accessed February 13, 2017. http://www.terrorhaza.hu/en/permanent-exhibition/second_floor.

Than, Krisztina. 2017. "Ruling Fidesz Party Wants Soros-Funded NGOs 'Swept out' of Hungary." *Reuters World News*, January 11. Accessed January 25, 2017. http://www.reuters.com/article/us-hungary-fidesz-soros-idUSKBN14V0P2.

Thomson, Susan. 2011. "The Darker Side of Transitional Justice: The Power Dynamics behind Rwanda's Gacaca Courts." *Africa* 81 (3): 373–90.

Tismaneanu, Vladimir. 1998. *Fantasies of Salvation: Democracy, Nationalism, and Myth in Post-Communist Europe*. Princeton, NJ: Princeton University Press.

Torpey, John. 2003. Introduction to *Politics and the Past: On Repairing Historical Injustices*. Edited by John Torpey. Lanham, MD: Rowman and Littlefield, 1–34.

———. 2006. *Making Whole What Has Been Smashed: On Reparations Politics*. Cambridge, MA: Harvard University Press.

———. 2015. "The Political Field of Reparations." In *Historical Justice and Memory*. Edited by Klaus Neumann and Janna Thompson. Madison: University of Wisconsin Press, 63–73.

USHMM. "About." Accessed June 7, 2015. http://www.ushmm.org/museum/about/.

———. "About the Mandel Center." Accessed February 16, 2017. https://www.ushmm.org/research/the-center-for-advanced-holocaust-studies/about-the-center-for-advanced-holocaust-studies.

———. "Art and Architecture." Accessed January 25, 2017. https://www.ushmm.org/information/about-the-museum/architecture-and-art.

———. "Confront Genocide." Accessed July 7, 2015. http://www.ushmm.org/confront-genocide/about.

———. 2016. "Museum Condemns White Nationalist Conference Rhetoric." November 21. Accessed February 16, 2017. https://www.ushmm.org/information/press/press-releases/museum-condemns-white-nationalist-conference-rhetoric.

———. 2016. "Press Kit." Accessed July 7, 2015. http://www.ushmm.org/information/press/press-kits/united-states-holocaust-memorial-museum-press-kit.

"USHMM Design Concept Proposal." 1986. Presented by the Design Concept Development Committee, Stuart Silver, Chairman, January 31. USHMM Archive.

Wagner-Pacifici, Robin. 1996. "Memories in the Making: The Shape of Things That Went." *Qualitative Sociology* 19 (3): 301–21.

Wagner-Pacifici, Robin, and Barry Schwartz. 1991. "The Vietnam Veterans Memorial: Commemorating a Difficult Past." *American Journal of Sociology* 97 (2): 376–420.

Waldorf, Lars. 2006. "Mass Justice for Mass Atrocity: Rethinking Local Justice as Transitional Justice." *Temple Law Review* 79 (1): 1–87.

Weinberg, Jeshajahu. 1994. Address at Conference of the Annual Association of American Museums, Seattle. USHMM Archive.

Wieseltier, Leon. 1993. "After Memory: Reflections on the Holocaust Memorial Museum." *The New Republic* 3 (May): 16–26.

Wilde, Alexander. 1999. "Irruptions of Memory: Expressive Politics in Chile's Transition to Democracy." *Journal of Latin American Studies* 31 (2): 473–500.

Winter, Jay. 1995. *Sites of Memory, Sites of Mourning: The Great War in European Cultural History*. New York: Cambridge University Press.

Wright, Thomas C. 2007. *State Terrorism in Latin America: Chile, Argentina, and International Human Rights*. New York: Rowman and Littlefield.

Young, James E. 1993. *The Texture of Memory: Holocaust Memorials and Meaning*. New Haven, CT: Yale University Press.

———. 2005. *At Memory's Edge: After-Images of the Holocaust in Contemporary Art and Architecture*. New Haven, CT: Yale University Press.

———. 2016. *The Stages of Memory: Reflections on Memorial Art, Loss, and the Spaces Between*. Amherst, MA: University of Massachusetts Press.

Zelizer, Barbie. 2002a. "Finding Aids to the Past: Bearing Personal Witness to Traumatic Public Events." *Media, Culture and Society* 24 (5): 697–714.

———. 2002b. "Photography, Journalism & Trauma." In *Journalism after September 11*. Edited by Barbie Zelizer and Stuart Allan. London: Routledge, 36–48.

Zurita, Raul. 2011. "Of the Memory and the Dream." In *Museo de la Memoria y los Derechos Humanos* museum guide. Santiago, Chile: Ograma, 26–31.

INDEX

ABOUT THE AUTHOR

AMY SODARO earned her PhD in sociology at the New School for Social Research and is currently associate professor of sociology at Borough of Manhattan Community College/City University of New York. Her research focuses on memorial museums, and she has published essays on the US Holocaust Memorial Museum, the Kigali Genocide Memorial Centre in Rwanda, the House of Terror in Budapest, the Jewish Museum in Berlin, and the 9/11 Museum. She is coeditor of *Memory and the Future: Transnational Politics, Culture and Society* (2010) and an issue of *WSQ* on the topic "At Sea."

Printed in the United States
By Bookmasters